M000272436

By Silver Moon and Silver Light, All I Desire Is Mine Tonight

Human beings have always lived in harmony with the cycles of the Sun and Moon. The annual cycle of the Sun turns the Wheel of the Year—we watch the days grow longer as summer approaches, then shorter as the autumn leaves are buried under the cold winter snow.

The monthly lunar cycle is more subtle than that of the Sun, but is just as powerful. The increasing energy of the waxing moon is perfect for spells designed to attract positive change, while the waning moon is the time to banish negative patterns and habits. The full moon is conducive to most types of magick and is the traditional time to celebrate the Moon goddess.

Moon-centered worship may be as much as 70,000 years old according to some scholars. Moon goddesses are an integral part of modern Pagan spirituality. But lunar ritual work can also incorporate the "man in the Moon"—the God. For those interested in expanding their ritual workings, this book includes an appendix with a comprehensive listing of lunar goddesses and gods from diverse cultures.

Magick and Rituals of the Moon includes recipes, rituals, and other creative and even whimsical ways to celebrate the changing lunar cycle. You'll discover dozens of ways to work with lunar energy:

- Perform rituals to honor all phases of the Moon
- Make a magickal mirror for spellwork and divination
- Craft your own traditional besom (broom)
- Cast spells for love, prosperity, banishing negative habits, and more!

Connect with lunar deities and work magick with the tides of lunar energy—and live in harmony with the ever-changing faces of the Moon.

About the Author

Edain McCoy became a self-initiated Witch in 1981, and has been an active part of the Pagan community since her formal initiation into a large San Antonio coven in 1983. She has been researching alternative spiritualities since her teens, when she was first introduced to Kaballah (Jewish mysticism). Today, she is part of the Wittan Irish Pagan Tradition and is a Priestess of Brighid within that tradition. An alumnus of the University of Texas (BA in history), she currently pursues parttime graduate and undergraduate studies at Indiana University. Edain has taught classes in guided meditation and automatic writing, and occasionally works with students who wish to study Wiccan and Celtic Witchcraft. She is an ordained minister of the Universal Life Church, and is a member of The Indiana Historical Society, The Authors Guild, The Wiccan/Pagan Press Alliance, and is a former woodwind player for the Lynchburg, Virginia Symphony. A descendant of the infamous feuding McCoy family of Kentucky, Edain also proudly claims as a forefather Sir Roger Williams, the seventeenth-century religious dissenter.

To Write to the Author

If you wish to contact the author or would like more information about this book, please write to the author in care of Llewellyn Worldwide, and we will forward your request. Both the author and publisher appreciate hearing from you and learning of your enjoyment of this book and how it has helped you. Llewellyn Worldwide cannot guarantee that every letter written to the author can be answered, but all will be forwarded. Please write to:

Edain McCoy
c/o Llewellyn Worldwide
P.O. Box 64383
Dept. 0–7387–0092–4
St. Paul, MN 55164-0383, U.S.A.

Please enclose a self-addressed, stamped envelope for reply, or $1.00 to cover costs.
If outside U.S.A., enclose international postal reply coupon.

Magick & Rituals *of the* Moon

Edain McCoy

2001
Llewellyn Publications
St. Paul, Minnesota, U.S.A., 55164-0383

Magick & Rituals of the Moon. Copyright © 1995, 2001 by Edain McCoy. All rights reserved. No part of this book may be used or reproduced in any manner whatsoever, including Internet usage, without written permission from Llewellyn Publications, except in the case of brief quotations embodied in critical articles or reviews.

SECOND EDITION
First Printing, 2001
(previously titled *Lady of the Night*)

Cover Design by Gavin Dayton Duffy
Cover Art by Katherine Ace
Interior Art by Tom Grewe and Anne Marie Garrison
Interior Design and Editing by Marguerite Krause

First edition, three printings, 1995.
Library of Congress Cataloging-in-Publication Data
McCoy, Edain, 1957–
     Magick & Rituals of the Moon / Edain McCloy. — 2nd ed.
        p.   cm.
     Rev. ed. of: Lady of the night. c1995.
     Includes bibliographical references and index.
     ISBN 0–7387–0092–4
     1. Moon—Miscellanea. 2. Magic. 3. Neopaganism—Rituals. 4. Goddess religion. I
Title: Magick and rituals of the moon. II. McCoy, Edain, 1957-Lady of the night. III.
Title.

     BF1623.M66 M37   2001
    133.4—dc21   2001018651

Llewellyn Worldwide does not participate in, endorse, or have any authority or responsibility concerning private business transactions between our authors and the public.

    All mail addressed to the author is forwarded but the publisher cannot, unless specifically instructed by the author, give out an address or phone number.

Llewellyn Publications
A Division of Llewellyn Worldwide, Ltd.
St. Paul, Minnesota 55164-0383, U.S.A.
www.llewellyn.com

Printed in the United States of America

Other Books by the Author

Witta: An Irish Pagan Tradition

A Witch's Guide to Faery Folk

How to Do Automatic Writing

Celtic Myth and Magick

Sabbats: A Witch's Approach to Living the Old Ways

Entering the Summerland

Inside a Witches' Coven

Mountain Magick

Making Magick

Celtic Women's Spirituality

Astral Projection for Beginners

Bewitchments

Forthcoming

Enchantments

Table of Contents

Illustrations, Tables, and Charts

The Silver Lady in the Sky

Lady Moon, Lady Moon, where are you roving?
Over the sea.
Lady Moon, Lady Moon, whom are you loving?
All that love me.
— Richard Monckton Milnes

A bright silver-yellow disk rides low in the night sky, casting its diffuse rays ever wider as it slowly rises in the darkness, climbing higher and higher into the star-lit heavens. Under its gentle light a world half in darkness notes its passing. Many do not consciously register the moment when the silvery glow catches their eye, their minds tracking quickly to other concerns. But for countless others, the event cannot be so easily passed over.

On a secluded grassy hillside a small group stands in a circle holding silver goblets upward to catch the nurturing rays. They gaze skyward lovingly, offering praise and thanksgiving.

In the small backyard of a quiet suburban neighborhood, a woman stands alone, opening her arms to the night sky, her naked body bathed in the moon's gentle white glow. With a shiny silver blade she pulls down the light, and directs its luminous energy into herself.

In an urban highrise towering over a busy city, a lone man contemplates the rising orb. In front of him is a small altar. He tosses jasmine and lotus incense on hot coals, and inhales deeply, connecting himself to the power of the silver light. He whispers an invocation which only he and the great night mother can hear, and he smiles, knowing she is with him.

With bedroom windows open to the moonlight, a young couple wanting a child makes love under the full, fertile rays which wash sensually over their conjoined bodies.

In an eldercare home in a small town, an old woman pleads the need to retire early and retreats to her rooms. Alone, she opens the blinds and looks up with a smile as if greeting an old friend. Her wrinkled lips mutter the words of a long-known, heart-felt prayer.

In a large city, two friends meet in a park to meditate together under the silver-golden streams which light the dark corners of the verdant park as if it were the peak of twilight.

Far away, in a toy-laden bedroom, two children notice the silver Lady of the night wandering past their nursery window. Drawn inexplicably to the awesome sight, they rise from their beds and go to the window to watch her in silence.

All of these people are expressing the inborn Pagan nature that is a part of our collective genetic memory, a quality never more manifest than in the deep pull we have all felt toward the moon — the mother of creation and ruler of the night — since the dawn of time. Some of us are conscious of the ways in which our Pagan expression is manifested. Others feel only the stirrings of something long forgotten, but nonetheless powerful and alluring, something which, if only for a moment, draws the attention skyward. The moon, our first satellite and night light, captivating humankind since humanity's birth, was our first calendar, our first mystery, and her nightly appearance the first occurrence which could be counted upon in a scary, primitive world. She pulled the tides, measured the fertility cycles of women, guided the migration of animals and insects, inspired songs and poems, called to lovers, and was a bold catalyst for magick.

The moon is also our oldest spiritual focus. Since ALL religion is based on myth, the cosmological sequences discussing the creation of the heavens and the earth (which include the moon) are the very oldest tales in existence. We turn to these ancient stories again and again, and we listen in awe and wonder long after the "in vogue" scientific theories of creation have come and gone.

So just where did the moon, this heavenly miracle, come from? One modern scientist once went so far as to say that the moon could not exist because its presence simply could not be scientifically explained. Perhaps this is part of her allure. She does exist, and has since long before humankind walked the earth. Mythology attempts to explain the existence of the moon, and nearly every culture has its own story about how the moon was formed. These stories vary greatly, but all share one common thread — that the moon was one of the first-born things of creation. In some myths, she is the very first, the great mother from whom life flows and to which all life someday returns.

It is this mythological link which Pagans today still honor, and to which they are most strongly drawn. When asked about their first experience with Paganism and/or Witchcraft, or their first inkling that they might be interested in a spiritual path older than the ones offered daily by the larger culture, a great many cite the moon as that catalyst. They speak of sitting alone looking up at the night sky, of watching the moon wax and wane and feeling that somehow they ought to be attuning to her subtle changes. They sensed that something within themselves was missing, being neglected; something was hidden which they should find and be able to understand and express. Instinctively, they all looked first to the moon to fill that unnamed void.

Our moon is small when compared to the large role it has played in human history. Just twenty-seven percent the size of the earth, it takes 29.53 days to make its elliptical orbit around the earth, keeping the same face to us at all times. During that turning it waxes and wanes from a thin, barely perceptible crescent into fullness, and then slowly wanes again. It passes through cloud banks, is obscured by storms, peeks through treetops, lights the darkness, and sometimes, just like a playful mother, initiates a game of hide and seek with us. She smiles upon us with her bright face, ever hiding from us her dark side, nurturing us by offering a wee sense of security and order in an otherwise chaotic world. Little wonder that our planet's first religions focused upon her.

Moon-centered worship — not to be confused with worship of the the moon itself — is believed to be the single oldest common human event. Some scholars estimate that organized moon-focused spirituality may be as much as 60–70,000 years old. By comparison, the Sabbats, the solar festivals of the Pagan year, are at best 12,000 years old (the Winter and Summer Solstices being the very oldest).

Interestingly enough, some of the earliest moon deities were male, principally in the Middle East and among the Celts. Perhaps the reason for this was that the sun, connected with summer and therefore to growth and plentiful game, was seen as feminine. Or maybe, somewhere deep in the dark reaches of the psyche, our primitive ancestors realized that men just might play a role in procreation, and there once was a prevalent belief that it was the moon which actually caused impregnation.

Over time, the obvious connection between the cycles of the moon and women's fertility cycles moved the moon clearly into the realm of the feminine. Eventually the mystery surrounding the moon came to reflect an expression of a Triple Goddess: maiden, mother, and crone, all three divine faces, eternal and one, ever-changing, but always the same. She is a phenomenon almost worldwide in scope. Only her multitude of names changes from culture to culture. (A list of Moon Goddesses and Gods

The Symbol of the Triple Goddess

The waxing, full, and waning moons

from around the world appears in Appendix A.) Because of the moon's relationship to the female fertility cycle, most of the deities are feminine, although male deities are also well-represented. The majority of moon deities still known to us today come from civilizations which have preserved their original lunar calendars (i.e., The Middle East, Africa, Polynesia, China).

Many Cultures in Europe and Polynesia took their day to day — or rather night to night — relationship with their moon Goddesses a step further and designated which Goddess ruled which part of the lunar month. Each reigned for approximately three days and nights. Some modern Pagan traditions have attempted to reclaim these ancient divisions, most notably the Anatolian Wiccan path, a Greek tradition that has attempted to purge itself of Roman influences. The table on page xii lists more than one deity for some time periods. This denotes differences in archetypal concepts within the Anatolian and other Greek traditions. The differences have also been attributed to divisions in political culture and to accepted concepts of polar rulership in Greek spirituality. Most of these Goddess names will be familiar to modern Witches.

With the rise of patriarchy, the male domination of the world (approximately 5,000–7,000 years ago), the night and all of her attributes began to be devalued and, with the darkness, the moon and the Goddess fell in status. Rather than being seen as half of

Days of Lunar Month Ruled	Anatolian Goddess who Rules the Days
1–3	**Persephone,** a Goddess of initiations, new beginnings, grains, sowing, and changes who ventures to the Underworld once a year
	Athena, one of the best-loved Greek Goddesses whose temple still stands in the city which bears her name; she is a Goddess of love (though not a sexual love like Aphrodite's), protection, the arts, and a warrioress who oddly represents peace; the patron Goddess of the city of Athens; archetypally linked to initiatory rites
4–6	**Artemis,** virgin Goddess of nature and the hunt, a mutable symbol of the potential of feminine power; sister of Apollo
7–9	**Kore,** an archetypal link between childhood and womanhood, symbolized by the beginning of the menstrual cycle and awakening sexuality; also seen as another form of Persephone
	Disponia, a beautiful maiden/mother Goddess who symbolizes the loss of youth; archetypally linked to menarche and first sexual contact, a patron deity of feminine coming of age
10–12	**Hera,** a creative deity linked to mental prowess, creative inspiration, and communication; the consort of God King Zeus
13–17	**Gaia,** the earth mother, the supreme creatrix, and divine principle of fertility and abundance
	Selene, a sexual image of a full moon/mother Goddess, sister of the sun God Helios; archetypally, the bestower of immortality
18–20	**Demeter,** a harvest and Underworld Goddess and the mother of Persephone. Also the patron Goddess of seers and mothers of older children
21–22	**Hestia,** an archetypal link between motherhood and cronehood, symbolized by menopause; a Goddess of the home and of fire
23–25	**Medusa,** a crone Goddess, the embodiment of old wounds and fears which must be released in order for us to move on to other planes of learning, and an archetypal link between the earth world of existence and the water world of death; archetypally a link between the divine and human worlds
26–29	**Hecate,** a crone Goddess of wisdom, death, change/rebirth, and the Underworld/Otherworld; a patron Goddess of magick in many Wiccan traditions

the whole (i.e.; God/male and Goddess/female, both needed for creation and completion), the night was seen as the realm of demons and evil folk (read "Witches"). New folklore arose around the moon, a curious mix reflecting both the old beliefs and the new revulsion for the moon, and displaying both the old awe and the new fear of lunar power.

Among the more popular of extant moon lore are the beliefs that:

- An owl calling to the full moon on a clear night portends a death in the neighborhood.

- Cats cannot live unless periodically exposed to moonlight, and a cat who always wishes to go out under the full moon should not be let back into the house.

- Eclipses, a time when the shadow of the earth falls across the moon's surface, were once thought to be expressions of anger from some stellar deity. Later they were linked in popular folklore to insanity and natural disasters. (This was a dreadful forecast; lunar eclipses can happen up to four times a year.)

- The transformations of werewolves (humans cursed to shapeshift into vicious wolves) were thought to be triggered by the full moon.

- In Slavic countries, werewolves were called Vlkodlaks and were blamed for eclipses.

- The Seneca Indians believe that the moon was created from a wolf spirit; this is why wolves insist on howling at the moon.

- If the winter new moon rises far in the north it will be a cold month; if it rises far in the south it will be unusually warm.

- If the moon is resting on its back at the start of its fourth quarter, it will be a rainy week.

- A cloudy morning during a waning moon will create a sunny afternoon.

- If the moon is red when it rises, expect rain the next day.

- Changes in the moon's appearance occurring on Sunday mean heavy rains or flooding.

- New clothes first washed on the full moon will not wear well.

- Stained linens can be whitened under the full moon's bleaching rays.

- The happiest marriages are those which take place at the first full moon in the month of June.

- Weaning a child on a waning moon will make the child sickly.

- Planting on a waning moon will yield a poor crop.

- A child born on the dark of the moon will die before reaching adulthood. But a child born on the full moon will live a long, healthy life.

LADY OF THE NIGHT

- If a pregnant woman is exposed to the moon's light her baby will go insane as an adult and be given to night wanderings and nightmares.

- Pointing nine times at the moon in one night will prevent one's admittance to Heaven.

- Riding a white horse under a dark moon produces a month of nightmares.

- Mushrooms gathered on a full moon are cursed by faeries and should not be eaten.

- Faery rings, dark circles of grass in which humans can become entrapped in the faery world, are at their most dangerous under a full moon.

- You must have silver money in your pocket when the new moon begins in order to ensure a prosperous month to come.

- Over-exposure to the moon when it shines in daylight can lead to illness or madness.

- Only the most pure of heart should venture outdoors on the night of the dark moon; others risk falling under the dominion of the Devil.

- Vampires, animated corpses which feed on the blood of the living, have their greatest need on the moon's wane.

The persistent belief that the full moon causes lunacy may have come from observances of Pagan worship during the dangerous years of Witch persecutions, when only the crazy or foolhardy were believed to be willing to risk death by openly honoring the old ways. The wild dances of joy and abandon that once characterized these coven meetings may have been misconstrued by unseen observers as moon-induced madness.

Modern Pagans still dance and sing and celebrate the full moon, and all of her other faces as well. We still look to the night sky for guidance and inspiration. We still honor her and keep the old ways she taught us, usually without fear of discovery and retribution. Like Pagans of old, we in this new generation are rediscovering the magick and lure of the shining silver Lady of the night, seeking always to recapture the old ways and make them meaningful for today.

From myths and folklore, we are able to glean insight into past moon-oriented Pagan spirituality. All around the world, many moon festivals still exist around which the seeking Pagan can begin to build these new traditions. (A list of some of the major moon festivals or holidays which either honor the moon itself or are timed by her appearance, appears in Appendix B.)

Lady of the Night is intended to be used as a guide and handbook to moon worship, ritual, and magick. Its spells, rituals, and suggestions for celebration can be used as they are, but it is hoped that they will stimulate your creativity and move you to construct your own solitary or group rituals, which will be deeply meaningful to you and those with whom you work and worship.

The book is organized by the moon's phases and is directed mostly at solitaries; moon worship was, in many cultures, traditionally more of a solitary or family event as compared to the large, communal solar festivals. However, since covens, groves, and other groups are most likely to meet together at the full moon, a group ritual is included in that chapter. Each phase offers history, lore, rituals, and ideas for lunar celebrations for yourself and others, whether or not they are Pagan. The last chapters provide samples of moon magick, including advanced natural magickal techniques, which are very lunar oriented.

To this end, and to all seekers of the old ways, this book is lovingly dedicated.

E. M.
Midwinter's Eve, 1993

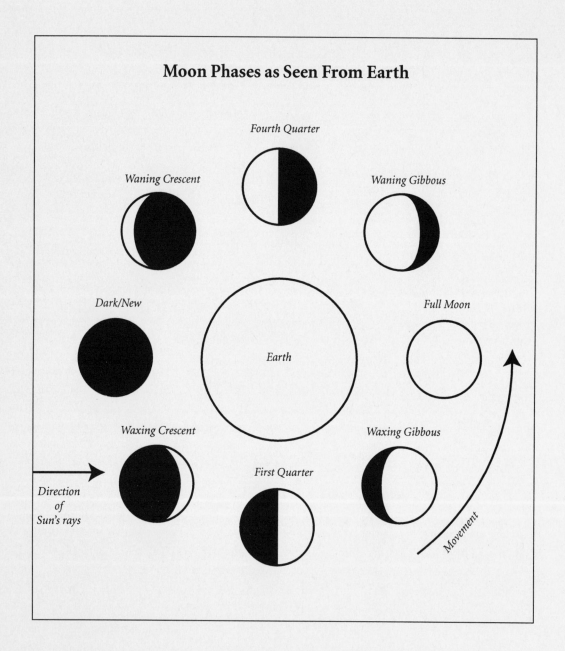

Phases of the Moon by Common Name			
Waxing Moon From new to full Phase lasts approximately two weeks	*First Quarter* From new to half-full Phase lasts approximately one week	*New Moon* First day of the new cycle	Cycle of waxing (maiden/virgin) energy
		Crescent Moon Four days into the new cycle	
	Second Quarter From half-full to full Phase lasts approximately one week	*Waxing Quarter* One week into the new cycle	Cycle of full moon (mother) energy Also the realm of male moon deities
		Gibbous Moon Three and a half days before fullness	
Waning Moon From full to dark Phase lasts approximately two weeks	*Third Quarter* From full to half-dark Phase lasts approximately one week	*Full Moon* Mid-cycle	
		Disseminating Moon Three-and-a-half days past full	
	Fourth Quarter From half-dark to dark Phase lasts approximately one week	*Waning Quarter* Three weeks into the cycle	Cycle of waning (crone) energy
		Balsamic Moon Three or four days before total darkness	

PART I

The
Mother

The Full Moon Esbat

At these words they threw back their shaggy heads
and howled their delight,
And by so honoring her they became beautiful.
— Rebecca Worrell

The full moon is a popular feature in legend and folklore. From childhood we are asked to look up and see the human-like features on her face, and we wonder at her power when we discover that she actually pulls the tides of the mighty seas. Logically we conclude that, since our own bodies are ninety-eight percent water, she must also have some mystical pull on us.

The time of the full moon, commonly called the Esbat, is Paganism's celebration of the heavenly mother Goddess. The Esbat has long been seen by Pagans of many cultures as a peak night of Goddess power and an efficacious time for ritual and magick. The word Esbat comes from the French *esbattre,* meaning "to frolic," and it gives us an insight into the joyful group workings which have become a popular part of our modern Pagan celebrations. This is a good sign; only a few years ago, in all but a few traditions, a dull solemnity generally characterized the Esbats. Solemnity is a radical departure from the way our ancestors viewed their full moon festival.

The word Esbat is also the word from which we get the term "estrus," the fertile period of all female mammals other than humans. Even though human females are the only ones with monthly cycles (most animals have them once or twice yearly), the word has come to mean that which occurs monthly. All monthly gatherings timed by the moon are technically Esbats, but we Pagans tend to apply the name only to the time of the full moon.

The full moon and the mother Goddess she represents have had a sad history in the past several thousand years. Because of the patriarchy's fear and jealousy of the mother's power and hold over her children, a concerted campaign of extermination was mounted against her. This was accomplished by murdering any of her daughters and most of her sons who were caught outdoors on the night of the full moon, especially if they were found in the woods, or if any "odd" incident (such as a cow which stopped giving milk) occurred the next day.

This period is known in Paganism as The Burning Times. During eight centuries of terror, European and North American Witch persecutions and killings took the lives of untold numbers of people. No one was immune from accusation, not Witch, Christian, or Jew. Any charge of Witchcraft would undoubtedly bring about a capital conviction.

Since that time mothers have been blamed for everything wrong with the planet, including most of the problems of their adult children. Mothers aren't perfect, nor do even the best of them live up to all our expectations; because of these inadequacies some people find they have difficulty relating to the mother aspect of the Goddess.

The following are some simple exercises you can try to help you overcome these feelings. If you find your problems run deeper than the fundamental programming of a misogynistic culture, you may want to consult a mental health professional to further assist you.

1. Spend time remembering that in Paganism the deities are not perfect, nor are they as all-powerful as those in the mainstream religions. Try to focus on this conundrum: if a Goddess is not perfect, can you expect more of your human mother?

2. We often hear talk today of the hurt child living within each of us. Before we can start working on something as intimate and tricky as our relationship with our mothers, both the earthly and the divine, we must overcome those hurts. It doesn't matter if others think your grievances are valid or not. It is your feelings on the issue that matter, and they are always valid, right or wrong.

Spend as much time as possible in meditation and reflection on your past. At what times did you feel hurt, rejected, scared, or insecure? Don't deal in generalities. Pinpoint as many specifics as possible.

After you have done that, look at each event from a broader perspective. Step back from it and examine it critically. Decide just how many people, including yourself, may have been responsible for the occurrence. Was your mother really involved? Was she even aware of a problem brewing? If not, by doing something differently could she have prevented the problem you faced or the embarrassment you endured? If she was aware and purposefully chose her actions (or inactions), what might have been her motivation? Was it to deliberately hurt you, or to teach you? Did she see the issue as trivial? Was it trivial, to everyone but you?

Be realistic with your answers. Accept the blame when all or part of it is due. On the other hand, don't fall into the trap of considering yourself a victim or you'll only feel worse.

For those times that you feel your mother was at fault for letting you down, form a clear image of the pain in your mind and mentally pour into it all your rage and resentment. Then let it go. Holding on to pain won't change it, but you can change the ultimate effect it has on your life. Visualize yourself burying the pain-filled image and then turning around and mentally hugging your mother in forgiveness. Remember, she is/was human, and just because she is/was a parent does/did not mean she was divinely decreed infallible.

This exercise sounds much simpler than it really is, but it is worth the effort.

3. In other relationships, it is the mother (or the father) who harbors some resentment from the past toward you. Whether you feel that it is or is not justified is a moot point.

While you cannot force anyone else to let pain go, you can release it from your own side. Follow the exercise above and release your anger at your parent's disappointment in you. Holding on to it will only hinder your spiritual growth.

4. Meditate on all the nurturing images you can call to mind, then try to recall how many women — and men — in your life have offered these gifts to you. The word "mother" (or "father") is not merely a biological title. It is the name for a person who loves and cherishes you. Parents may make mistakes, but they ultimately have your welfare at heart.

It is possible for us to have more than one mother. Some adoptive children have searched for and found their birth mothers and now have wonderful relationships with them as well as with their adoptive parents. Likewise, some birth parents are less worthy of the title "mother" than many casual acquaintances.

You can get along with your birth or adoptive mother and love her dearly, and still have other mothers in your life. These women might be relatives, older friends, mentors, or teachers. When I was a teen I had an older friend who I often referred to as "mom." She enjoyed the flattery of the title and I enjoyed making her happy. She never talked down to me; I felt quite grown up when I was with her. But like a mother, she did not stand idly by and allow me to engage in stupid or dangerous antics. Like a loving parent, she would do what she had to to correct or stop me, and perhaps even tell my mother what I was doing.

It should not be hard to make the leap from loving these nurturing women in your life to relating to the mother Goddess, embodied by the moon, who loves and cares for all her children equally.

5. Make up a list of traits you as a child would have thought essential for the ideal mother. This list probably would include such gems as allowing you to go to bed whenever you wanted and eat chocolate cake for breakfast.

After you list those qualities, make a counter-list of the drawbacks such an upbringing could have presented — fatigue and illness, for example. Compare your mother to the list and see where she stands.

Then make another list describing your image of an ideal mother today. How have your ideas changed? If you are a mother (or a father — they can nurture, too), are you meeting those needs in your own children? How are your fantasies of perfection met in yourself? How were they manifested in your mother, both in the past and, if she is still living, now?

Our ideas about ideal parenthood can change dramatically over time. What bothers you today may seem trivial years from now. The great wit Mark Twain, commenting on his own father, observed that when he (Twain) was a boy he was appalled at the ignorance and backwardness of his father. As an adult he couldn't believe how smart the old man had become in only twenty years.

You may also want to have some fun playing around with the various images of TV moms. Try to picture what life would be like with each of them raising you and how you would be different today under their tutelage. Every TV mom from Donna Reed to Peggy Bundy is fair game in this exercise.

6. If you are not a parent, read parenting magazines, which are aimed primarily at women, to understand the concerns of today's mothers. These may offer you some new insights into the things your own parents did and didn't do for you and why they made those choices.

7. If you are a mother or father, spend some time alone mentally focusing on the love you have for your child. If you are not a parent, focus on a cherished pet, a little brother or sister, a niece or nephew, or another living being you cherish and for whom you are partly responsible. Let the feeling of love become as tangible as a physical object you can hold in your hands.

Now picture your mother and transfer that love into her image. This is not to be a manipulative magickal act, intended to change her attitude toward you, but one which allows you to experience her feelings for you in a powerful way and help link you as parent and child.

After you can clearly see this feeling manifested in your own mother, transfer it onto an image of the mother Goddess.

The Calendar of the Night Sky

Moon calendars, carved in stone, have been found that date back more than 200,000 years. Some cave painting calendars are more than 50,000 years old; they became more sophisticated and widely used 30,000 years ago. This probably makes our genetic memory and awareness of the moon older than any other collective conscious thought.

Many cultures still use a lunar calendar. The dating usually starts with the new moon nearest to the Winter Solstice (though some cultures start their new year at a new moon in autumn), and the months are celebrated at their peak on the night of fullness. There are approximately thirteen lunar months in each solar year; most societies who use these lunar timetables make periodic adjustments so that their months stay reasonably confined to certain seasons of the solar year. The one notable exception is the Islamic calendar, which was based on an ancient Persian system of timekeeping. It makes no adjustment at all for the solar year. Because of this the months travel slowly forward in relation to the solar calendar with each passing year.

Many cultures named their moons after things or events represented by the month in which they fell. Studying the names given to each moon can tell us much about what these old societies valued and how they viewed their Wheel of the Year.

Listed on pages 7 and 8 are just a few samples of the many, many naming systems that have been applied to the lunar months over the centuries.

Naming Systems for the Lunar Months

Celtic Tree Lunar Calendar	Appalachian Folklore Moon Names
Beth (Birch)	Snow Moon
Luis (Rowan)	Seed Moon
Nion (Ash)	Budding Moon
Fearn (Alder)	Leaf Moon
Saille (Willow)	Blossom Moon
Huath (Hawthorn)	Strawberry Moon
Duir (Oak)	Oak Moon
Tinne (Holly)	Blackberry Moon
Coll (Hazel)	Corn Moon
Muin (Vine)	Vine/Thistle Moon
Gort (Ivy)	Apple/Pear Moon
Ngetal (Reed)	Blood Moon
Ruis (Elder)	Holly or Blue Moon

New England Folklore Moon Names	Native American (Northeast) Moon Names
Wolf Moon	Snow Moon
Snow Moon	Hunger Moon
Worm Moon	Crow Moon
Pink Moon	Egg Moon
Flower Moon	Planting Moon
Strawberry Moon	Flower Moon
Buck/Hot Moon	Storm Moon
Green Corn/Barley Moon	Ripe Moon
Water Moon	Cherry Moon
Harvest Moon	Dying Grass Moon
Hunter's Moon	Hunting Moon
Beaver Moon	Frost Moon
Cold Moon	Sleep Moon

Although the Jewish calendar is now identified with a mainstream/patriarchal religion that worships only one father God, the names of the months of its year were taken from a very ancient Babylonian Pagan calendar, making it one of the oldest lunar calen-

Additional Naming Systems for the Lunar Months

Old Norse Runic Half Months

Eoh (Yew)	Peorth (Womb)
Elhaz (Elk)	Sigel (Sun)
Tyr (Pillar)	Beorc (Birch)
Ehwaz (Horse)	Man (Humanity)
Lagu (Sweet Waters)	Ing (Waxing Energy)
Odal (Home)	Dag (Daylight)
Feoh (Prosperity)	Ur (Strength)
Thorn (Defense)	As (Divinity)
Rad (Motion)	Ken (Illumination)
Gyfu (Gift)	Wyn (Joyfulness)
Hagal (Confinement)	Nyd (Necessity)
Is (Static)	Jara (Eternal)

American Wiccan or Eclectic Wiccan Calendar
(beginning with the cycle nearest Yule)

Wolf Moon	Meade/Ale Moon
Storm Moon	Wort Moon
Chaste/Virgin Moon	Barley/Wine Moon
Seed Moon	Blood Moon
Hare Moon	Snow Moon
Dyad Moon	Oak Moon
	Blue Moon (a variable)

dars still known and in use today. It uses a twelve month system (354 days to the lunar year) and makes an adjustment to conform to the solar year by adding a "leap month" seven times every nineteen years in the third, sixth, eighth, eleventh, fourteenth, seventeenth, and nineteenth years.

By contrast, the Norse divided their lunar months roughly in half, beginning around the time of the Autumn Equinox. When a solar calendar was adopted the Winter Solstice became their new year. Twenty-four designations made the calendar fit neatly into the solar year.

Over the past several decades a lunar calendar based on the general seasons common to most of the inhabited regions of upper North America, and on the archetypal meaning of those seasons, has been widely adopted. Usually called the American Wiccan or Eclectic Wiccan Calendar, it has been discussed in books by noted Pagan authors such as Silver RavenWolf, Pauline Campanelli, and Zsuzsuanna Budapest.

Like the American Wiccan Calendar, numerous moon systems name only twelve of their moons and make the thirteenth the Blue Moon. This is always a variable date. Since there are just under thirteen full lunations which must be placed within the twelve months of the solar year, one month will likely end up with two full moons. It is this moon which gets the honor of being the Blue Moon for the year. Opinions vary on how it is to be celebrated. Perhaps the best approach is to look upon it as a bonus, like the thirteenth pastry in a baker's dozen. Do something different, experiment, make it a night of surprises and excitement which you or your coven will look forward to with healthy anticipation.

All of the above-mentioned calendars can work adequately for almost anyone, but adopting them wholly can have drawbacks if you do not live in the region in which they were developed. In order to work best, a lunar calendar should not only have personal meaning to the Witch using it, but also make sense in relation to his or her world. For example, a lunar calendar based on the seasonal changes of eastern Canada loses relevance when transported to central Africa or southern New Zealand. If you or your tradition have no lunar calendar with names already attached to the months, and do not feel drawn to any of the existing ones, you may wish to create your own based on the seasonal manifestations of the place in which you live. Remember that all lunar months had to be named by someone sometime, and that they all had a beginning in which they struggled for legitimacy. In the end, the only legitimacy that counts is your participation.

I have found that many Witches are more comfortable with these individualized calendars because they make sense to both the conscious and subconscious minds. If you adopt a calendar with a November "Snow Moon" but you live in a place where you are not likely to see snow fall until January — if at all — it becomes very hard to force your mind to accept a ritual built around snow.

I currently live in central Indiana, which has a very balanced four-season climate. Starting with the lunar month that begins nearest to the first of December, I name my thirteen months like this:

- **Light Moon** — for the many expressions of a festival of lights at this season

- **Snow Moon** — a definite January occurrence

- **Cardinal Moon** — for the winter red bird who stays here all winter and is our official state bird

- **Fever Moon** — by now we all have cabin fever; we're tired of being cooped up indoors and ready for spring

- **Changing Moon** — around March we never know if we'll have spring or winter weather on any given day

- **Crocus Moon** — for the small flower which is traditionally thought of as the first official sign of spring

- **Rain Moon** — there is always a chance of flooding here in late spring

- **Green Moon** — for the verdant foliage of the midwest

- **Damp Moon** — for those humid midwestern nights

- **Corn Moon** — for the August corn and grain harvest, principal crops of Indiana

- **Fire Moon** — descriptive of the blaze of autumn color which fires the local trees

- **Apple Moon** — for the abundant harvest season of the Indiana farmland

- **Feast Moon** — for the Thanksgiving season

While I was living in southern Texas I did not name my moons, but if I had they would have had an entirely different flavor:

- **Dark Moon** — for the dark days of Midwinter, even though the difference in the number of hours of light each day and dark each night is much less than it is farther north

- **Blue Norther Moon** — January is the time of the periodic Blue Norther, an arctic cold front that can drop temperatures by as much as forty degrees in less than an hour

- **Wet/Cool Moon** — winter in south Texas is usually more like a damp spring in other parts of the country

- **Calving Moon**— in honor of the spring calving which takes place on the many Texas ranches

- **Fiesta Moon** — for the spring fiestas, originally from Mexico, that are celebrated joyously in the region

- **Marriage Moon** — for the union of the Goddess and God at Bealtaine

- **Heat Moon** — in honor of Midsummer, when the hot southern sun reaches its highest point in the sky above, a time to celebrate the powers of both the light and the dark

- **Dry Wind/Dust Moon** — for the dry windy days that can blow in dust storms

- **Fire Moon** — the dryness and the intense heat always brings the risk of a brush fire or two

- **Cotton Moon** — in honor of the cotton harvest

- **Cyclone Moon** — named for the unpredictable hurricane season

- **El Muerte Moon** — the moon of death which falls near Samhain and the Mexican Day of the Dead

- **Coyote Moon** — the Native American trickster lives wild in south Texas and is symbolic of the great unknown as the year ends

If you do use or adopt these or other systems of named-moon months, your tradition probably dictates to a certain extent how they are to be added to your rituals. However, there is no law carved in stone which says you cannot be creative with the moon's energy. You may wish to add related items to the altar, tell a folktale about the moon which corresponds to its name, give to an organization which is involved with this aspect (i.e., a wildlife sanctuary for a month named for an animal), or invoke the title to get a real feel for its meaning. To do this simply concentrate your mind on the qualities of the name. See them forming like a ball suspended in front of you, then inhale and draw them in.

For instance, if this is your hunger moon, draw the qualities of hunger into yourself. Allow yourself to experience the chilling, weakening fear of starvation. Feel yourself a part of the world of our long-dead ancestors, who could not refill their larders in winter from a grocery store full of food. If supplies ran out, there simply was no more food until it could be hunted or grown in spring; none for your family, and none for livestock or pets. This exercise can give you a whole new understanding of why a certain moon got its name. If you wish to follow up your experience with a gift, there are many organizations that feed the hungry. They would love a donation of either time or money.

When you are done with the invoked energy, exhale it back into a ball floating in front of you, and mentally allow it to dissipate and become grounded harmlessly into the earth.

The Lunar Eclipse

A lunar eclipse occurs when the earth moves directly between the sun and the full moon, casting its shadow over her face. From the earth it appears as if the moon is being slowly consumed by the huge curved mouth of some giant heavenly beast. The word itself refers to that which is obscured or overshadowed, and comes from the Greek *ekleipsis*, meaning to "fail" or to "pass over."

Ancient people feared an eclipse and saw it as a bad omen, a time when the Gods were expressing their anger, threatening to take away the most visible, stable object known to early cultures. Long after science was able to explain the phenomenon, people the world over were still uneasy when their night light began to disappear before their watching eyes. In some folk legends an eclipse was conceptualized as the wolf of the heavens eating and then regurgitating the Lady of the sky. In others, it was seen as a great battle between the forces of good (light) and evil (darkness), and the outcome was always uncertain.

We modern Pagans know that there is no more evil in the darkness than in the light. We need both for balance and survival, but we can take those images of light and dark and make use of them in personal eclipse rituals.

If you are lucky enough to have a total eclipse happening on a night when you can watch it from beginning to end, you can use the energy to "eclipse" something you wish to eliminate from your life.

Before the moon begins to be eaten away, invest in it the essence of something of which you want to be rid. This can be a bad habit, a mountain of bills, something you dislike about your personal appearance, or anything else that plagues you. Just make sure that in eliminating this unwanted problem you will not be harming anyone or infringing on someone else's rights or free will.

Use the power of your mind to invest the problem in the moon by feeling all the hatred you have toward the problem, then mentally projecting it upward to the moon's surface. The more energy you pour into this preliminary effort, the more effective the spell will be. Stop projecting when you see the first sign that the shadow of the earth is falling over the lunar surface.

Watch as the moon, and your problem, is consumed by the great wolf of the heavens. Literally feel it being eaten out of your life.

At the moment when the moon's surface is completely obscured by shadow, utter words which confirm your belief that your problem is now gone. In the case of wanting to be rid of bills you might say:

> *Big Bad Wolf, scavenging in the night,*
> *Eating away the moonlight bright,*
> *Eating the scourge which once held me tight,*
> *I am free of my bills, I walk in the light.*
> *As I say, so do I see,*
> *By my will, So Mote It Be!*

Your words do not have to rhyme, but poetry, no matter how trite or silly, always makes us feel as if we have given an extra boost of power to the enchantment. Many old grimoires and experienced Witches recommend this practice.

As the shadow passes over the moon, revealing its light again, see this as symbolic of the new light of freedom from your difficulty shining on you.

The newly-emerging light at the end of the eclipse can also be used as a focal point for potent visualizations designed to help you uncover something that is hidden or is blocking some aspect of your life from moving onward. Imagery and visualization are the keys that unlock all magick. What single image has a more universal appeal to the psyche than light? Daily we speak of light chasing away shadows, illuminating the darkness, and bringing the light of a new day. When we catch on to a confusing concept or have a brilliant idea we say that we have "seen the light." When we have undergone a particularly tough experience we say that we can now "see the light at the end of the tunnel." The light of the newly emerged full moon can be tapped to work for us in the same way.

For example, if you are having trouble making a difficult decision, feel stuck in a dull routine, cannot overcome an illness, or cannot make your divination work on one particular question, you can spend the minutes when the shadow of the earth is falling over the moon in mentally sending the difficulty into the shadow. Visualize the blockage which surrounds you being lifted and sucked into the darkening sky. At the precise moment that the moon is completely engulfed by shadow, affirm to yourself that the blockage is gone. You may want to use words or a chant such as the one on the next page.

Gone, gone is the wall of constraint.
Here, now, a new dawn I do paint.

After the moon is completely uncovered, go to your divination device, your job search, your static relationship, or whatever else you felt was blocked, and see if you don't have a new perspective. If not, don't despair just because there won't be another total eclipse visible in your area for three more years. The feeling you experienced in this mini-rite will be fresh in your mind for some time. Simply call it to mind, putting into it all the emotion you used originally. Again, your imagery is the key to success.

You may also want to experiment with the unusual experience of having present the energies of the mother Goddess, symbolized in the full moon, as well as the crone Goddess, symbolized by the darkness of the total eclipse. This exercise can truly drive home the point that the Goddess with all her many names and faces is one.

This exercise works best if you can be outside, but it is not absolutely necessary. Sit under the full moon where you can see its light. You can view her from your own living room window if you like. Start about half an hour before the shadow of the earth will begin to fall across the surface. Allow yourself time to attune to the energies of the full moon and the loving mother Goddess. As the shadow begins to obscure the moonlight, allow yourself to feel the power of the crone that is manifest in all darkness. Yet, underneath the dark surface, know that the full moon still shines brightly. Only our own shadow hides her from sight, a shadow seen only from the perspective of the exact point in the universe where you now sit. Think of this as a metaphor for all the inner-blockages which sometimes prevent us from connecting with the Goddess.

As the shadow passes and the moon grows full and bright again, recall that behind the visage of every old crone is the heart of a young mother.

The Ceremony of Cakes and Ale

The Ceremony of Cakes and Ale is a very old lunar ritual, although the precise form we use today may date back no more than a few hundred years. Religions change and evolve with the people who practice them, and the rites we use today will probably be largely unrecognizable to people a few hundred years in the future.

Cakes and Ale involves the blessing and sharing of wine/ale or meade and bread or cake. In Paganism these symbolize several aspects of the Goddess and her world.

The concept that what one consumes will be made manifest is another old Pagan belief whose roots are buried deep in antiquity. People in many cultures used to consume parts of their felled warriors, enabling the dead to be reborn into their own clans or tribes. Native Americans would eat the heart of a brave animal they killed, in order to take on its characteristics and keep it propagating. In the Irish myth cycles we see the faery queen Edain consumed by Etar and reborn as a mortal child.

Symbolisms of Cake and Ale

Cake	Ale
matter	spirit
flesh	blood
earth	heavens
Underworld	Otherworld
earth plane	astral plane
stability	movement
physical body	astral body
action	thought
birth	conception

When we consume the Cakes and Ale offerings we take into ourselves a part the universal Goddess. We unite in ourselves the essences of spirit and matter. We can also look upon the bread as the earth Goddess and the ale as the blood of the God of the heaven whose life force will be spilled onto the earth each autumn so that life can continue for us. This last was a popular concept in Celtic and Briton society, where ritual regicides occurred on a regular basis.

Crescent and round cookies served with apple wine are
appropriate for hosting the Ceremony of Cakes and Ale

So deeply meaningful is this rite to the human psyche that virtually all religions have adopted some form of the ritual. The Jews offer special blessings over wine and bread as part of their Sabbath services. Christians observe communion, in which they invest the cake and ale with the essence of the blood and body of Jesus.

Because eating, like any bodily function, can be a significantly grounding act, it is usually performed just prior to the closing of the circle.

Meade, a honey ale from the Celtic traditions, is a traditional drink of the Esbats, but wines have also been used frequently. Meade, related to the Irish word *midhe,* meaning center, represents the spirit around which all life revolves. Connoisseurs of meade cultivate their brews as carefully as makers of fine wine, and jealously guard their secret recipes. There is even a meade society which tries to gather these recipes from around the world and preserve and publish meade lore.

The following is a much-simplified recipe for meade. I have made it public before because it is so easy to do; it eliminates the lengthy fermentation process. You can add grain alcohol or leave it out depending on your personal tastes.

SHORT CUT MEADE

½   gallon water
1½ cups raw honey
¼   cup lemon juice

⅛   teaspoon nutmeg
⅛   teaspoon allspice, rounded
½   cup Everclear or other
        grain alcohol

Slowly heat all ingredients together — except the alcohol — in a large stock pot. As the honey melts, an oily crust will form on the top of the meade. You can leave it there — some feel it adds to the full-bodied texture of the meade. Others will tell you to skim it off. Do not allow the meade to come to a roiling boil. When it is well blended, remove from the heat, stirring occasionally until it settles. When it has cooled, add the Everclear and serve.

New Pagans often question just what types of beverages can be used in this rite, especially those who prefer not to drink alcohol or who are not partial to meade. For non-alcohol substitutes you can use milk or egg nog, both lunar-associated foods, or some type of juice. Apple, grape, and cranberry are the most "lunar" of the choices available. In autumn, apple cider makes a timely substitute. Lemonade also works well, unless you deeply associate the color yellow with solar rites. Also remember that there is no rule which says you cannot use plain old water infused with the essence of the Goddess as your ale.

The following is a non-alcoholic egg nog recipe which you might like to try. Eggs, like the honey in meade, are deeply associated with the moon.

NO-COOK EGG NOG

12	pasteurized eggs, separated	⅛	teaspoon salt
1	lb. confectioner's sugar	1	teaspoon vanilla
2	quarts whipping cream	1	cup water
¾	teaspoon ground nutmeg	3	cups rich milk
			(evaporated or whole)

Mix the egg yolks, sugar, and salt together and let stand in the refrigerator overnight so that the flavors can "marry." Next day, beat the egg whites until they are just stiff, then mix them in with the rest of the ingredients until slightly thick. Serve chilled.

What we think of as being a cake, a sweet flour-and-sugar concoction, does not have to be used in the rite. In fact many Witches do not use this type of cake in their Esbat rituals, unless they are part of covens which will be celebrating a rite of passage along with the Esbat. These passages include, but are not limited to, birthdays, initiations, coming of age (spiritual adulthood), and handfasting (marriage).

For the cake you can use regular cake, but you can also use breads, rolls, donuts, sweet rolls, crackers, or cookies. Cookies, cut in the shape of crescent moons and decorated in lunar colors, are probably the most widely used cake. The crescent is the symbol of the moon in many traditions of Paganism as well as in astrology. It matters not that the moon is full; this symbol is instantly recognizable by most everyone — Pagan or not — as being related to things lunar.

Here are two recipes you might want to try using for your "cake." The first is a simple, but very flexible, sugar cookie recipe. The dough can be easily cut into crescent shapes.

LUNAR COOKIES

2	cups all-purpose flour	1½	teaspoons vanilla
¼	teaspoon ground nutmeg	1	beaten egg
⅛	teaspoon ground allspice	⅓	cup vegetable oil
1¼	teaspoons baking powder	¼	cup milk
¼	teaspoon salt		

Thoroughly mix all the dry ingredients and the oil together in a large mixing bowl. Beat all other ingredients together until they appear light and fluffy, then put them in the mixing bowl with the other mixture and stir them together. Set the mixture in the refrigerator to chill for at least two hours. If you can leave it overnight it will be easier to handle. When you are ready to roll out the dough, divide the chilled mixture into four equal sections. One section at a time, roll the dough out onto a generously-floured cutting board until it is about ⅛- inch thick. Cut out crescent shapes with a cookie cutter or sharp knife and place the cut-outs on an ungreased cookie sheet. Bake at 400° for 7–8 minutes. The cookies will be a bit stiff and will be starting to change to a very light golden color. Do not bake cookies until browned or they will become hard and brittle. Recipe makes about 2½ dozen.

Honey Cake is a dessert which Jews traditionally serve on their spiritual new year, Rosh Hashanna. In keeping with the old adage that "we are what we eat," they believe that sharing and eating this cake ensures all who partake a sweet and happy year to come. As mentioned before, honey is also associated with the moon.

HONEY CAKE

2½	cups flour	1¼	cups granulated sugar
½	teaspoon baking soda	½	cup safflower oil
2½	teaspoons baking powder	1	cup raw honey
1	heaping teaspoon allspice	1¼	cups unsweetened
¾	teaspoon ground cinnamon		orange juice
1	teaspoon ground ginger	2	cups raisins (optional)
⅛	teaspoon nutmeg	2	cups walnuts (optional)
4	beaten eggs		

Grease and flour a 9" x 13" baking pan. Combine all ingredients, stirring until they are well-mixed. Pour into the greased pan and bake for 45 minutes in an oven pre-heated to 350°. This cake is traditionally served unfrosted, but you can make a glaze for it with confectioner's sugar and orange juice. Drizzle the glaze over the cake while it is cooling.

Many books on Witchcraft offer visions and versions of this ancient ceremony. All are good and embrace the values of Paganism as well as those specific views of the tradition or writer who made them public. Below you will find two more for you to read and contemplate. These Cakes and Ale rituals can be used as they are, incorporated into the rituals you already use, adapted to personal taste, or worked into any other non-Esbat time when you wish to unite with and honor the divine in this manner.

A Solitary Ceremony of Cakes and Ale

Before beginning the main body of your ritual, have your cake and your ale, in whatever form you prefer, sitting on or near your altar. Open your circle in your usual manner and do all of your other Esbat ritual work first. When you are ready for the Cakes and Ale, center them on your altar. Stand before them with arms held upward and address the Goddess:

> *Blessed Mother of us all, I stand before this altar on this, the night of your full moon, when your energies drench your earth with the light of your pale, loving eyes, to offer you my love, my allegiance, and my blessings, and to reaffirm that I am your child. Tonight I will consecrate and consume the cake of your earth and the ale of your heavens, that I might carry your essence within me, that your love and will might be carried by me into the mundane world.*

Take a piece of the cake and hold it in your receptive hand (the non-dominant one, the hand you do not write with). If you are outdoors or near a window, allow the moonlight to wash over the cake.

> *Mother* (or insert the name of a moon or mother Goddess with whom you feel an affinity), *I thank you for the bounty of your earthly body which sustains me with food. From your womb flows all life and all manner of life's sustenance. Allow me to use this symbol to fill myself with your boundless presence. Be in and of me always.*

Eat a bite of the cake, then break off another small piece and hold it up in your power hand (the one you write with, the one that is dominant for you). You are going to give this portion as a libation, a traditional offering both to the Goddess and to the nature spirits and animals that may be nearby:

> *Though I am a solitary Witch, I know that I am never really alone in my honor of you. This bit of life-giving grain from your womb I give back to you now in humble thanksgiving for your many gifts of love. May you and your creatures of the wild partake and enjoy.*

If you are outdoors, set the libation of cake on the ground. If you are inside, have a plate ready to collect the offering so that you can place it outside later. Next, hold up the ale in your receptive hand. Again, if you are outdoors, allow the moonlight to reflect over its watery surface. Spend a moment watching the play of light on the wet surface:

> *Mother, I thank you for the mysteries of your watery realm which sustains my spirit and imagination, for this blood of your womb which brought forth all life. By your blood all living things are blessed and made sacred. Allow me to use this symbol to fill myself with your boundless presence. Be in and of me always.*

Take a sip of the ale, then transfer the receptacle into your power hand, saying:

Like a single drop of water blends in the great sea, I too am not alone. Like the single droplet, I am part of the ebb and flow of life, death, and life renewed. I am myself and also a part of the whole. These precious drops of life-giving water from your great womb I give back to you now in humble thanksgiving. May this symbol of your blood give life renewed to all who partake with pleasure.

If you are outdoors, pour a bit of the ale onto the ground near the cake. If you are inside, transfer the liquid into something that you can take outdoors later. Now take the ale receptacle in your receptive hand and the cake in your power hand and say:

Behold, the Triple Goddess is one! Maiden, Mother, and Crone. Earth and heaven are one! The womb and blood. I am one with them. I am the child of the Goddess. In me may she always be manifest.

Dip a piece of the cake into the ale and allow the cake to soak up some of the liquid. Think of the unity of the Goddess, of her earthly womb and heavenly blood being united inside you, ready for any acts of creation. Then eat a portion of the unified part. By doing so you are signifying your willingness to be a vessel for the manifest creative power of the Goddess as you leave your circle and move back into the mundane world. End your ritual with words such as:

Behold, I am Goddess. Behold, I am the Creative Principle. Behold, I am divinity. I am alone, yet I am one with all that is. I am a drop in the ocean and I am the tide which rises, falls, and rises again. The Triple Goddess is one. She lives in me. I live in her. Forever and Always. Merry Meet, Merry, Part, and Merry Meet Again. So Mote It Be!

You may now eat whatever portion of this mini-feast you wish, or you may simply sit quietly and meditate on the ritual you just performed. Afterwards, you are free to close your circle in your preferred manner.

A Ceremony of Cakes and Ale For Two or More Persons

Before beginning the main body of your ritual, have your cake and your ale, in whatever form you prefer, sitting on or near your altar. Open your circle in your usual manner and do all of your other Esbat ritual work first. When you are ready for the Cakes and Ale, appoint someone to center them on your altar.

The Leader of the rite, as chosen by the coven or grove, should stand before the altar with arms held upward and address the Goddess:

Leader:
> *Blessed Lady Goddess, mother of all life, we thank you on this night of your fullness for the bounty of your earthly body on which we stand. We offer you all the adoration that grateful children have to give.*

The members of the coven, moving clockwise around the circle, should call out offerings of praise for the group. The example below can be expanded or combined, or multiple parts assigned, so that all present can participate equally:

Coven Member #1:
> *We give you our love.*

Coven Member #2:
> *We give you our allegiance.*

Coven Member #3:
> *We give you our blessings.*

Coven Member #4:
> *We reaffirm that we are your children.*

Coven Member #5:
> *We affirm that you are our beloved Queen.*

Coven Member #6:
> *We acknowledge that we were born of you.*

When the complete circle has been made, the Leader motions for the coven members to gather closer to the altar:

Leader:
> *Tonight we consecrate and consume the cake of your earth and the ale of your heavens, that we might carry your essence within us, that your love and will might be carried by us into the mundane world. By this sharing we also tie tight the bonds which hold us together in spirit on the Old Path.*

Covenors:
> *Blessed Be the cake of the earth. Blessed Be the mother.*

The Leader takes a piece of the cake and holds it in his or her receptive hand. If your group is meeting outdoors or near a window, allow the moonlight to wash over the cake.

Leader:

> *Mother* (or insert the name of a moon or mother Goddess with whom your group feels an affinity or regularly worships), *we gratefully thank you for the bounty of your earthly body which sustains all creation with the fruit of your being. From your womb flows all life and all manner of life's sustenance. Allow us to use this symbol to fill ourselves with your boundless presence. Be in and of us always, as a mother is part of her child.*

The Leader eats a small bite of the cake, then breaks off another small piece and holds it up in his or her power hand. You are going to give this portion as a libation, a traditional offering both to the Goddess and to the nature spirits and animals who may be nearby. The cake is then passed clockwise around the circle so that all covenors can partake. As each member passes it on something should be said to the effect of:

Covenor passing bread:

> *From one to another we are all linked. The bread sustains all life. It is in the giving and taking of sustenance that we continue the sacred, never-ending chain of life. Eat hearty, my sister* (or brother).

When the cake is returned to the Leader, he or she places it back on the altar and takes a piece which s/he holds up:

Leader:

> *Blessed Be this coven, the microcosm of the Triple Goddess. We now stand in a world between all points of time and space. This bit of life-giving grain from your eternal womb we give back to you now in humble thanksgiving. May you and your creatures of the wild partake and enjoy.*

All:

> *Blessed Be!*

If you are outdoors, set the libation of cake on the ground. If you are inside, have a plate ready to collect the offering so that you can place it outside later.

Next, the Leader holds up the ale in his or her receptive hand. Again, if you are outdoors, allow the moonlight to reflect off its watery surface. Spend a moment observing the play of light on the liquid:

Leader:

> *Mother, we thank you for the mysteries of your watery realm; they sustain our spirit and our imagination. This is the blood of your womb, which brought forth all life. By your blood all living things are blessed and made sacred. Through it all things are born, and by it we shall all return to you. Allow us to use this symbol to fill ourselves with your boundless presence. Be in and of us always.*

Covenors:
> *Blessed Be the blood of the heavens. Blessed Be the mother.*

The Leader takes a sip of the ale, then transfers the receptacle to his or her power hand, saying:

Leader:
> *As single drops of water blend in the great sea, we are not alone. We are a small pool, part of the ebb and flow of the vast sea of cycles, of life, death, and life renewed. These precious drops of life-giving water from your great womb we give back to you now in humble thanksgiving. May this symbol of your blood give life renewed to all who partake with pleasure.*

The chalice is then passed clockwise around the circle so that all covenors can partake. Each member should be free to honor the Goddess with the cup in his or her own way. Remember that there are many reasons one might not wish to drink from a communal cup; those reasons should be respected. Also, a member of your group may be a recovering alcoholic who does not want to drink spirits, or may be dangerously allergic to the sulfides used to preserve wine (sulfides have landed me in an emergency room more than once). Each member should offer some personal honor to the Goddess. This gesture can take many forms. A portion of the fluid can be poured on the ground or it can be drunk. Someone else might wish to kiss the cup or lift it heavenward. Another might wish to speak a line or two by way of a special toast. All will be honoring the Goddess in ways that are meaningful (and safe) for them. These personal choices should always be respected. As each member passes the cup on, something should be said to the effect of:

Covenor passing chalice:
> *From one to another we are all linked. The blood of the Goddess was the first sea in which we all swam when our lives began, and it will be to her we all return when this cycle ends. In the sharing of this blood we affirm that we are all brothers and sisters in the never-ending chain of life linking one to the other, moon after moon, generation after generation, forever and always.*

When the chalice returns to the Leader, he or she should pour a bit of the ale onto the ground near the cake. If you are inside, transfer the liquid into something you can take outdoors later.

The Leader should dip a piece of the cake into the ale. Allow the cake to soak up some of the liquid:

Leader:
> *Behold the unity of the Goddess. She is all, and she is one. May her earthly womb and heavenly blood be united and manifest in us, ready always for any and all acts of positive creation.*

The Leader should eat a portion of the unified part.

Covenors:

Behold, the Goddess is all. The Lady is one.

Leader:

By this act of union we are signifying our willingness to be vessels for the manifest creative power of the Goddess as we leave our sacred circle this night and move back into the mundane world.

All covenors should approach the altar one at a time and take turns dipping a piece of the cake in the ale and eating it (again, providing they wish to consume the wine). As they eat, or make any other honorary gesture they see fit, they should verbally acknowledge the meaning of the act with any brief words they may choose.

When everyone is back in his or her place, the Leader turns inward, facing the center of the circle like the rest of the coven:

Leader:

Behold, the moon is full. The Triple Goddess is one!
Maiden, Mother, and Crone.

Everyone, including the Leader, now turns facing outward:

All:

Earth and heaven are one! The womb and blood. The earth and the heavens. And we are one with them. We are the children of the Goddess. In us may she always be manifest.

Leader:

From this sacred space we will return to the mundane world. Hopefully we will leave wiser and more loving, like the mother we honor here tonight. She lives in us. We live in her. Forever and Always. So Mote It Be!

Covenors:

So Mote It Be!

Everyone turns inward again and joins hands:

Leader:

Merry meet.

Covenors:

Merry part.

All:

And merry meet again.

Leader:

    In the name of our blessed Lady and Lord ...

All:

    Blessed Be!

Drawing Down the Moon

Invocation, the act of bringing divine energy into a human vessel, has always played a leading role in Esbat celebrations. Whether one is a solitary or part of a coven, the popular and ancient ritual known as Drawing Down the Moon is always a central part of the festival. In this rite the spirit of the mother Goddess, who is represented by the full moon, is invoked into a physical body — usually that of a high priestess or some other female. While the essence of the divine is present in the woman she can lead the coven ritual, speak for the Goddess, and channel magick with increased efficiency.

The companion ritual to Drawing Down the Moon, Drawing Down the Sun, is less well-known, and usually takes place at solar festivals (i.e., the Sabbats). This energy is almost exclusively channeled into the body of a high priest or another male.

In recent years feminist Witches have attempted to reclaim the image of the old sun Goddesses and have increasingly drawn the almost forgotten feminine side of the sun into themselves. Yet Pagans of both sexes tend to balk at the idea that a man should be able to successfully accomplish the same thing with the forgotten masculine side of the moon.

While it is somewhat understandable that women, who have so long been shut out of the inner-circles of religious power, should want to keep this single event to themselves, it boggles the mind that men would not want to share in this potent energizing rite.

There is no reason why a man should feel excluded from the practice of Drawing Down the Moon. As mentioned in the Introduction, nearly all cultures gave the moon a masculine face before her relationship to women's cycles was recognized. As Pagans, we supposedly subscribe to the idea that power is just power, waiting to be characterized and used by the magician. So why can't our heavenly bodies be treated in the same manner?

For male solitaries experimenting with lunar energy, this rite should become even more important. A solitary man is usually taught to call down the moon Goddess to his circle, or perhaps into his chalice, but never into his own body. She is present, her loving energy captured in a pool of moon-drenched water, but he is not able to experience what it is like to become a part of her.

Granted, we may not be able to fully experience rites that have been deeply associated with the opposite sex, simply because humanity has, for centuries, collectively placed many heavy layers of gender identity on them. But both men and women can gain some new insights and have some success with either Drawing Down experience.

Men who want to experiment with the practice can begin by getting to know more about the ancient moon Gods. Start by reading the list of moon deities in Appendix A; find one with whom you feel a connection. Then head for your nearest library or bookstore and search through books on mythology and folklore for more detailed information. Be warned; these myths can be hard to find. Our society so loves to compartmental-ize everything so that even the most mainstream person thinks of the moon as being wholly feminine and the sun as wholly masculine. Women who have searched for specific information on sun Goddesses have faced this same dearth of resources.

The next step would be to take the solitary Ceremony of Cakes and Ale and create one based upon it which honors both the moon God and Goddess. This would require no more than the addition of foods to represent the masculine elements of fire and air, to be consecrated in the same manner as the cake and ale. For fire foods, you might wish to try those which are red, yellow, or orange/gold in color, like oranges, tomatoes, or lemons. Hot and spicy foods made with curry or cayenne also conjure up fiery images. For air you might want to go for the light and frothy, like mousse or whipped cream dyed a lunar color.

When you feel comfortable with the idea that the moon also has a masculine energy, you can take your favorite Esbat ritual and rewrite the Drawing Down the Moon rite to accommodate your alternative perspective and bring down the moon God with whom you have built a relationship.

If you work within a coven don't be surprised if you meet some resistance to what your fellow covenors might feel is very unorthodox behavior. If you can't reach an agree-ment with them you might want to compromise; offer a step-by-step method to intro-duce the idea that men can carry within themselves the power of a moon deity. For instance, start by allowing your priestess to draw a moon deity down into you. By using her as a channel for the moon God/dess you will bridge somewhat the gap of mental resistance in the group mind. Later on, you can try a ritual where a man draws the God/dess into another man.

Women will likely be your greatest opponents, but you might be able to win them over by offering to reverse the situation at the next Sabbat; allow a priest to draw the essence of a sun God/dess into a woman.

For both sexes it is best to begin your experiment by using the image of a sun Goddess (for women) and moon God (for men). This helps bridge the gender gap in a way that makes it easier to take the first step. Later you can begin to fully invoke the essence of a deity of the opposite sex.

Although I am a die-hard feminist at heart, I see only good coming out of this shar-ing of invocation rites. It can do nothing but create an atmosphere of greater under-standing and empathy between the sexes. Deep within our psyches we all have attributes that are both masculine and feminine. In order to be sane, balanced, and whole, I believe we must acknowledge and honor both aspects.

The next chapter offers sample Esbat rituals that use both males and females as ves-sels for the moon's divine energy.

Lunar Correspondences

As with everything else in Paganism, there is a list of correspondences of animals and objects which resonate with the energy of the moon. These can be used to help you align with her by focusing on them or by placing them around your altar as decorations.

The two most important lunar correspondences are the number nine and the metal silver. Nine has been the numerical correspondence for the moon since at least the medieval period when the Kaballists (students of Judeo-Christian mysticism) assigned it to the sephira (the conceptual realm) of Yesod (the moon) on the Tree of Life. It is the natural multiple of three which represents the three faces of the moon: maiden, mother, and crone. Like the Triple Goddess, it was a number which always magickally comes back to itself over and over again. As such, it is a symbol of creative power and energy of the moon Goddess.

To test the theory for yourself, multiply any number by nine, add the digits of the resulting sum, and you will get nine again. It will never fail. For example, multiply 2 x 9 and the result is 18. Break apart the 1 and 8, add them together, and again you get 9. Multiply 5 x 9; you get 45, and again, 4 plus 5 is 9.

As a lunar symbol, the precious metal we call silver probably pre-dates the similar use of the number nine. It was assigned to the shiny Lady in the sky just as gold was likened to the sun. Hence, silver became a feminine symbol associated with the oceans, tides, and the moon Goddess. Witches often wear silver jewelry at Esbat celebrations; in some covens it is a requirement.

Page 27 presents a more extensive list of moon correspondences. You will find many uses for these in magick and in altar decorations, and you will see references to them when you study the folkstories and faery tales of the past, where much Pagan lore was hidden to preserve and protect it from the Witch hunters.

Unconventional Ways of Honoring the Lady

Never underestimate the power of the full moon to inspire frivolity and mayhem in the hearts of Pagan and non-Pagan alike, and don't ever feel that if you cannot hold your ritual on the exact night of the full moon, or if you have no Pagan group with whom to work, you are cut off from meaningful ways to honor the Lady.

One of my most cherished full moon memories goes back several years to when I was employed as a long-distance telephone operator, working the night shift. On this night our calls were sparse, as well as strange, and there weren't too many of us left on staff by midnight. The Thanksgiving decorations had been trashed earlier that day to make way for the Christmas glitter and, being bored, the woman in the next cubicle and I pulled the sad and torn things from the trash can and taped them up all over our work stations. She then pointed out that the moon was full so, quite naturally, that must be to blame for the unusually bizarre calls we were receiving.

The supervisors strolling past admired our silly collage, which soon segued into a running joke about the new reindeer decorations that all had the appearance of being drunken dogs with antlers.

Deciding there was more to celebrate here than the calendar alone could tell, the woman and I decided to include HAPPY FULL MOON notices on our salvaged decor.

The capricious spirit of the Esbat spread rapidly through the operator center and soon everyone — the bosses included — were wearing the cast-off decorations as

Moon Correspondences

Stones/Minerals
Amethyst
Aquamarine
Beryl
Bloodstone
Geode
Lodestone
Mother of Pearl
Moonstone
Olivine
Pearl
Sapphire
Selenite
Silver
Tourmaline
White Chalcedony

Miscellaneous
Breasts
Colors Purple and White
Cotton
Crescents
Glass
Heart Symbols
Horns
Hanukkah Menorah
Mirrors
Moths
Numbers 3 and 9
Star of David
Stomach
Water Wells
Women

Food/Drink
Ale
Apple
Butter
Carob
Cheese, White
Coconut
Eggs
Honey
Ice Cream
Lettuce
Meade
Melon
Milk/Cream
Mushroom
Passion Fruit
Pomegranate
Potatoes
Pumpkin
Turnips/Tubers
Yogurt
Water
Wine

Animals
Canines, Wild
Cow
Crow
Felines, All
Groundhog
Hen
Hare
Horned Animals, Most
Horse
Nightingale
Nighthawk
Opossum
Owl
Raven

Flowers/Herbs
Aloe
Blueberry
Camellia
Camphor
Eucalyptus
Heather
Irish Moss
Jasmine
Lily
Lily of the Valley
Lotus
Magnolia
Meadowsweet
Milkwort
Moonwort
Pine
Poppy
Roses, All
Sandalwood
Wintergreen
Wormwood

Trees
Apple
Birch
Blackthorn
Dogwood
Hawthorn
Lemon
Maple
White Ghost Gum
Willow

crowns, broaches, and anything else that could be made from them. The foreign language board, whose purpose was to notify us which languages were available to callers, began to read like a "special of the day" advertisement: *French, Russian, Thousand Island*. Between calls we drew moons on all our accouterments, made werewolf jokes, and entertained extremely unprofessional anti-boredom devices such as doing "The Wave."

Although I was stuck at work with non-Pagans, that night was one of the most delightful Esbats I ever experienced. It was even more special to me because the mini-celebration grew spontaneously, and in it I could actually see the Lady pouring her mischievous magick over all of us.

Even if you are a solitary with no contact whatsoever with other Pagans, you can find many creative ways to celebrate the Lady that include others, but are not offensive to anyone else's religious beliefs. In fact few, if any, of your friends even have to know why you feel compelled to throw a MOON PARTY.

I have always loved books. As a very young girl, one of my favorites was a storybook adventure in which the Hanna-Barbera cartoon characters were trying to fly to the moon. Huckleberry Hound led the group, which included such luminaries as Yogi Bear, Boo Boo, and Quick-Draw McGraw, in the building of a rocket that would fly the group to the moon and back. They built their contraption on a mountaintop with the aid of several friendly mountain goats, animals which, incidentally, are symbolic of the God. The night before take-off the characters held a lunar party, complete with crescent moon decorations, moon-shaped food, and a decor of muted lunar colors.

The image of that moon party has always fascinated me. When I came to Paganism, I realized just how great an idea such a gathering would be for a solitary Witch, or for anyone else who wanted to put a new spin on an old idea. Covens could also use the idea for open gatherings when they were trying to introduce their families and friends to their spirituality.

Pick a night for your party when the moon is full. Send out invitations which simply state that you are having a Moon Party to honor the moon. Make the invitation as intriguing as possible. People are always looking for new ways to celebrate anything and everything and will probably be curious as to just what a moon party will entail. See the sample invitation on page 29 to glean ideas for creating your own.

The next step is to decide whether your party will be outdoors or indoors. Then plan your decor. Add as many lunar symbols as possible, both Pagan and secular, that can be easily related to by all present. Several years ago I discovered that an old Hanukkah Menorah, the nine-branched candelabrum used for the celebration of the Jewish Festival of Lights, makes a great moon-centered item. It has nine branches, the number most often associated with the moon, and a Star of David, the six-pointed star which, although today it symbolizes the Jewish religion, is probably the very oldest symbol of the creator in existence. It is the union of the four alchemical symbols for the elements — although the occult science of alchemy post-dates the origin of the Star of David.

Candles in white, purple, or silver provide a festive touch, as do shiny silver ornaments. Stars created to top Christmas/Solstice trees can also be gotten out and used, as can strands of holiday lights, particularly in lunar colors. Or you may want to adopt a color scheme of white, red, and black, the colors of the Triple Goddess from the Celtic and English traditions.

Pucker Your Lips and Come Howl With Us

Saturday, March 5
7:30 p.m. until ???

at the home of

Mark Greenwood and Edain McCoy

Why?

Because it's the night of the

FULL MOON

(Do we need any other reason?)

Feast on Lunar Lemon Pies, bay with the Wild Coyotes, let
Loretta the Gypsy Witch Queen peer into your future, and
imbibe the authentic and highly intoxicating
Twinkle Moon Punch,
the official drink of the mysterious Twinkie People of Luna 9
(perhaps served to you by an authentic intoxicated Twinkie or Twinkette)

Bring a date, your imagination, and
any friendly aliens you meet on the way.

Remember, the Moon is full and anything
—*ANYTHING*—
can (and probably will) happen!

Moon-Madness-Inspired Costumes Optional

Example of a flyer or invitation for a Full Moon Celebration.

You can cut out cardboard crescents and hang them about the room or yard. This was done in the Huckleberry Hound book, and is still the most vivid visual image I have of the story.

The menu can be fun, too. You may want to make a lunar punch in moon-oriented colors, or use cream drinks. Look at the list of food correspondences earlier in this chapter to find other edibles ruled by the lunar light.

You can also make non-moon-corresponding foods that you creatively tailor to have a moonish appearance. Frost a cake with silver icing, shape or cut hor d'oeuvres into crescent shapes, or pock-mark other foods to look like lunar "craters." As crazy as it sounds, all the effort will add to the atmosphere and greatly amuse your guests.

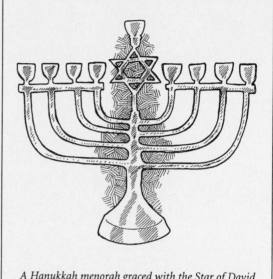

A Hanukkah menorah graced with the Star of David (also called the Seal of Solomon) makes a deeply fulfilling Pagan symbol of the moon. Its nine branches represent the lunar number nine, and the star is one of the oldest symbols of the creator/creatrix known to humanity.

You may also wish to adopt a theme with a moon-orientation, such as a wolf theme. Make "howling at the moon" the central activity. Or adopt a theme of moon-madness and allow the unexpected and bizarre to be the hallmark of the event. You can even make the event a costume party with moon overtones. Dress as a moon Goddess, a Witch (how hard could that be?), a ghost, a wolf, an owl, a silver-painted alien, etc. Or display your wit by coming as a lunatic, a common English label for someone who is insane, derived from the Latin word *luna,* meaning "moon."

In order to please as many people as possible you should also include the regular party activities that your particular crowd enjoys, such as music, dance, and good conversation. You can add moon fun by telling scary moon stories, similar to telling Halloween ghost stories. You can relate moon myths that might interest your friends, or play "pin the crater on the moon."

If you are a science fiction buff you might show old movies about "moon men" or tell stories about invasions from the moon. Ask everyone to come dressed in their own conceptions of a moon person. The decor can be taken straight from the pages of the corniest sci-fi novel you ever read.

The full moon is related to that which is hidden; therefore it has become the symbol for diverse occult practices, especially divination and other psychic work. Everyone loves a free fortune-telling, even if they feel it is only in fun. Set yourself or a Pagan friend up as the local Gypsy Witch, and have a go at all takers. You might surprise your guests as well as yourselves with your divinatory accuracy.

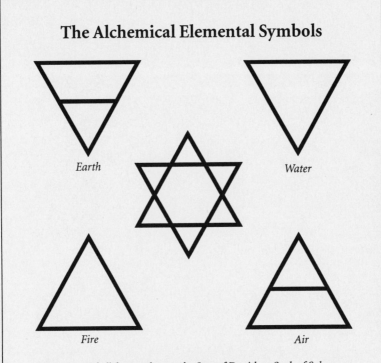

The Alchemical Elemental Symbols

Earth

Water

Fire

Air

The union of all four makes up the Star of David, or Seal of Solomon, one of the oldest symbols of the Creator.

Your own creativity is what will make your moon party an interesting and enjoyable event, one that your family and friends will look forward to repeating.

The Goddess too will no doubt be pleased with your efforts. Remember always that the word Esbat means "to frolic." She likes to see her children happy in her moment of fullness. We are all the sons and daughters of this joyful mother of life.

Two Esbat Rituals

They dined on mince, and slices of quince,
Which they ate with a runcible spoon;
And hand in hand, on the edge of the sand,
They danced by the light of the moon,
The moon,
The moon.
They danced by the light of the moon.
　　　　　— Edward Lear, *The Owl and the Pussycat*

Two complete full-moon rituals are presented in this chapter, one for solitaries and another for groups. Whether you are alone, with a large group, or part of a Pagan twosome, you will need to prepare for your Esbat ritual by gathering your tools and arranging them on your altar in your regular working spot. Working outdoors is nice if you can be assured of quiet and privacy, but there is also nothing wrong with holding rituals indoors. Sometimes this is even for the best. For instance, when it is excessively cold you cannot possibly concentrate all your energies on the task at hand. Stay warm indoors and trust that the moon's energy can penetrate even the thickest walls.

Gather all of your equipment beforehand, including items you will need for any spellwork you intend to do. Lay everything out on your altar in whatever manner your tradition or your own inner-sense of direction tells you is right. Don't forget to bring the food and drink for the Ceremony of Cakes and Ale. Once the circle is cast it should not be broken to run after the things you have forgotten. Such disorganization will not only spoil the effect you want inside the circle, but will drain off much of the power you are trying to raise.

If you are new to the Craft and still unfamiliar with ritual/magickal tools and the methods and purpose of circle-casting, a brief introduction will be provided in this chapter. You should also seriously consider delving into books that focus solely on Pagan ritual, in order to fully understand what you are trying to do with your rites and how it is to be accomplished. If you can find a book written from the perspective of the particular tradition you wish to follow, all the better. Centuries of experimentation have taught us what usually works best, although there is leeway (especially for the solitary) for unique interpretation. Also take a look at Chapter 13, which discusses the art of ritual in more depth.

Esbat rituals follow this basic form:

1. Casting the circle

2. Calling the quarters, elementals, or watchtowers, and doing other preliminary work

3. Statement of purpose and blessing of the moon Goddess

4. Inviting the Goddess and/or God to the circle

5. Aligning with the energy of the full moon and her deities

6. Acknowledgement of any specific energies given to this month's moon by your tradition or by your own choice

7. Seasonal poetry, songs, etc., to honor the God/dess

8. Drawing Down the Moon

9. Receiving a message from the invoked deity

10. Working any magick needed, or using guided meditations to align with the God/dess

11. Sending out the cone of power

12. Releasing the invoked God/dess

13. The Ceremony of Cakes and Ale

14. Dismissing the quarters and other beings called to the circle

15. Closing the circle

Everyone approaches lunar rites in a slightly different frame of mind and with varying expectations. Every person's concept of the exact purpose of his or her Esbat ritual is slightly different, and every individual and coven will want to add their own touches. Therefore, within this framework literally thousands and thousands of possibilities for Pagan spiritual expression can be explored. This is as it should be. The way you align yourself with the lunar energies, the magick you wish to do, and the deities you wish to call upon all make your rituals uniquely your own, and stir your spirit in meaningful ways which nothing dictated by others can ever match.

The Pagan Altar

The first "tool" of Witchcraft is the altar. The altar is the center and grounding point of your rites, the axis around which they revolve. The word "altar" comes from the Greek *altare* meaning "high place." When moved into our circle it becomes the resting place of the divine energies that are present in ritual. On a more practical level, an altar is a place to neatly and safely lay out needed tools and other equipment where they are easily within reach.

An altar does not have to be a fancy invention, just functional. It can be round, square, or rectangular, tall, squat, or tiered. You may create it from a large flat boulder, a special cloth spread on the ground, an inverted box, or from a table or dresser top. What you choose is not as important as how it works for you. Find something of a size and shape with which you are comfortable, then consider any mundane functions or origins that might color your feelings about its use as a sacred spot. In my private rituals I use a small occasional table that was handcrafted by my great-grandfather. Although he probably would not have whole-heartedly approved of my choice of religion, I nonetheless feel a connection to the many ancestors who came before me when I use this tangible link to the past as a resting place for my tools. On the other hand, if you know that a table has been used for a purpose that strikes you as negative, whether anyone else would agree or not, don't use it. The association you have with this altar will shade your consciousness during your ritual and interfere with your higher purpose.

Set your altar inside the area where your circle will be cast. You can orient it to whichever direction you like. Often this is dictated to you by a specific tradition stating that such-and-thus is the best way to arrange an altar for a certain ritual. Choosing an orientation from personal taste is fine, too. You may prefer to have your altar facing the moon, but remember that the moon travels swiftly across the night sky and, if you orient your altar to her at the beginning of your ritual, she may be significantly out of physical alignment by the time you are finished.

Ritual Tools of the Craft

While ritual/magickal forms and methods remain virtually identical from tradition to tradition, ritual tools and the directions, elements, and attributes associated with them can vary greatly.

The purpose of any ritual tool is twofold: first, it aids in the direction and projection of the energy that the Witch has raised, and second, the presence of specific items representing all the elements creates an energy balance within the circle. These elements were believed for many millennia to be the basic building blocks of all things, both in thought form and physical form.

The familiar ritual tools we know in Paganism today came into Witchcraft in the very late Middle Ages through Pagan contact with Ceremonial Magick. This type of magick, based upon Judeo-Christian mysticism, involves the use of tools, called elemental weapons, to manipulate and control elements and discarnate intelligences summoned to the edge of the astral plane to meet the magician.

Before the advent of elaborate ritual tools, Witches probably used only what could be found in nature — stones, bonfires, twigs, etc. — as catalysts for focusing energy and intent in magickal and ritual experiences. Exactly which objects these old Pagans used and how they used them is a mystery likely never to be solved. We do know that the tools of the craft today have been around for several hundred years and work very well

An Esbat Altar

for many of us. The symbolic associations make sense to the modern mind as we seek to capture a fragment of an ancient religious practice.

However, not every tool speaks in the same voice to all. Different traditions have adopted different sets of tools. Some paths adopt tools based on cultural associations (example: using a torch instead of a candle to represent the element of fire), others use mythology or personal tastes, and others prefer the stark simplicity of that which is found in nature. Some traditions dictate to the Witch what tools should be used and how they should be arranged on the altar, but the Witch is always free to use his or her personal choices when alone. Some eclectic covens allow members to bring their own tools for the elements and lay them out together on a large altar wherever the one who owns them feels they should be.

Unfortunately, these divisions in ideology have separated more Pagans by petty bickering than they have brought together in honor of the old Gods. The diversity that is world spirituality seems to have that contrary effect on people who are otherwise quite rational and open-minded in their dealings with others. The bickering is especially evident where the elements of air and fire are involved. One tradition sees a sword as slicing through the air and thus an air-related item; another sees the steel forged in fire and so uses it to represent the element of fire.

Today, many Pagans — both covens and solitaries — use some sort of ritual tools to represent the four directions (also called "quarters" or "watchtowers") and their corresponding attributes. Read as much as you can about the various tools. Try to get a feel for each tool and why someone once assigned it to a particular element. If you do not already have personal tools, don't rush out to buy them. You might be able to find perfectly good substitutes. For example, a pointed finger can direct energy with just as much power as a ritual knife, perhaps more, since it is intimately a part of you. Spend time reflecting on just what you really need and want before making a costly decision.

Rest assured that there is no right or wrong where tools are concerned. The only question is what one tradition or individual feels is best for it/him/herself. All tool/directional/elemental associations work if the Witch using them believes they do. Belief is the foundation upon which all successful magick is built.

Below is a list of some of the many items that have been used to represent each element. Some are listed twice because various traditions classify them differently. The direction representing each element varies so greatly from one tradition to the next that no attempt will be made here to give those attributes, which are decided upon by means as diverse as weather patterns, mythological associations, and astrological phenomena. The elements, although they are often assigned different symbols and directions, have virtually the same general meanings and attributes in all the many traditions of modern Witchcraft.

Water (feminine) — Water is the realm of the psychic, the dream world and inner-space. Its energy is related to children and/or childbirth, pregnancy, art, inner-transformation, divination, purification, the emotions, healing, romantic love, manifesting, death and rebirth, past-lives and new beginnings. Some of the tools associated with water are: wine goblets, water, wine, meade, ale, rings, wine casks, barrels, silver, shields, hollow coconuts, buckets, cauldrons, eggs, dried apples, chalices, cups, pans, teakettles, mugs, pitchers, bowls, hollow horns, holey stones.

Earth (feminine) — Earth is the realm of stability, growth, germination, and the eternal mother Goddess. It is related to fertility, prosperity, grounding and centering, money, dance, motherly love, planting and harvesting, the home, and pets and livestock. Some of the tools associated with earth are: disks, shields, wood, carved wood blocks (pentacles), stones, clay, bowls of rich earth, salt, gemstones, thick tree branches, the double-headed axe, green plants, wheels, sewing equipment, crystals, the pentagram, drums, necklaces, clubs, tree bark, herb roots, drums, bronze, bows, breads, whole grains, fruit, gold coins, currency.

Air (masculine) — Air is the unpredictable realm of the mind as characterized by the phrase "the winds of change". It is related to the intellect, study, travel, writing, electronics, communication, the astral realm, music and sound, weather magick, and power-raising. Some of the tools associated with air are: staffs, tridents, stangs (two-forked tridents), athames (ritual knives), wands, swords, feathers, incense, slingshots, pikes, single-headed axes, picks, spear and javelins, daggers, earrings, leaves, small twigs, nests, wind instruments, smoking pipes, copper, arrows.

Fire (masculine) — Fire is the realm of physical and psychic transformation, and of passion. It is related to protection, exorcism and banishing, sex and sex magick, work, purification, masculine power, personal energy and strength, and all ritual fires and candle magick. Some of the tools associated with fire are: candles, balefires (ritual bonfires), blades forged in flames, wands, red or orange stones, pikes, matches, flint, ashes, wheels, torches, bracelets, solar disks (made from the symbol of an equal-armed cross), besoms (brooms), gold, spears, obsidian.

Spirit (no gender association) — A fifth element is spirit, most often called by its Vedic Indian name, *akasha*. Spirit is in and of all the other elements. It transcends and supports them. In Native American traditions spirit is always honored in the direction of "above." Pagans often conceptualize it as the unifying force animating all other elements. The Germanic equivalent of *akasha* is *aether*, used in Teutonic Paganism, and more and more often in Celtic circles.

Protecting and Containing Your Ritual Energy

When a Witch is within the confines of a cast circle, he or she stands at the very center of the universe, a place apart from the known world, poised in a space that stands "between the worlds." Inside the circle the Witch can easily reach out into the unseen realm and use the energy produced there to manifest desired outcomes in the mundane world.

All magick and ritual, no matter how simple and short, should be done inside the protective walls of a circle. This is not only a magickal tradition of great antiquity, but also common sense. From ancient times this symbol of eternity and completeness has been utilized for protection and containment. Although the circle is cast mentally and therefore exists on what we think of as the astral plane, it creates a true and solid, physical outer barrier that unwanted energies, which may be attracted to the high vibrations of your working, cannot cross. It also serves as an inner barrier, preventing the energy you are working so hard to raise from leaking out before you are ready to release it to its intended purpose.

Some new Witches ignore the emphasis on using a well-cast circle, particularly when they are attempting a short ritual or simple spell. The habit becomes ingrained, and they continue to work without one. The novice's self-confidence increases each time a ritual or spell is completed without any ill effects. This lulls the new Witch into a false sense of security. As the novice improves in the skills of visualization and energy raising, his or her higher inner-vibrations — a resonance increasingly in tune with the energy of the astral world — will attract an increasing number of entities to feed upon that energy. This draining of your power will diminish the efficacy of your spells at best, and at worst could cause you psychic harm.

When I was a novice, my primary working partner was my best friend, Avigail, also a newcomer to the Craft. While we did not completely ignore the process of casting a circle, we went about it in a very haphazard manner, anxious to get to the "real stuff."

Everything went along fine for us in our bumbling attempts, until we decided to try a scrying divination exercise we had read about. We went out to a wooded area, cleared it of prickly cactus and broken glass, then plopped down some seating pads and our bowl of inky water. In our usual haste to get started, we took some basil and tossed it about us in a rough approximation of a circle. Then we sat down to scry.

The two of us were so close and so in tune with one another that it never took long for things to happen when we forced our collective will. We had not been at the scrying too long when the telltale white clouds formed over the bowl, telling us the exercise was working. Neither one of us allowed our eyes or concentration to leave the center of the bowl, but I was very aware of Avigail sitting across the "circle" from me.

Then I thought I saw something. I expected it to be a picture or a symbol forming inside the bowl, which is how scrying works. But as I watched I saw a hideous, mis-shapen hand, the details of which I have tried to forget over the years, reaching up out of the bowl, like the product of some B-rate horror writer's distorted imaginings. As stunned as I was, I didn't break my focus, and decided that it must not really be there because I could sense no reaction from Avigail. In another minute or so, the horrible thing retracted back into the depths of the bowl and the clouds vanished.

I don't know who mentioned this disturbing vision first, myself or Avigail, but even-tually the story came out, both of us adding enough detail to convince the other that we had seen exactly the same thing.

Neither one of us has experienced anything like that again, nor have we ever ana-lyzed it beyond the knowledge that we conjured up some sort of lower astral being. All we knew then was that our protection was sadly lacking, and that the consequences of our stupidity could have been quite serious. I am thankful that our calmness, born solely of ignorance, did not mutate into panic, for fear is a nutritious food on which lower astral creatures thrive and grow.

Practice, and good teachers, taught us better habits. We eventually learned that the preliminaries to any ritual are just as important as the ritual itself, not only for protec-tion, but to start pushing all the right inner buttons, alerting the deep mind that a pro-found change is about to take place.

A circle should not be broken once it is cast, although some traditions allow the cut-ting of an opening in the energy field with an athame, which allows one to pass safely through. However, unless it is absolutely necessary, it is best not to move in and out of the circle once it is in place. Frustratingly enough, animals and small children seem to be able to move freely across a circle's perimeter without ever disturbing the energy or risk-ing harm to themselves or others. This may be attributed to the fact that children, like animals, have not learned to divide their thinking into the supposed spheres of real and unreal. Children naturally see all types of psychic phenomena and are quite comfortable with them, until society teaches them otherwise.

To cast your circle you should first select a tool to help you. Or you may choose instead to use your forefinger or even the palm of your hand. Stand quietly for a moment in what will be the center of your circle, first making sure that all the things you will need for your ritual or spell are present. When you are ready, raise your arms skyward and feel yourself filling with spiritual energy. Walk to the edge of your circle (begin at any point you or your tradition chooses) and point your finger, tool, or palm at the ground. You can touch the ground if you wish, but this is not necessary.

Begin by visualizing protective energy coming from the end of your finger, tool, or palm, creating an impenetrable wall of protective, containing light. See it rising as an intense, translucent blue-white sphere. Persons psychically sensitive enough to actually see the subtle body of a cast circle say this is its color. Continue moving clockwise around the perimeter until you are back at your starting point. Return to the center, or as near to it as you can get if your altar is there, and spend a moment or two visualizing the energy surrounding you. Know that you are protected and that your efforts will be contained until you are ready to send them forth.

If you are part of a coven this form may be modified slightly to include everyone. For example, some covens allow all persons present to follow the high priest, priestess, or other leader around the circle, each adding his or her energy to the circle wall.

Whether alone or in a group, many Witches like to add some physical reminder of the circle's boundaries and will outline its perimeter with stones, herbs, salt, candles, torches, or other markers. If you do this, always keep in mind that a circle is not created by these objects, but by the energy and efforts of the Witch who creates it anew each time it is needed. (Recall the experience with the basil circle.)

Salt is frequently used in combination with water to bless a newly-cast circle, another very old custom of Witchcraft. Salt has a grounding effect, that is, it will neutralize or absorb negative energies, and is perceived as being stable and sturdy. Water, since ancient times, has been seen as the element of purification, still used today for offering blessings, initiation, and absolution in virtually all spiritual paths, both Pagan and non-Pagan.

Another practice, traditionally occurring just after the opening of the circle, is the "calling of the quarters." This involves summoning the powers and beings of the four elements as personified by each direction (quarter). This may also be called summoning the watchtowers, invoking the elements, calling the hosts, or calling on the spirits or elementals of the quarters. Every tradition has its own way of doing this and its own jargon for identifying these beings. At its most basic, the calling of the quarters includes approaching each direction with the tool representing it and its element, awakening its power to assist your rites and protect your circle, and inviting — but never commanding — all elemental spirits to be present. Usually an invoking pentagram is drawn at each quarter as it is called. Such pentagrams, cast in the air in front of the Witch doing the calling, can be done whenever any energy is being drawn in or down. Spellwork makes much use of this symbol, and of its twin, the banishing pentagram, used whenever energies are being dismissed or sent away.

The calling of the quarters can be worded in any way you or your tradition wishes. The following is one example. It begins in the west because that is the starting point preferred by my tradition.

Taking the tool which represents west and, in this case, the element of water, walk clockwise to the western boundary of the circle, saying:

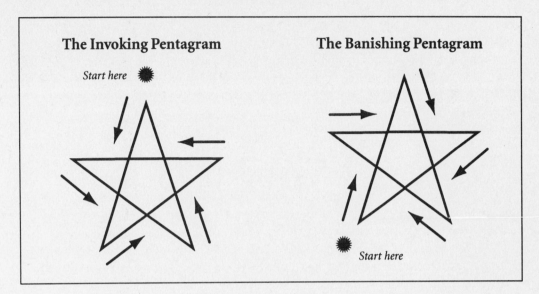

The Invoking Pentagram

Start here

The Banishing Pentagram

Start here

Blessed Be the powers of water — Mutable, sensual, and feeling. Hosts of the watery realm of the west, you are welcome here at this sacred place in this sacred hour. Come join us that we might together honor the Lady of the Night and her consort, our Lord.

Raise the tool and visualize a great distant portal opening in the western sky, spilling free the astral world entities whom you have invited.* Return to your altar and replace the western tool. Next, pick up the tool for the north. Walk clockwise with it to the northern boundary of your circle and summon that quarter:

Blessed Be the powers of earth — Stable, secure, and fertile. Hosts of the dark realm of the north, you are welcome here at this sacred place in this sacred hour. Come join us that we might together honor the Lady of the Night and her consort, our Lord.

As you did in the west, hold high the tool and feel the universe opening to allow the entities you have summoned to appear. Again, return to the altar and replace the tool of the north. Still moving clockwise, pick up the tool of the east and of air and carry it to the eastern quarter, saying:

Blessed Be the powers of air — Free, thinking, and ever-changing. Hosts of the light realm of the east, you are welcome here at this sacred place in this sacred hour. Come join us that we might together honor the Lady of the Night and her consort, our Lord.

---

*For detailed instructions on how faeries and elementals can be more than just observers to your rituals and magick, consult my earlier work, *A Witch's Guide to Faery Folk* (Llewellyn).

Repeat the process of replacing the eastern tool and picking up that of the south. Walk to the southern edge of your circle and call to the quarters again:

> *Blessed Be the powers of fire — Passionate and transforming. Hosts of the warm realm of the south, you are welcome here at this sacred place in this sacred hour. Come join us that we might together honor the Lady of the Night and her consort, our Lord.*

You must now walk again to the altar. Replace the tool of the south and walk once more to the west, or to whichever point you began. This will complete your circle. Raise your arms and offer another invitation, one that includes all friendly, well-meaning entities:

> *Blessed Be all children of the Lady and Lord in whatever form they take, in whichever land they inhabit. All who love the Lady are welcome here tonight to share in the joy of the Esbat. Offer me* (us) *your blessings and protection as I* (we) *share with you the lunar feast from the womb of our bounteous Lady* (a reference to the libations, or ritual offerings, of the Ceremony of Cakes and Ale). *Come feast. The hour is nigh, the moon is high. Let all who gather here be merry, safe in our mother's loving embrace. So Mote It Be!*

At the conclusion of any spell or ritual the excess energy should always be grounded to prevent it from running amok and causing you to feel jittery or "haunted." This includes the energy you projected to create your circle space. At the end of your ritual, after the quarters have been dismissed — always in the opposite order in which you called them — you are ready to ground the circle. To do this, simply reverse the process you used to create it. Take the same tool you chose to use in the creation process and retrace your steps, moving counterclockwise. Visualize the energy returning to the ground, or returning into your tool. Use your psychic senses to feel it dissipate.

Some traditions like to finish the grounding process with an old custom called "sweeping away the circle," a practice probably dating to the medieval period. They take a besom and sweep over the circle's perimeter just after the energy has been grounded. This is symbolic of casting away any negative energy that may have been attracted to the working; on the practical side it also obliterated the physical evidence that the coven had been there, a wise safety precaution in the age of Witch hunts.

Solitary Full Moon Ritual

Because this book has been written largely with the solitary practitioner in mind, you may find what could be perceived as small gaps in the ritual texts. This was not an oversight. The open-ended form allows you to fill in your own expressions, songs, gestures, needs, or any other material you feel is appropriate and that is best suited to help you invoke the divine.

Although many covens regularly meet at the Esbats, they have come to be viewed by some as a private time during which the individual is invited to connect with the universal forces of nature alone. This does not mean that covens forgo their joyful celebrations. It does mean that there is no rule which says that you cannot also have your own private Esbat ritual in which you connect with the psychic and emotional forces of the full moon in a personal, introspective way.

Once you have cast your circle, called the quarters, or performed any other preliminary rites you wish, you should stand before your altar and open the main body of your ritual by stating its purpose out loud. Many cultures believe that to vocalize an intent, or to verbally call to any deity or elemental, automatically sets up a chain of vibratory responses that accomplish much more than merely thinking the ideas through. Here is an example of how you might state the purpose of your Esbat ritual and bless/evoke the mother Goddess:

> *Blessed Be Lady moon, mother of all life. I invite your presence in my circle tonight. Join with me in the joyous enchantment of this Esbat night. For behold, I stand here in the light of your love to worship in the ancient way and to spin moon magick. Like my ancestors before me, I seek to invoke your primal creative power, that my rite shall be successful. Hear me now, my mother, as I bless your bounty and your goodness. Bless me in turn with your eternal tenderness. Wrap me in your warm silvery light. Hold me forever in the protective embrace of your boundless arms. So Mote It Be!*

Spend a few moments feeling your connection to the energy of the full moon and the mother Goddess. Allow yourself to feel surrounded with her attributes. It is also customary to light a candle in her honor. Red is the color associated with the mother in the Celtic traditions; others use white, silver, or green. If you are unsure about the color you prefer — no matter what the ritual is intended to do — white is the safest choice. Other traditions prefer to light an incense to her made up of herbs and fragrances that have lunar associations. Good choices are jasmine, sandalwood, lemon, wintergreen, lotus, or gardenia.

Even though the Esbat ritual is generally a time to honor the Goddess, the God should not be forgotten. Welcome him to your circle also:

> *Lord of the Night, join me now in this sacred space. Your Lady rides high in the starry sky and will soon be in and of me. Come now to join me in the ancient holy rites. So Mote It Be!*

Spend a moment or two becoming aware of the presence of the God within your circle. Feel his energy as an integral part of the atmosphere in which you stand. Light a candle to honor him. Gold, orange, red, and yellow are the colors most often associated with him in his guise as the consort of the moon Goddess. If you prefer incense to a candle, good choices are eucalyptus, ambergris, or myrrh. All three of these scents have lunar associations which are as much masculine as feminine.

If you are a solitary man planning to Draw Down a moon God, you might want to call upon the Goddess instead and ask her presence in the circle to await the God, a reversal of what has so far been presented. The text of the evocation need not change drastically:

> *Lady of the Night, join me now in this sacred space. Your consort rides high in the starry sky and will soon be in and of me. Come now to join me in this holy rite.*

At this point it is traditional to honor the mother moon with songs, seasonal/lunar poetry, or acknowledgements of any moon attributes special to the particular month. For example, if this is your tradition's Corn Moon, honor the Goddess as the corn mother (or Corn Father if you are trying to invoke a lunar God). Spend time aligning with the fertility/harvest aspect of her.

None of these additions necessarily need to be solemn in nature, unless that is the feeling this particular night engenders in you. Your poems can be silly, your songs bawdy, and your images of the lunar month as bizarre as you care to make them. If you wish to cast your circle in a cornfield and throw yourself joyfully into the forest of its stalks to dance wildly with a corn deity, then do so. If you play a relatively portable musical instrument, bring that into the circle with you and improvise as the lunar spirit moves you. In this world-between-worlds you will find many new inspirations to compose tunes to enhance your meditative state, honor the deities, or express a magickal wish.

After this, you are ready for the rite of Drawing Down the Moon. You may use any tool you like to direct the moon energy down into you. Some like a pointing tool such as an athame or wand, others prefer the feminine symbolism inherent in a chalice or cup filled with liquid — usually the meade/ale from the Ceremony of Cakes and Ale that will close the circle. Men attempting to Draw Down the Moon for the first time will probably find that the masculine associations of the athame or wand will work better for them.

If you do not already have a tool you use regularly for Drawing Down the Moon, you should pick one now and be consistent with it, as the energies absorbed by it over time will make each subsequent moon invocation easier to do.

Begin by standing as near to the center of your circle as is possible, then turn to face the moon. Allow its light to flood over your face. If you are not outdoors, try to be near a window. If this is not possible, simply look up and visualize the moon's power coming in through your ceiling, bathing you in its light. If you are using an athame, etc., raise it and point it at the center of the moon. If you are using a chalice, hold it in front of your face so that you can see the moon's light, or your perception of it, reflected on the surface of the liquid inside. Women might make a statement of alignment such as:

> *Blessed mother Goddess* (or insert the name of a moon Goddess with whom you feel a connection), *your silvery, fertile light washes over me, permeating my being with your eternal, vibrant life energy. Enter now this consecrated* (state the name of the tool you are using, verbally adding any attributes of the tool you feel moved to explain) *and prepare to merge with me, your loving child. Come into me, my mother. I now Draw Down the Moon into me, her earthly vessel.*

Men, especially those new to the Craft, might wish to call on a moon God rather than a moon Goddess. In either case, the imagery is largely the same. Moon Gods originated in a time when the moon itself was thought to be the cause of pregnancy, and therefore the fertility image of the mother moon Goddess would remain the same. The alignment statement might consist of:

> *Blessed father God* (or insert the name of a moon God who appeals to you), *your silvery, fertile light washes over me, permeating my being with your vibrant life energy, your creative potential. Enter now this consecrated* (state the name of the tool you are using) *and prepare to merge with me, your loving child. Come into me, my father. I now Draw Down the Moon into me, his earthly vessel.*

Whether you are invoking a Goddess or a God, mentally see the tool you are using filling with divine moon energy. Visualize it happening and know that it is real. You must open yourself completely to the God/dess's presence in order to fully invoke him/her. While this sounds simple enough in theory, it can be extremely difficult to do. Letting go completely and allowing another entity to become a part of us is something we have been taught since childhood to consider dangerous. With your first effort you will have some success with invocation, but it will take practice to become proficient.

When you feel the moon deity's essence has entered your tool, you are ready to bring it into yourself. If you are using an athame or other pointing tool, or if you are a man using a chalice, pull the tool to your breast. If you are a female using a chalice you may use the breast or the womb as the entry point.

> *I Draw the Moon into Me. I am divinity incarnate.*
> *I am the God/dess, S/he is me.*

You may chant this quatrain over and over until you feel the divine energy has filled you completely. Feel the God/dess spirit entering you and the sensation of the two of you becoming one. If you have done this correctly, you will begin to feel different. Some people report a feeling like static electricity coming into the circle while this is happening. Others experience a tingling or a sense of "displacement" as they make room in themselves for another being.

When you feel you have absorbed all the energy from the tool, you may put it back down on your altar. If you are a woman you might want to affirm your role as Goddess with words such as:

> *I am Goddess, fertile and powerful. Let all positive and pleasurable acts commence, for these are my sacred rites, my gifts to my children. Let laughter ring from the dark hillsides. Let all hearts be light and all earthly cares foresworn. Let magick be afoot, for this is my will.*

A man might wish to slightly alter the text:

> *I am God, fertile and potent. Let the rites of my full moon commence. Let them be positive and pleasurable, for these are my sacred rituals, my gifts to my children. Let laughter ring from the dark hillsides. Let all hearts be light and all earthly cares foresworn. Let magick be afoot, for this is my will.*

Since you are not with a group there is no need to let the God/dess speak to you. Simply close your eyes and feel him/her within. Allow yourself to feel whatever gentle message of love and inspiration s/he has for you.

While it is a very rare occurrence, it is possible that you may sense the presence of messages or ideas that are not at all positive, even some which might be disturbing. Unless you can identify these as things you need to hear whether you like them or not, you need to expel the alien energy immediately and close the circle. Whatever is inside you is not divine, or else is being distorted by some unresolved inner conflict you may have about the rite of which you might not even be aware. Record your feelings and experiences in detail and spend some time alone seriously considering what went wrong. Wait at least another month before trying again.

While you have the essence of the divine within you is the best time to perform magick for yourself or others. You will find spells for things such as healing, fertility, romance, and peace are especially efficacious under the influence of the full moon.

You can also raise your cone of power as the God/dess, a peak of energy deliberately manifested by the Witch(es) working the magick. The lore surrounding this cone is as interesting as the practice itself. Many Pagans believe it is the origin of the pointed hat seen *ad nauseum* in drawings of wizards and Halloween witches. This is a misinterpretation — like many the general public has about magick — in that the cone was not worn, but was built in the air around the Witch(es). This old custom involves the projection of energy, as manifested in the cone, with a specific goal in mind. Dancing, chanting, singing, and drumming are the preferred ways to raise the cone. When you feel it peak over your circle, release it to do its job. Mentally send it out, physically backed up by a releasing gesture such as relaxing your muscles, flinging wide your arms, or spinning to "push" it away.

When you have concluded your magick, it is time to release the invoked energy. To reverse the Drawing Down the Moon process, simply hold your tool against the place you used as an entry point and visualize the God/dess energy flowing out of you and back into the tool. Raise the tool towards the moon. Visualize the energy returning from whence it came, and feel yourself returning to normal consciousness. You can use some inner chant, or hum a melody if you like, whatever you feel is a fitting background for the event.

Some people, especially if they are newcomers to the Craft, do not feel comfortable with any invocations. This is fine. No spiritual practice is universal, and many of us were probably attracted to Paganism in the first place by the lack of authority figures telling us what we have to believe and do. These hesitant persons can still experience the full moon energies of the lunar mother by using guided meditation to explore an inner-world in which the mother is present.

To do these inner-explorations you will need to get comfortable within your circle and allow your thoughts to slow. Then guide yourself through a mental world such as the one outlined below. Make it as real as possible. See all the action from your own point of view. The first few times you perform such an exercise you may feel very detached from the action. With a little practice you will discover that the inner world is as real as the outer world, and your self-explorations will become cherished parts of your rituals.

It is sundown on a clear late summer day, and you are strolling through a beautiful orchard. Pears and apples hang heavy and luscious on the boughs above you as if anxious for the fall harvest. Everywhere you look you are surrounded by the bounty of mother nature. Off in the distance is a cornfield, with golden green ears sprouting from each stem, begging to be picked. Beyond that is a verdant melon patch near a silver-blue lake.

You saunter along without a care in the world when, without warning, you hear a low growl coming from just ahead of you. Looking up, you find yourself virtually eye to eye with a large, brown, she-bear. Though your heart is hammering like that of a frightened rabbit, the bear does not appear to be a threat. She stands poised at the edge of the orchard, staring deeply into your eyes.

Mentally you send her your best wishes, hoping she will sense you mean her no harm and go on about her business, but she makes no move to leave.

After a moment she places her front paws back on the ground and walks over to you. Even though you now tower over her, you are acutely aware that she could rear up at any moment and rip you to ribbons with her scythe-like claws.

Then, to your great surprise, she circles you and begins rubbing against you like a gentle kitten. Impulsively you reach down to pet her huge head. With your hands entangled in her thick neck fur, she begins to pull you out of the orchard toward the isolated hills on the other side.

Trusting the bear, you allow her to lead you through the hills to the mouth of a dark cave. The entrance is egg-shaped and, though it is dark, it is somehow warmly inviting. You wonder if this is the bear's home and if so, why she has brought you here?

As you edge closer to the mouth of the elliptical opening the bear remains where she is, seemingly unconcerned about what you will do next.

You step into the cave and take a moment to adjust to the darkness. Some instinct draws you further and further in. You move cautiously along the darkened walls until you notice, far up ahead, a strange light. Thinking it may be another way out you move toward it.

When you reach the light you are shocked to discover that it comes from a room whose crystalline walls shine from deep within with all the colors of the rainbow. More surprising is that, in the middle of the room, a woman sits on a crystal throne. She is dressed all in blue and appears heavily pregnant. Around her head is a crown of silver studded with emeralds and moonstones. In her hands is a scepter of solid silver with a large clear stone on the end, and in her lap is a jewel-encrusted silver chalice which emits a tantalizing, honey-like scent. It seems to radiate an aura of power which is almost visible in the shimmering, silvery air around you.

The woman herself seems ageless. She could be twenty or fifty. There is a keen sense of intellect about her, an omniscience that seems to emanate from deep within her serene countenance. Her sharp blue eyes stare into yours without expression of any kind.

You smile timidly at her. She returns the greeting with a warm enthusiasm as she motions you to come near to her, her chalice offered for the taking.

Greet the mother with the traditional words "Merry Meet" and allow your inner-senses to finish dictating the direction of the meditation. Allow the mother to teach you either by showing or telling you something you need to know, or simply stand near her, getting comfortable with her presence. When it is time to go, thank the Goddess for her company in any way you feel is appropriate. When you are ready, head back out of the cave to the place in the orchard where you began this inner-journey. After you are there you can return to your normal consciousness by any means you choose. Always know that you are welcome at any time in this inner-world, and that your Goddess will always be waiting for you here.

Men wishing to experience the imagery of a lunar God before attempting the rite of Drawing Down the Moon can work the path of a similar guided meditation:

You are walking on a rural path near the edge of a thick forest. It is midnight, but the full moon above you lights the lane with a soft glow that keeps you surefooted. The woods are beautiful, bathed in the moon's glow, and you stop for a moment to listen to the soothing sounds of the night. Somewhere in the distance an owl hoots, soon answered by its mate. The brush occasionally rustles with the sounds of scurrying feet as a nightingale sings nearby. It is a very satisfying scene, one which feels distantly familiar to you.

As you peer into the trees you notice a light coming from deep within the center of the forest. Thinking it is a fire, you feel a moment of panic that this beautiful woodland might be spoiled by flame. But as you keep watching, you see that the light remains steady, contained.

Curiosity compels you to follow the light. and you head into the woods after it. As you get closer you can clearly see that it is unlike any fire you have ever seen. The glow is silverish and mellow, not the yellow crackling illumination you are used to seeing.

Soon you walk into a clearing and see not a fire, but a luminous silver glow. Within it stands a man. He is naked from the waist up; from the waist down the blue cloth that covers him is partially obscured by the peaceful light. Despite the peace of the light his muscular body radiates an animal power, like that of a nighthawk searching for its prey. His hair is long, the color of rich, fertile earth. On his head is a silver crown studded with golden jewels.

As you look above his head, you see that the light you mistook for fire does not so much radiate from him as to him. A thin pale beam reaches up from his head, linking him to the yellow moon that appears to be centered directly over him.

You stare at him in wonder.

In his hand he carries a long staff. Its moonstone handle reflects the silvery light and the shaft appears smoothed by untold years of use. Like him, it seems to radiate a power all its own.

All about the glade are animals which seem wholly unafraid of him. There are bucks, hares, raccoons, even an owl or two.

You have never seen anyone like him before and you are tempted to flee from this apparition which radiates such intense power. His ageless silver eyes bore deeply into your soul, and you feel that in this instant of observation he has learned all about you — past, present, and future.

Despite your nervousness, you sense no harm will come to you and you raise a hand in friendly greeting. The man does likewise and offers a warm smile in return. With a sudden move, so swift it is almost beyond your visual grasp, he thrusts his staff into the ground and beckons you near.

Greet the moon God with the traditional words "Merry Meet" and allow your inner-senses to finish dictating the direction of the meditation. Allow the God to teach you either by showing or telling you something you need to know, or simply stand near him, getting comfortable with his presence. When it is time to go, thank the moon God for his company in any way you feel is appropriate. When you are ready, head back out of the oak woods to the place in the rural pathway where you began this inner-journey. After you are there, you can return to your normal consciousness by any means you choose. Always know that you are welcome at any time in this inner-world, and that your God will always be waiting for you here.

The next step in your Esbat ritual will be to hold the Ceremony of Cakes and Ale (the complete text is found in Chapter 1).

Afterward be sure to dismiss the quarters, and to thank the Goddess and God, and any other deities you called upon. You may then close your circle in your usual manner.

It is always wise to record the feelings and experiences you have in any ritual, and is almost a must when you do magick. Men experimenting with the invocation of a male moon deity will especially want to keep records. Even though the masculine, just like the feminine, is but one half of the whole, you will find that the character and feeling of your Esbat circle will be markedly different when you draw down a moon father rather than a moon mother. Write down what you feel and why. If you work with a coven, or hope to in the future, you may want to use your own experiences and findings to help encourage your fellow covenors to experiment with these and other non-traditional energies.

Group Full Moon Ritual

This ritual is designed for two or more persons. Groups of two, even of three or four, often hesitate to identify themselves as a coven. But since the word coven comes from the same root word as "convene," meaning to "come together," without specifying numbers, small groups are also covens — often very good ones, because the participants frequently know each other very well, and there is little room for the immature power-playing that often destroys larger groups.

As always, everyone should have their parts memorized, and all tools, decorations, magickal needs, Cakes and Ale, and any other items you will need should be in place.

When all are assembled and ready to start, cast your circle and call your quarters in your usual manner. The Leader of the group should stand before the altar and make the opening statement of purpose and call on the Goddess. The Leader can be a high priest or priestess, or anyone else chosen to lead the ritual by the group. If there is more than one Leader, they should divide the Leader's text between them.

Leader:

> *Blessed Be Lady moon, mother of all life. Come to our circle tonight, join in the joyous enchantment of this Esbat night. For behold, we stand here in the light of your love to worship in the ancient way and weave magick by the moon. Like our ancestors before us, we seek to invoke your primal power that our rites and petitions will be successful. Hear us now, our mother, as we bless your bounty and your goodness. Bless us in turn with your eternal tenderness. Wrap us in the secure protection of your warm silvery light. Sustain us forever in your boundless arms.*

All:

> *Welcome the Lady. So Mote It Be!*

Spend a few moments allowing all present to feel a connection to the energy of the full moon and the mother Goddess. This also helps to foster a sense of group mind and purpose which can be further enhanced by attempting to breathe in unison. Don't force this, as over-exertion in this effort can be more distracting than inspiring, but try to let it evolve naturally, taking cues from the Leader.

Even though the Esbat ritual is generally a time to honor the Goddess, the God should not be forgotten. Welcome him to your circle also. The Leader may call to him in any direction the group deems appropriate and may hold upward any tool which they associate with the God.

Leader:

> *Lord of the Night, beloved consort of our mother, join us now in this sacred space. Your Lady rides high in the starry sky and will soon be in and of those assembled here. Come now to join us in the ancient holy rites.*

All:

Welcome the Lord. So Mote It Be!

Spend a moment or two becoming aware of the presence of the God within your circle. Feel his energy as a part of the atmosphere in which you stand.

At this point it is traditional to honor the mother moon with songs, seasonal/lunar poetry, or acknowledgements of any moon attributes special to this particular month. Allow all who wish to add something to this part of the ritual to do so without ridicule or criticism. Keep in mind that, even though we may be part of the same tradition, we all experience our spirituality in different ways. Also, do not censure the lighter side of the festivities. If a fellow covenor wishes to express a bit of "moon madness" in his or her choice of readings, music, etc., let it be.

When all have had their say, you are ready to Draw Down the Moon. One person, the Chosen One, should have been selected ahead of time to have this honor, and another, the Invoker, selected to Draw Down the moon into the Chosen One. Many covens prefer to invoke the Goddess into a high priestess or other senior woman of the coven, assisted by a man. If no man is present, another experienced woman is usually selected. Aligning with any foreign energy takes practice and familiarity with Craft customs. This is why elders are usually selected for these rites.

You may use any tool you choose to direct the moon energy down into the Chosen One, but many covens stick to the long-standing tradition of using a blade, such as an athame, for this task.

The two who are to be actively participating in this rite should move as close to the center of the circle as possible. All others should take their places round the circle's edge. To symbolize the light of the divine which will soon be entering the circle, give everyone an unlit candle to hold. Assign someone to pass them out just before the actual rite of Drawing Down the Moon commences.

The Chosen One should stand in front of the Invoker and should be facing the moon as much as is possible. Those working indoors will have to make an educated guess as to the direction of the moon. The two participants should align their breathing while focusing their attentions on the lunar energy bathing the circle.

The Invoker should raise the athame high over the head of the Chosen One, holding it firmly in both hands, with its point up.

Invoker:

Lady of the Night, your loving children await your presence. Fill this vessel with your silvery warmth and your loving countenance. Bless us with your presence, our eternal mother, bring your eternal wisdom to us this night.

Covenors:

Come to us, Lady. Your children await.

The Invoker should raise the athame and point it at the center of the moon.

Invoker:

> *Blessed mother Goddess* (or insert the name of a moon Goddess with whom your group feels a connection), *your silvery, fertile light washes over* (name person to be Drawn into), *permeating her very being with your eternal, vibrant life energy. She is chosen from among us, honored to be the instrument of your presence here this night. Enter now this consecrated athame and prepare to merge with her, your loving daughter, representative of our collective soul. Come into her, our mother, and grace this sacred space.*

Covenors:

> *Grace this sacred space, our mother. We now Draw Down the Moon.*

The Invoker should mentally see the tool filling with divine lunar energy. Visualize it happening and know that it is real. Everyone present should also be adding the energy of group will to the event. The members of the coven who are standing at the perimeter of the circle may wish to hum together a special melody in honor of the Goddess, or to utter a low chant as the transformation of the Chosen One takes place. Some covens use drumming, an act long known to aid the process of shifting one's consciousness. The choice should be made by all and no one should be so uncomfortable with it that they cannot function with the majority.

When the Invoker feels the divine moon essence has entered the athame tool, s/he is ready to bring it into the body of the Chosen One. To do this, bring the point of the blade down and rest it against the forehead or breastbone of the Chosen One, allowing the energy of the Goddess to be transferred to her.

Invoker:

> *I Draw the Moon into you. You are divinity incarnate.*
> *You are the Goddess.*

Covenors:

> *Behold, the Lady stands before us.*

Invoker(lowers the blade and steps back to the edge of the circle with the others):

> *Behold the silver light of the moon personified. Her divine radiance lights the darkness of our circle.*

The Chosen One should walk to the altar and pick up the Goddess candle, then turn to face the group.

Invoker:

> *Her light is passed from one to another, like the love in her heart which spreads over us this night.*

The Chosen One should use the Goddess candle to light the unlit candle held by the person nearest her. Moving clockwise around the circle, each person should light the candle of the person standing next to him or her with words such as:

Covenor passing light:
> *Blessed Be the light of the moon. Love shared is the only love which is real.*
> *Take her love and multiply it by passing it on.*

When the circle is completely lit, the Chosen One replaces the Goddess candle on the altar. She then stands in front of it, facing the coven.

Invoker:
> *Will you speak to us, Blessed Lady?*

The opening lines of the Goddess's speech are usually pre-written for the Chosen One. This will get the creative link with the divine lunar energy flowing and may inspire other words of wisdom. After the opening speech, the Chosen One should not feel obligated to continue speaking unless she feels true inspiration and believes that the words will bring help and goodwill to all gathered. This is another reason why someone with integrity and experience in the Craft is usually chosen for this task. It is all too easy for someone untried to be tempted to use this merger as an excuse to express anger or jealousy, or to attempt to sway other coven members to their point of view on an issue with which you have been collectively wrestling. Such immature behavior is easily recognizable by all, is very destructive, and should be stopped immediately. The Chosen One should proceed with the opening speech:

Chosen One:
> *Behold, I am your Goddess, the fertile and powerful mother of all living*
> *things. Let all positive and pleasurable acts commence, for these are my*
> *sacred rites, my gifts to my children. Let laughter ring from the dark hill-*
> *sides. Let all hearts be light and all earthly cares fore-sworn. Let magick be*
> *afoot, for this is my will.*

Covenors should place their candles securely on the altar, or on some other steady surface while the rest of the ritual progresses. For safety, you may not want to clutter the altar with fire, especially if it is going to be used to arrange a spell. If you have globed candles, they can be set down behind you, outlining the circle's perimeter, or they can be stuck into the ground if there is no dry brush which might ignite. For indoor rituals I have seen tin wash buckets and similar inflammable containers used to hold these candles. They can be placed under the altar until they are needed again.

While you have the essence of the divine present is the best time to perform any group magick. You will find that spells for such things as healing, fertility, romance, and peace are especially efficacious under the influence of the full moon. After you have raised and sent the cone of power and concluded your magick, it is time to release the invoked energy. Covenors should gather up their candles and take their places back around the circle. The Invoker and the Chosen One should again move into the center of the sphere.

To reverse the Drawing Down the Moon process, simply hold the tool against the place used as the entry point and visualize the God/dess energy flowing out of the Chosen One and back into the tool. While this is taking place, the coven members should begin to extinguish their candles. Pinch them out one by one, starting with the last one lit, and moving counterclockwise around the circle until all are dark. As the light dims the Invoker should send the lunar energy back up to the moon with words of thanks:

Invoker:

> *Bright mother of the night, we thank you for your bounteous presence. As you turn again from mother to crone to maiden, and back to mother again, may we always be aware of your shining beacon of silver, the constant reminder of your eternal presence among us. So Mote It Be!*

Raise the tool back toward the moon. Visualize the energy returning from whence it came, and allow the Chosen One to feel herself returning to normal consciousness.

All:

> *Blessed Be the mother.*
> *Blessed Be the eternal faces of her silver light.*

As these last lines are spoken, the Invoker should move to the altar and extinguish the Goddess candle.

The next step in your Esbat ritual will be to hold the Ceremony of Cakes and Ale (complete text to be found in Chapter 1).

Dancing, singing, circle games, and pleasant conversation can follow, but avoid giving in to the temptation to discuss coven business. This is sacred space and the mundane mechanics of your practice are best left for other meetings.

Afterward be sure to dismiss the quarters, and to thank the Goddess and God, and any other deities you called upon. You may then close your circle in your usual manner.

While everyone in your coven probably keeps his or her own Book of Shadows, it is nice to appoint a scribe to keep the group's impressions of the ritual. They should be taken down as soon as is reasonably possible after the rite. The scribe will be the first to know about any dissatisfaction within the group. He or she should do everything in his or her power to work out any rising difficulties before they become unsolvable and destroy the group.

Covens and the Invocation of Lunar Gods

If you are experimenting for the first time with worshipping a lunar God and Drawing Down his energy into a man, you must carefully prepare and re-write the entire Esbat ritual to reflect this change. The first time you do this will no doubt make a lot of people, males and females alike, uncomfortable. Change is hard to accept and adapt to and, when the inner-worlds are involved, breaks from expected patterns can disrupt the flow of energy and inhibit the involuntary responses to which you have accustomed yourselves.

On the other hand, no spiritual advancement can take place without the occasional experiment. The risks involved in a less-than-perfect ritual are small when compared to the gains of expanded awareness.

A coven wishing to try the invocation of a lunar God into a man should begin their exploration as did the solitary man, by studying the lore of the extant moon Gods. This should be done together, if possible, so that all participants in the group will have a chance to express their feelings on the matter. If you regularly make a practice of acknowledging sun Goddesses, or if you occasionally Draw Down the Sun into women, your task of making the mental realignment will be much easier.

You will also need to re-write your ritual to reflect the honoring of a masculine rather than feminine deity. This will involve calling on the blessings of the moon God, and evocation of the presence of his consort, the Goddess. Remember to honor the God as the father of life, and allow all the imagery of fertility and love to remain the same.

Use the athame to make the invocation, and start by allowing a woman to be the one to Draw Down the God, just as men usually have that honor when the Goddess is drawn into a female. Draw the blade to the breastbone near the heart, the area of the body associated with emotion, a lunar attribute. Allow the God to speak through the chosen man just as you allow the Goddess to speak through a woman.

After the ritual is concluded, the group should meet again as soon as possible to openly discuss the ritual and magick done. The most prevalent expression will be of the very "different" atmosphere that a lunar God furnishes. As mentioned before, some will appreciate the contrast, others most vehemently will not.

Your coven will now be faced with deciding how to handle future Esbat rituals. Will you never again invoke a lunar God? Will you only occasionally invoke a lunar God? Is this imagery something that will upset the magickal workings to such an extent that it is not worth considering further? Does the potential for spiritual growth justify the time needed to gain expertise in this area? How long would it take your most die-hard male–sun/female–moon adherents to mentally adjust to the change?

A wise old cliche tells us that the first time for any new experience never equals the high expectations given it in fantasy. Therefore you may want to give the Drawing Down of a lunar God one more try just so that you will all know for sure exactly how you feel about the practice. Try re-writing the ritual, changing as many points as possible to conform to a group vision of how things should be improved, and give it one more effort.

Whatever you decide, be aware beforehand that your coven will never be the same again. You may have to split into two groups to accommodate the desires of all. This is not necessarily a bad thing. You can still come together as one large group for certain festivals (different covens often meet together for special occasions), and in the mean-time you will have two good covens, each operating from knowledge and experience and who have made informed decisions.

Pagan diversity is to be cherished, not avoided. It is through diversity that we become stronger.

Non-Western and Seasonal Full Moon Festivals

Even the most meaningful of rituals can become stale without the occasional new spark of interest to fuel the flame. Solitaries or covens wishing to put a new spin on their Esbat rituals might want to look at the list of moon festivals given in Appendix B with an eye toward ways to adapt some of the unfamiliar customs of non-western Witchcraft. This serves two purposes: first, it keeps alive valuable Pagan lore which might otherwise be lost, as has so much already; and second, it enriches the group with a new learning experience which just might prove to be something you will wish to keep as part of your regular Esbat rituals.

For example, you might wish to set aside an Esbat for honoring Ch'ang-O, the Chinese moon Goddess. Start by getting to know her. Read about her myths. Then read about Chinese divination practices, which are part of her celebration. These are easily found in many books on divinatory techniques or Chinese astrology. Note also that her festival falls on the full moon nearest the Autumn Equinox. This positioning deeply links her to the harvest season. In honor of this you may wish to decorate your altar with decidedly Asian foods, particularly rice, since paying homage to deities of staple grains has been a part of virtually every culture on the planet.

Covens are in a unique position to experiment beyond the scope of who or what they choose to invoke/honor. With the creative impetus of the group mind, covens can test full-scale rituals that take them directly into the practices of non Euro-based Paganism. With a little ingenuity and research your Esbat rituals need never grow dull; there is an entire world of Paganism to explore. Don't worry that somehow this will intrude on the integrity of your path. No culture has ever existed in a vacuum. Deities and spiritual concepts knew no political boundaries in the ancient world, so there is no reason why they should respect these arbitrary demarcations in our time.

For instance, the interest of your group might be tweaked by southeast Asia's Festival of Youth, which takes place on an autumn full moon. On this night children are given full responsibility for the power of light. This is an excellent time to bring young-sters into your circle and allow them to begin to take on some adult responsibilities. Show them how to make Asian paper lanterns; instructions can be found in many good craft books for children. Allow them to decorate the circle area for the group and, in the ritual, to light the circle candles. Charge the kids with their care until the circle is closed. This festival would also make a beautiful time for a Coming of Age Rite. This is the time when one's tradition deems youngsters to be of an age to accept the responsibilities of adult spirituality. The age varies from twelve to eighteen, depending on the group and on the family's feelings about the ceremony. During this ritual the young person is initiated formally into the coven and given gifts to commemorate the event, which usually take the form of tools the person can use throughout his or her religious life.

Never feel that any Pagan idea cannot be used by you just because it is outside of what is generally termed your "tradition." The moon is the oldest focus of spiritual impulse known to us. Deep in our genetic memory, all of these rites have a place in the universal consciousness. It is your right, and even your duty, to use them if you feel moved to do so.

Honoring seasonal moon festivals is another way to introduce and experiment with mostly non-European Pagan practices.

The majority of the major full moon festivals about which we still have knowledge show a pattern of being timed not only by a lunar calendar, but also by their relationship to the solar year. For example, for many cultures in the northern hemisphere, lunar harvest festivals often took place at the full moon nearest the Autumn Equinox, regardless of the month of the lunar year in which it fell.

For today's Pagans, this timing presents no barrier to celebration. Days that mark the changing seasons (the Sabbats) are ancient Pagan festivals in their own right. At these times covens and solitaries from many traditions ritually observe the turning of the Wheel of the Year, and honor the part of the life-cycle of the Goddess and God that each represents. Incorporating the old moon festivals into new expressions of solar-centered worship can add an interesting dimension to old rituals.

Begin planning for your dual festival by studying the aspects of various moon festivals (a list appears in Appendix B), and select a few that appeal to you or to your coven the most. Next, look to see how they correspond to or contradict your usual perception of the season. For instance, a fertility festival in autumn is almost unheard of in western Paganism, but not in many other parts of the world. Your gut reactions may steer you away from your original selections. This is fine. In Paganism one should never do anything inherently uncomfortable regardless of the reason. Your feelings are always valid, subject to change, and should be respected by you and any others with whom you work.

After you have settled on a moon festival with which to experiment, you will need to write your Esbat ritual, incorporating both the association of the moon festival with the symbolism of the season in which it occurs, as interpreted by you or your tradition.

Using the Mother Moon Pilgrimage of the Maori people of New Zealand as an example, we can begin to experiment with ways in which such festivals can be made creatively meaningful to Pagans following Celtic/Anglo-Saxon/Teutonic ways.

In the three above-mentioned traditions the night of the Autumn Equinox is a moment of balance, after which the energies of darkness overtake the light. It is a time when the inner-pace slows, when the Goddess becomes crone and the God prepares to die when the last of the harvest is cut. But at the same time that we are experiencing autumn, in the southern Hemisphere the Maori are celebrating the Spring Equinox. On the full moon immediately following the Equinox, their mother moon is honored as the guardian of the upcoming harvest who awakens the earth from her winter's slumber. They pay homage to her by making a pilgrimage to the highest mountain available and making offerings.

For your Esbat ritual, cast your circle in the highest elevation available to you. This can be anywhere which seems "high": a hillside, an attic, or a rooftop. Honor the mother moon both as mother (as presented in the full moon and the Maori association) and the crone (as presented by the season). Then open your full-moon ritual in the usual manner. But this time, instead of merely honoring the full moon and Goddess in your usual manner, use the Maori custom for honoring the Goddess for the coming harvest. Even though the earth in the northern hemisphere is preparing for sleep, you can thank the Lady for the promise of the coming spring, and thank her, in her Maori aspect as guardian of the harvest, for your successful harvest.

Though the images can be sometimes confusing when combining festivals in this way, doing so will underscore the eternal nature of the Goddess. Like the three faces of the moon, our Lady is always changing, yet is always the same Goddess. She is always with us, blessing the harvest in one hemisphere and the planting in another.

PART II

The Maiden

The Waxing Moon

*In ever-widening arcs, the light
strives to embrace me.*
— Rebecca Worrell

The waxing moon is the realm of the gentle, carefree spirit of the maiden Goddess. She is the princess of springtime, the Imbolg bride of the sun, whose newly awakened sexuality leads to her sacred union with the God at Bealtaine.

We love the maiden as much as we envy her free spirit. The future is before her and, in her world, all things are possible. We connect with her spirit easily each day, without even being consciously aware of her presence. The maiden is present in the laughter of every little girl, in the deep, innocent sleep of your own daughter, and in the star-clouded eyes of a young woman with her first crush. We are a part of her when we smile happily upon the nervous bride, rejoice over a pregnancy, or celebrate the joy of a new birth.

For those who do not feel an affinity with the maiden, consider using the exercises below to help you connect to her youthful spirit.

1. Go to a place where children or young people gather and watch them. Because of the recent media focus on child molestation and kidnapping, use common sense in deciding how long and closely you observe, lest your innocent intentions be misinterpreted.

At a very young age there is little difference in the social behavior of males and females. The differentiation will come later when society starts subtly making its demands known. These little ones all have the spirit of the maiden Goddess within them. They are trusting, curious, and vulnerably open.

Notice how children move. Everything is either a game of grand fun or a challenge to be mastered. Try to catch a sense of the free spirit that dwells within them.

If you are observing teenagers it is better to focus solely on the females. By now the change in behavior and outlook is complete; you will find very little of the maiden Goddess in adolescent boys. Notice how the young ladies' eyes twinkle expectantly when they talk to each other, how they cherish their very existence, how they are bursting to be women. Hear their laughter and, most importantly, notice their furtive glances at the young men who pass by. The maiden is awakening to womanhood and is full of curiosity, hesitations, and high hopes.

2. If you have nieces or nephews, or friends with small children, offer to give the parents a break and take the youngsters on an outing. Try to choose a place that will unleash their imaginations, like the zoo or a stage play for children.

Watch and listen as they fall into the spirit of the occasion. You will be amazed at how easily children can let reality slip away, and become the animal they see or the stage character they admire. When they fall into these roles you may have to call to them more than once to snap them out of their make-believe world. This is a grim reminder to us as to just how far we have let the larger society shape our thinking and root us firmly in the non-magickal here-and-now. If we could recapture even a fraction of the mind-set of a child, our magick would be powerful indeed.

Encourage the children's role-playing and allow it to evolve into the making of personal myths, which can help the child grow up feeling self-confident and personally empowered. Learn from this process and try to recapture it for yourself. Remember that kids still possess our long-lost capacity for easy self-transformation, and the zestful energy and belief that the future is theirs for the taking. To them, all things are possible.

If you have children of your own, this is a great way to learn to empathize with them and form a stronger bond between you. Perhaps you can spare them some of the hurts you endured and prevent them from losing the magickal powers with which they were born.

3. Spend time remembering yourself as a teenage girl, or focus on a sister or an old girlfriend. Remember the feelings, the urgent desire to grow up and enter womanhood fully. Recall the excitement over your first date, first kiss, and first sexual experience. These encounters are the world of the maiden Goddess.

In the Pagan solar calendar the maiden is associated with the Sabbats of late winter and early spring. At Imbolg she is the bride of the returning sun God. At Ostara her sexuality awakens and she turns all her interest to her new consort. At Bealtaine her sacred marriage to the God is celebrated with flowers, feasting, and the weaving of the May Pole, which symbolically enacts their sexual union.

The terms maiden or virgin can be confusing for Pagans since the old meaning of the word — which applies to this aspect of the Goddess — has been lost in the obsessive need to control the bodies of the earth's women. A virgin was a woman who had no master or husband. Like the famous Vestal Virgins of ancient Rome, she was free to do as she pleased with regard to taking lovers, and was financially supported by the culture in which she lived. She was described by society as being either "complete" or "intact," meaning that she did not need any other person to make her whole. Somewhere in history the idea of being intact was grafted onto the hymen, the thin fleshy covering over an unentered vagina.

In the Pagan world one reference had nothing to do with the other. In fact, if you look at the mythology and folklore that provide Pagans with much of our cosmology, it is the virgin aspect of the Goddess who gives birth to the God(s), not the mother aspect. Read virtually any book on the seasonal celebrations of Witchcraft and you will find many references to festivals which honor the virgin Goddess as bride and mother of the young God. These are very old cycles of stories, regardless of the cultures from which they come. Even Christmas, that thinly-disguised version of Yule, incorporates the image of a virgin mother giving birth to a God.

The early waxing moon is almost as much a focal point of Pagan worship as is the full phase, and some covens will meet in those days between her newness and the appearance of her waxing quarter. Covens also sometimes meet at the first visible sign of the new moon, the gentle silver of a waxing crescent barely perceptible in the night sky.

The energy of the waxing moon is associated with matters of gain and increase. For centuries, farmers have mated livestock and planted crops on the waxing moon to ensure growth. In modern-day Texas, I know of several ranchers who adamantly refuse to brand cattle at this time because they fear the mark will spread and become overly large with the growth of the moon.

Certainly the cattle could wait for their branding until the approved moon phase, but there are numerous other beliefs about activities one should undertake only as the moon waxes; respecting every one could make living difficult. These include:

- starting a garden
- mating animals
- opening a bank account
- entering a new business venture
- making investments
- buying land
- building/buying a home
- giving charitable gifts
- canning
- getting routine medical exams
- studying
- making herbal medicines
- marrying

As you can see by this abbreviated list, if one rigorously adhered to these folktales, one's life would be restricted by half. Sadly, many people who should know better get obsessively caught up in the wax/wane game.

A friend and I once met another Witch with whom we found we had much in common. At the time my friend and I had rejected the idea of working with a larger coven and were keeping to ourselves. The woman we met also was a veteran of several failed covens. The three of us happened to know of several others in the area who shared our bad experiences with local covens, and so we decided to arrange a time for all of us to meet, get to know each other, and see where the chemistry might lead. Finding a time for eight busy people to meet was difficult enough, but it was made more so by this woman's insistence that the meeting must take place only during the waxing phase of the moon.

Eventually we all did meet, but because we were trying to accommodate the moon's phase rather than our own convenience, nearly all of us were rushed, sandwiching the gathering in between other commitments, and any good chemistry that we might have had fizzled before it even had a chance to get started.

While the energy of the moon can be a powerful tool for magick, never allow it, or any other spiritual belief, to prevent you from living your life. Pagan spirituality is supposed to be liberating, not restrictive. If you really feel you want to work as closely as possible with the moon's phases in as many areas of your life as possible, a little creativity will allow you to do this without losing out on anything special. With careful changes in wording and visualization, virtually any need or spell can be adjusted to correspond to the moon's current phase without constraining you in any way. For example, if you need to do a spell for more money (needing the influence of increase) and the moon is waning (the influence of decrease) you can simply word your magick to ask for a decrease of poverty rather than in increase in prosperity. You would also want to adjust your visualization accordingly. Instead of seeing your bank book with the numbers growing, you would want to see your bills being marked paid and disappearing, thereby leaving you more disposable cash. (See Chapters 11 and 12 for more ideas on how this adjustment works.)

The waxing moon is also a time when many occult teachers recommend that students work on tasks that might be aided by the extra boost of energy inherent in this phase. Astral projection, the art of sending one's consciousness traveling from the body, is one such practice. Another is that of scrying, a method of divination which involves gazing into a reflective surface until pictures form. Some also claim that the divination tools such as pendulums, the Ouija Board, and automatic writing are easier to work with on the waxing moon.

The waxing moon, because it is a time of looking forward, is a good time for divinations about the immediate future. Unlike the elaborate divinations designed to give you a peek at all the many influences that can affect your future, and all the past contributors to your problem, you can use your Runes (stones with old Norse letters carved into them) to get a simple peek at what the day ahead holds for you. If you do not have Rune stones, you can make reasonable substitutes either by finding similar-sized stones (about an inch and a half long, three-quarters of an inch wide, and fairly flat) and marking the Rune symbols on them with a felt-tipped pen, or by making Rune cards by cutting card-sized rectangles from posterboard and drawing the Runes on them.

Just after you awaken, while you are still in that half-dreamy state, take your Rune bag and, while focusing your mind on the day ahead, pull out a single stone. Over time you will be able to develop your own interpretations of the stones, especially if you are familiar with the Runes or you practice in a Teutonic tradition. Until that time, use the descriptions on pages 65–66 as a guideline.

Guidelines for Runestone Interpretation

(blank) **Rune of Odin** — This is the mark of unrevealed destiny, a sign that too many influences outside of your control are at work.

ᚠ **Fehu** — This is the sign of material well-being. Events concerning finances will be of importance.

ᚢ **Uruz** — This is the Rune of strength. Call on all your inner-reserves to get you through the challenges of the day.

ᚦ **Thurisaz** — This represents portals to new dimensions and experiences; or, it can stand for harmful intent on the part of others.

ᚨ **Ansuz** — This Rune is linked to Loki, a trickster God. It is also the Rune of signs and omens which may be difficult to interpret. Avoid snap judgments.

ᚱ **Raidho** — This stone indicates journeys; this can mean inner-transformations as well as physical trips.

ᚲ **Kenaz** — A Rune of regeneration which could indicate the opening of new possibilities and opportunities. It is also an indication of health and general well-being.

ᚷ **Gebo** — This stone indicates the giving and receiving of gifts and hospitality. It represents intense social intercourse.

ᚹ **Wunjo** — This is the Rune of joy. The appearance of this stone indicates that your day will be filled with happiness and satisfaction.

ᚺ **Hagalaz** — Fertile potential is indicated by this stone, which can mean the conception not only of life, but of ideas, concepts, and new beginnings.

ᚾ **Naudhiz** — A Rune of disharmony, of lessons to be learned, of needs not met. Brace yourself for a trying day. (Remember, the purpose of divination is to be forewarned so that you can alter your future. Nothing is predestined. Magick and visualization can lessen or eliminate a projected negative outcome.)

ᛁ **Isa** — The Rune of constraint and immobility could indicate that you may find yourself in a position of indecision, or be restricted by outside forces.

ᛃ **Jera** — This is the Rune of harvests realized. The fruits of past labors are likely to be plucked today.

ᛇ **Eihwaz** — A Rune of magickal potential. Spells performed today should produce good results.

Guidelines for Runestone Interpretation (continued)

Perdhro — This is the mark of secrets. Keep a wary eye out for things that are being hidden from you.

Elhaz — The Rune of protection. Take time to raise your psychic defenses this morning. (Again, magick and self-will can change bad potential.)

Sowilo — This represents the power of the sun. The key today is to "go with the flow" and let your natural abilities come to the surface.

Tiwaz — The Rune of victory; the mark of the successful warrior.

Berkano — The Rune of life and birth. Past magick may be realized today.

Ehwaz — This is the Rune of movement and duality. You are likely to be put in a position of being pulled in two different directions.

Mannaz — This is the Rune of the self; it indicates the influences of family, friends, and your past in the day ahead.

Laguz — The Rune of energy and growth. It could indicate a need to rest and recoup your energies, or to throw them behind an important project.

Ingwaz — This represents the grounding influence of the earth. Definitely a sign that you need to make time to reconnect with your homelife and your spirituality.

Dagaz — The Rune of balance and success. One is necessary for the other.

Othala — The Rune of retreat may mean that you need to back off from an upcoming battle. (If this Rune comes up, you may want to do a more complete divination to understand all that is involved.)

While it may be true that the waxing energy provides an added boost when you are learning any occult art, you should practice any skill at which you wish to become proficient, to the point of being able to do it anywhere at any time. The moon phases should only be a tool to get you started, not a crutch to lean on forever.

To learn to fully experience the waxing phase of the moon, we must allow ourselves to remember and love the curious, wide-eyed child who dwells within us all. The waxing moon is the daughter of each and every Pagan; she wants only to be loved and to enjoy life.

4

A Waxing Moon Ritual

Ever the wonder waxeth more and more.
— Alfred Lord Tennyson

The following ritual to honor the waxing moon and the maiden Goddess is intended for solitaries. Not many covens regularly meet on the waxing moon. For those who do, this ritual can be adapted for group use by assigning roles and/or by writing out spoken dialogue for the mental speeches, gestures, and/or alignments used by the solitary. Since solitary rituals are by their very nature inner- rather than outer-expressions, much of the work of the solitary takes place in the mind. By contrast, group rituals involve interaction, which naturally requires more movements, gestures, and spoken words. You would also need to expand the ritual to make the gathering worthwhile, to give everyone an active role, and to incorporate his or her input.

As always, you will need to gather your tools and set up your altar in your regular working spot. Working outdoors is nice if you can assure yourself of quiet and privacy, but there is nothing wrong with working indoors.

When you have your tools and any other chosen items ready, you may cast your circle in your usual manner and begin the main body of the ritual. (Refer to Chapter 2 for descriptions of, and instructions/ideas for, ritual tools, directional associations, circle casting, calling quarters, etc.)

Waxing Moon Solitary Ritual

Stand in front of your altar with arms spread and eyes looking heavenward. Breathe deeply and feel yourself aligning with the waxing lunar forces. Attune yourself to the growing energy that is all around you.

Either mentally or out loud call upon the maiden, stating your love for her and the purpose of your ritual. You can call her by any maiden-Goddess name you like. If you don't have a preference or haven't yet found the maiden image with which you feel most in tune, just call her "Gentle Maiden" or "Sister."

Blessed Be, Gentle Maiden. I, (state either your mundane or Craft name, if you have one), stand here in your growing light this eve to honor your newness, to cleanse my heart and reconnect myself with you at this moment of new beginnings. Bless the magick of this night with your innocence and love. Grant me the peace of your silent, heavenly realm.

At this point it is traditional in many paths to raise a glass of wine, water, or juice and offer the Goddess of the moon a toast of honor. The tool usually preferred is, naturally, the chalice. However, the chalice is deeply linked to the womb of the mother Goddess, and to the mysteries of the Otherworld crone. You might wish instead to offer up something more appropriate to the virgin, perhaps a bouquet of flowers, a special herb or plant, or some feed for an animal with moon associations. Another idea is to use a hollow horn, the symbol of the new crescent moon. Many drawings of ancient moon Goddesses (particularly Isis) depict her with these horns resting on her head. The decision is yours to make; no choice is inherently right or wrong.

Whatever you use to make the toast, your offering might sound something like this:

Blessed Be, Sister Moon, on this night when you rule the hearts and lives of your brothers and sisters on earth. Blessed Be your slender silver horns riding high on the night sky, and Blessed Be the animals of the forest who are most beloved of you. On this sacred night open wide the portal to your kingdom that I might know your ways. So Mote It Be!

It is an accepted practice in many traditions to light a candle in the maiden's honor. White, a symbol of purity, is the traditional color of the virgin in Celtic Paganism; other traditions use blue or silver. White, being the most neutral and fully-balanced color (it is actually the projection of all color reflections) is always a good choice when you are undecided about color use in any magickal operation.

You may wish to recite seasonal or ritual poetry that has meaning to your working, or to sing a song in the maiden's honor. Praise what she stands for and ask her to help impart those values into your life. The words might sound something like this:

Gentle Maiden, help me to understand, as I stand here under your waxing light, that no matter how old I grow there is always a future, there is always change, and I, like your three faces, will forever return to my own beginnings to start anew. Hopefully I will do this wiser than before. Impart to me your vast spirit of anticipation, your wonder at all that is, your joy in simply being. As I connect with your infinite energy, may I realize that there is value in the young. They are our collective future. And help me to know that this moment in time is but a small part of a never-ending cycle taking me swiftly to my end, and then back to where I began. Help me to see the worth of this moment now. So Mote It Be!

You might want to use an even more traditional elemental blessing, one which utilizes all four of the elements (or five, if you count the fifth element of spirit).

This blessing should come from your heart and be tailored to your current needs, goals, and level of spiritual development. Plan ahead how each element's attributes can be taught or enhanced by the maiden's powers of foresight and youthful enthusiasm. Take whatever tool you use to represent that element on your altar and walk with it to the direction that you, or your tradition, deems to correspond to that element. Move clockwise around your circle starting at any point you like.

For the element of air, associated with communication and intellect, you might say:

> *May that which is new, born of your youthful enthusiasm, be present in my creative consciousness, my planning for the future, and all my speech and understanding. Though I will cherish that which is old and familiar, may I never grow out of touch with the joy of things new, and may I embrace and respect all change as part of your eternal good will.*

For fire, linked to life, passion, and transformation, you might offer this:

> *May your joyful anticipation for the future be found in the steps my life takes, now and always. Take me where I need to be both spiritually and physically with a full sense of the wondrous adventure that is existence.*

The element of water, concerned with emotions, fertility, and purification, could be worded as follows:

> *May your divine presence purify my heart so that it will always be open to love when offered. May I always look to new relationships with the same enthusiasm for impending destiny that I had as a child.*

The element of earth is the realm of home, family, and prosperity:

> *May your sense of daring send me courageously into all my new ventures. Bless my home with your sisterly love, your friendship, and your divine guidance.*

If you wish to honor the element of spirit, raise your arms high and say something like:

> *My your youthful joy be in my heart and in my soul, carrying me through each moment of time in peace and transcendent understanding.*

End the blessing with words that express your blessings and good wishes for the maiden:

> *May your gentle light always shine brightly as your children turn to thee in love and adoration. May your gentle laughter always echo in the hearts of your children, turning us from sorrow to joy as we say — So Mote It Always Be!*

If you follow a tradition which honors each of the thirteen moons of the year as having a specific type of energy, now is the time to honor that aspect. For example, if this is your Wolf Moon, honor wolf energy with offerings, shapeshifting rites*, or promises to contribute to wildlife funds that aid wolves and other wild canines. Have something already on your altar to honor the wolf spirit that you might wish to call to your circleside.

After this, turn your attention back to the waxing moon. Spend some time attuning your inner-mind to its energies, or invoke her if you prefer, using the method presented in the full moon ritual for Drawing Down the Moon.

If you do not wish to invoke the maiden Goddess, but still wish to further connect with her in some meaningful way, you can use visual imagery similar to that of a guided meditation to create an inner-plane space in which to meet her.

To begin this exercise, breathe slowly and steadily. Slow your mind, allowing your thoughts to flow so far inward that you begin to feel separate from yourself. Then embark on your inner-journey. Allow it to go something like this:

It is just after dawn and you are walking through a dewy spring meadow. Early wildflowers are blooming underfoot and the yellow-green grass waves gently in the the light breeze. Off in the distance, a virgin woods sprouts new growth, and flowering buds decorate the once bare boughs where birds now twitter, brightly welcoming the new day.

You inhale deeply of the fresh air of morning, making yourself promise to remember to take time from your daily demands and constant concerns for the future to stop and enjoy these simple pleasures.

Suddenly, your eye is drawn by a flash of white which scurries past you on the ground. It is a small white rabbit.

You mentally send it blessings as you watch it run. At the edge of its den, it turns to you and winks. At first you want to dismiss the idea as silly. Then it winks again, as if challenging you to doubt.

You laugh with joy at the small creature as it turns to leave. You assume it is going to disappear inside its hole, but then it takes off at a bounding hop for the nearby woods. You watch it go and notice that it keeps stopping to look back at you, as if beckoning you to follow.

Feeling up for new adventures (and a bit like Alice about to stumble into Wonderland), you chase after the rabbit.

The rabbit slows when it enters the woods so that you can keep up. You continue to follow until the animal stops at the base of what has to be the tallest tree in the forest. It is an unusually tall willow, which seems quite out of place in the deep forest setting. Deciding the anomaly must be fed from an underground spring, you are about to abandon your game with the rabbit and return to the meadow when you notice someone sitting high on a curved bough.

---

*To learn this specialized technique refer to *Animal Speak* by Ted Andrews (Llewellyn).

To your utter surprise, a young woman is resting lightly on a fragile branch. She could be any age from fourteen to thirty. Although she is young, something about her seems ageless. Her silky yellow hair streams about her waist and her sea-green eyes seem to pierce right through you. She wears a long, flowing white gown. Her slender feet are bare, and around her head she wears a silver headband which holds a crest of silver upturned horns. You smile timidly at her; she returns the greeting with a warm enthusiasm as she motions you up in the tree with her.

Greet the maiden with the traditional words "Merry Meet" and allow your inner-senses to finish dictating the direction of the meditation. Allow the maiden to teach you, either by showing or telling you something you need to know. Or you may simply stand near her, getting comfortable with her presence.

When it is time to go, thank the Goddess for her company in any way you feel is appropriate. When you are ready, head back out of the woods to the place in the meadow where you began this inner journey. After you are there you can return to your normal consciousness by any means you choose.

You can now begin any spellwork you might wish to do. Keep in mind that virtually all spells can be tailored to fit the moon cycle, and all spellwork can be done with or without any invoked energy (i.e.; Drawing Down the Moon).

After the spellwork is done you should build and release the pent-up energy through dance, or by other some other method (see Chapter 2 for suggestions.)

By tradition, the movements of your dance for the waxing moon should proceed in a clockwise direction, which is symbolic of increase. This honors the growing energy of the waxing moon and aids magick that, on this phase, is most often done for matters of gain.

While the Ceremony of Cakes and Ale is generally not a part of waxing moon rituals, you should still offer some sort of sustenance to the beings you have called to your circle. This is especially true if you follow one of the Celtic traditions. Offer a libation to the animals, too. If you are inside, this portion can be set aside to be taken outdoors later.

You can then release any invoked energy you may have inside you, and/or dismiss any beings called to your circle. Thank the young Goddess for her presence and assistance:

I thank you, my Sister, for your gentle and loving presence, for your slender guiding light which will light my steps homeward and bless my dreams. Until next time, Merry Part. And may Merry we Meet Again. The rite is closed. Blessed Be!

Close the circle in your usual manner.

Waxing Moon Ritual Ideas for Covens

Since few covens regularly meet on the waxing moon (although a few do meet on the new moon), coven members who want to experiment with these energies have lots of room to be creative without stepping on the toes of those who wish to be enslaved to tradition. There simply are no communal traditions common to the waxing moon.

A few ideas for waxing moon rituals can be gleaned from various books on Pagan rituals, but you will find the majority focus solely on the full moon or, occasionally, on the new. The following is a list of possibilities you might wish to incorporate in a waxing moon ritual for groups. These ideas will stimulate your creative inspiration and provide you with a firm base for beginning your new venture.

- Begin the ritual in as much darkness as is practical. Light candles or other lights one by one throughout the rite, to symbolize the waxing energy.

- Allow the youngest member of the group to portray the maiden Goddess and offer blessing to the entire group. For example, you may have her hold a small cauldron or chalice containing salt water, and offer blessing to each person individually.

- Ask members to tell a story about their relationship with the maiden. Many will likely begin with stories of their childhood and discuss either their own lives or those of their sisters or female friends. Note how each individual's ideas have altered since their initiation into Paganism.

- Group guided meditation can be a powerful experience among people who work well together, bringing a greater sense of cohesion to your coven by uniting your group mind in ways you may never have thought possible. Adapt the meditation given in the solitary ritual in this chapter, or write your own. Compare notes when you are finished to see just how many of your numbers experienced similar visualizations and feelings. It is not uncommon for long-time group members to have startlingly analogous experiences.

- The maiden Goddess represents new beginnings and her waxing moon is a good time to bless upcoming events. You may even build a new tradition for yourselves from this association. For instance, you might allow the youngster who is portraying the maiden to offer special blessings to couples about to be handfasted (married), to teens going away to school, to someone about to begin a new business, etc. Anything new, different, or changing can be blessed by the maiden.

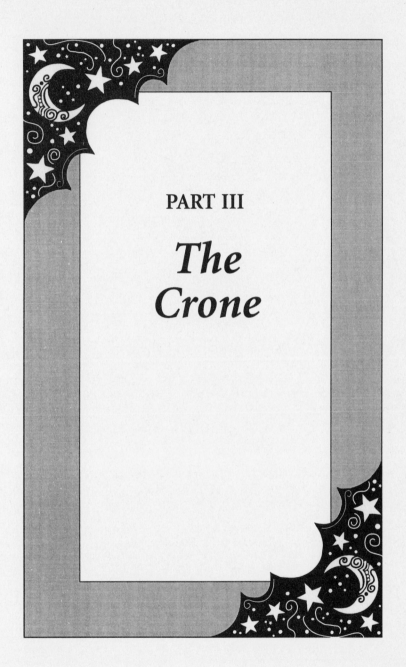

PART III

The
Crone

5

The Waning Moon

I will go with the old moon, but remember,
with her I shall also return.
— Rebecca Worrell

The waning moon is a time of release, of slowing down, a time when the peak of lunar energy is past, but its deeper mysteries remain to be uncovered. Like the undertow of the wave which recedes from the shore back into the sea, the waning moon pulls us into the darker realm of the Goddess. This is a time to cherish; there is only a short time to enjoy the ebb before the cycle begins again, bringing new waves to crest upon our shores in a never-ending symphony of push and pull.

The energy of the waning moon is believed by many Pagans to begin on the fourth night after the full moon and to last until the precise moment of total darkness. This single point of totality lasts for only a brief moment in time. It cannot be seen by the naked eye; an ephemeris would need to be consulted to determine this precise moment.

Waning moon energy is associated with the crone aspect of the Goddess, the powerful lady whose strength and wisdom has been feared and reviled for over 3,000 years. Her image has been denigrated, feared, and hidden. She is the prototype for the cackling, broom-riding, cauldron-stirring Halloween witch who eats children and casts spells of impotency over men and livestock. This general fear, and perhaps jealousy, has been projected onto womankind in general and old women in particular. It has been made an excuse for their ill-treatment and even their murder for many, many centuries.

This denigration of the crone has even found its way — albeit unintentionally — into Pagan scholarship. One writer in recent years has gone so far as to say that cultures which had crone Goddesses did not respect women or the elderly. This is purely a fear projection on the part of such writers; they reason that if the crone exists at all, she must therefore be bad, because she is old and unpleasant to look upon. Logic tells us that the opposite is true. Any culture that worshiped women (and all of them did at one point in time), particularly old women, certainly understood the crone to be a powerful deity, not in an evil way, but in ways different from those of her younger incarnations. She was not reviled, feared, or repressed until religions teaching monotheistic male worship went proselytizing among the common folk.

To be whole beings, we must embrace all aspects of our God/dess, including her dark side. This exploration need not be an unpleasant experience, nor need it be feared. On the contrary, it can be a beautiful and fulfilling experience, leading to a greater understanding of self, and of the lost Pagan mysteries we presumably seek. One of the best ways to realize this is through the Sabbats of the solar Pagan year which honor the crone. These are Samhain and the Autumn Equinox, when she mourns the annual demise and death of the God and prepares to travel back to the Land of the Dead so that her reincarnation as the maiden can take place at the Winter Solstice.

Some Witches flatly refuse to do magick on the waning moon, particularly as it draws closer to the point of total darkness. Their excuse is that these are dark forces best left undisturbed, that the crone is too unpredictable and vengeful to be trusted, that it is a negative time and no positive magick can be successful. Perhaps this is simply a fear projection. After all, wouldn't you be vindictive if you had been repressed and degraded for centuries?

This idea of the crone being dangerous is ridiculous! The crone is simply our own beloved Goddess in a different form. Such logic is like saying it's all right to love your mother until she becomes a grandmother, at which point you must ignore and/or suspect her. She is not negative. She is just changed, and change can be positive and produce positive results in the lives it touches. It is the same with the crone Goddess.

While intellectually many Pagans understand this distinction, in practice loving the crone is difficult for many, especially in youth-worshipping western societies. There are several things you can do to help yourself over this blockage to your completeness. They will take a little effort, but the results are well worth the trouble you will go to, as they will produce lasting, life-changing effects.

1. Next October go into any store which sells Halloween items and buy yourself the ugliest, most disturbing depiction of a Witch you can find. Unfortunately, they are not hard to come by. Take it home and hang it where you can see it every day. Meditate on its image while remembering how a once honored and positive image got this way. Never forget the fear and ignorance which caused this, but don't allow negative anger to rule your thinking.

Peer into the wart-covered face every day and try to see the beauty inside. Over time you will notice that she never ceases to surprise you with new revelations about herself. If the Witch has her cauldron with her, all the better. Archetypally this is the source of all life, the womb of the Goddess through which all things are born. Focus on this symbol; remember you have her to thank for your existence.

Also keep in mind that the Goddess will eventually change. She is eternal and will be young again, just as we each will be when the next life cycle begins for us. See beyond the crone to the maiden waiting to emerge and to the loving mother she was and will be again.

2. Find or create a guided meditation or pathworking* that takes you into the dark realms. A guided meditation is simply a story rife with archetypal symbolism which is

---

*For detailed information on pathworking and its construction see my earlier work *Celtic Myth and Magick*, or *Magical States of Consciousness* by Denning and Phillips (both Llewellyn).

read to someone in a meditative (also called an altered, slowed, or receptive) state of consciousness, allowing the person to experience rather than merely listen to the story. Guided meditations involving the crone can be somewhat hard to find as many Pagan writers shy away from these dark images. Rest assured there is nothing to fear from her. Rationally, there is more to fear in ignoring this part of ourselves and of our Pagan heritage. In your mind, allow yourself to approach her, learn from her, and, finally, embrace and thank her before you leave the meditative state.

3. Read oral histories which have recently been collected by historians. These descriptions of past events are taken down verbatim from older people who remember the incidents being discussed.

A crone figurine, with her cauldron, broom, and cat familiar, such as this, might be found at gift shops, discount stores, or autumn craft fairs.

Wisdom is the key word to remember when we wish to unlock the crone's long-kept secrets. She has a lifetime of experiences to share with us and she is much wiser than we realize, until we share her world. In ancient Pagan societies, old women were often the keepers of the history and knowledge of the tribe or clan. They were the storytellers, the mythmakers, the midwives, and the herbalists. Over a lifetime they gathered their wisdom to pass on to younger women who would one day take their place.

4. Look carefully at the faces of the elderly women you meet every day. Catch the twinkle in their eyes, the smile on their lips, and know they possess a sense of humor, a heart, and feelings as strong, as sensitive as your own. Look past the wrinkles to the face of the person beneath. Is she really so scary? Remember that she is likely someone's mother or grandmother, that she has a circle of acquaintances similar to your own and a lifetime of valuable experiences and stories to share if only you would let her.

5. Go beyond merely looking at older people to actually interacting with them. Speak to them, engage them in conversation. Don't talk down or allow your tone of voice to

become condescending. These are adults who have taken care of themselves for a long time. Treat them as though they are still fully human (which they are!).

Studies have shown that as a woman ages, western society tends to render her more and more invisible. She is unwanted. She makes people uncomfortable. She is a grim reminder of our own mortality. She is shoved, pushed, and ignored by the very people she devoted her life to raising and nurturing.

You might wish to volunteer at a nursing home or elder care center to further this contact with the elderly of both sexes.

6. Become involved with progressive retreats for the elderly such as Elderhostel. Elderhostel, and programs like it, are educational convocations for active older persons who wish to meet with others and learn new things. The programs, very innovative and never patronizing, are usually run and taught by people thirty or forty years younger than the participants. I have a friend who has worked with this program for years and finds it very rewarding. In line with the old adage that a good teacher is also taught by her pupils, my friend always comes away from these weekends as much richer for the experience as those she was hired to teach.

7. If you are lucky enough to have living grandmothers or great-aunts, or if your own mother is elderly, don't ignore these women. Make time to visit with them and allow them to become more than just a title applied to a soon-to-be-forgotten ancestor. They may have been the first people to hold you after your birth. My own paternal grandmother was the first person outside of hospital staff to hold and cuddle me. I even grew up to look startlingly like her. My maternal grandmother also gave her wisdom to me when I was very young. She taught me to cherish my family heritage and, thanks to her, I am sure I am one of the few thirty-somethings living in the 1990s who can dance the Peabody and the Charleston.

Grandparents can tell you stories about the past that rival all the excitement of the movies. Such stories are better not only because they are true, but because they are peopled with real characters, such as your own parents as children. Grandparents can also tell you stories passed down from their grandparents, providing the kind of link from one generation to another which has always been the lifeline of Pagan oral traditions. Without such stories our Pagan heritage would have been lost forever.

Folk remedies for many minor ailments are also part of our elders' vast collection of knowledge, and are marvelously effective. Unfortunately these remedies are falling victim to a systemized war to obliterate them. The medical establishment, which according to its own ethics ought to embrace anything which heals the human body; and the pharmaceutical industry, which is always looking for a fat profit, are the worst offenders. If we do not fight these power structures, assert our rights against them, and capture and record this ancient folk wisdom now, within a few short years it may be lost to us forever.

There is potent magick to be made on the waning moon, even when she wears her darkest face. Her energies are admittedly different than those of the waxing and full phases, but they are just as effective. Spells best worked on the waning moon deal with decrease, endings, and banishings. The waning phase is also best for the sort of protection magick that seeks to ground or return negativity which has been sent your way. It is a time of psychic slowing; its energies are compatible with the bending of time and the blending of one's self with other energies and intelligences. (See Chapter 11 and 12 for spells which utilize the moon's waning phase.)

Invisibility spells and rites, popular in many old cultures including the Celtic, are best learned during this phase because they use the imagery of blending with the universal. While most mythological references to invisibility are metaphors for astral projection (the expulsion of one's consciousness from the physical body), not all invisibility spells utilize this technique. Non-astral methods require learning to blend in with your environment, to merge with your surroundings and become unnoticed. In the wild, animals use this type of camouflage to their advantage every day. Often their survival depends on it. For humans it can be equally useful, particularly if you suddenly find yourself in a dangerous situation and there is no place to hide your physical self.

During the waning moon you can practice invisibility by getting to know the feel of the energy which emanates from your surroundings. Touch your walls. Are they papered or painted? Old or new? Do they vibrate from the running of appliances, or do they stand cold and stiff? Run your hand over your sofa and feel the texture. What color is it? Close your eyes; try to get a sense of the vibrations the color releases. What is the texture? Rough or smooth? What type of activities take place there, and how have they affected the energy flow? What is your initial emotional reaction to the fabric? What does the bark of the tree in your backyard feel like? What is your gut reaction to it? Throw your arms around it and hug it. What do you instinctively feel you would have to do in order to step inside and become a part of it?

Pick just one object with which to begin experimenting. As much as the natural places might appeal to the Pagan spirit, it is best to begin with something inside your own home. First of all, this item will have absorbed a large part of your own energy by living with you every day; it already shares an affinity with you. Secondly, indoors it is easier to have the total undisturbed privacy the experiment requires.

Once you have made your choice, settle yourself against the object with which you intend to merge. It is often best to practice this exercise naked until you are adept at doing it. Nudity allows you to use all of your body's senses to feel and become the object. Let's say you are using your sofa for practice. Take off your clothes, enjoy a pre-ritual bath if you prefer, then sit or lie on the sofa, contracting yourself into as small a position as is comfortably possible. Fetal positions are usually preferred. Close your eyes and sense the object beneath you. Feel it in every pore of your body. Let its subtle vibrations work their way into you.

Begin to allow your body to take on the energy of the sofa. Sense yourself becoming the color of the sofa, the texture, and then the shape. Feel the sofa absorbing you, welcoming you, shielding and hiding you.

After you become adept at merging with objects in your home, you can test your new skills in public (fully clothed, of course). Trying this exercise at a restaurant known for its prompt service is an excellent start. If the wait staff seems to overlook you, you will know that you are successfully concealing yourself.

While the non-astral invisibility technique seems simple, even hard to believe, it does work very well. Parapsychologists (scientists and psychologists who study paranormal phenomena) hypothesize that somehow persons adept at this practice actually are able to temporarily alter some of their molecular structure to truly become a part of their environment. Children do this easily — just ask any parent who has searched the house from attic to basement looking for a youngster who was sitting quietly playing on the floor of his room all along.

An intriguing documented case has been recorded by parapsychologist Christopher Chacon of the Office of Scientific Investigation and Research. One night a young boy who had been sleeping awoke to find himself partially transparent. Panicking, as anyone would, he ran screaming into his parents' bedroom. Without even thinking, he took the most direct route — right through the wall. During his rush he began to realize that what he was doing just wasn't possible. At this point his molecular structure, which had somehow been altered during sleep, returned to normal, and the boy become stuck in the wall of his parents' room. The fire department was called in to dismantle the wall and rescue the boy.*

Divinations performed on the waning moon work best when related to matters concerning our past lives, another province of the crone. Witches almost universally see her as the one who ultimately decides when, where, and how we reincarnate. Most good books on divinatory methods give at least one karmic (unresolved energy carried over from another lifetime) or past-life-revealing technique. One of my favorite techniques is a simple Tarot spread designed to answer a question about an immediate current-life problem which may have past-life roots. If the reading makes sense to you, then there is definitely a past-life connection. If it is pure nonsense, cards representing so many facets of life that there is no possible continuity, then this is likely a new situation for you.

To do this divination, shuffle and cut your Tarot cards in your usual manner. Before you lay them out ask the crone Goddess, either generically or by any name you prefer, to bless the cards and reveal any answers which may help you deal with your current situation or problem.

The layout follows a counter-clockwise pattern which symbolically cycles back through time. Begin laying out the cards in the manner shown on page 82.

Each position has a specific meaning:

1. This is the card of the self, the present-day you. The card should clarify your immediate concern, identify the heart of the matter, and perhaps reveal the real you in relation to the issue at hand.

---

*Interview from *The Very Scary Almanac* by Eric Elfman (New York: Random House, 1993).

2. This is the card of your most immediate fear or desire. It should reflect what you truly hope for as an outcome and/or reveal the fear which is preventing you from taking action.

3. The third card is the card of immediate causality, which reveals the present-life root of the current problem or issue.

4. The fourth card is the card of long-past causality. If a past-life connection for your current situation exists, it should be revealed here. The card should clarify the root of the issue in a way which is clearly understandable to you. If it fails to do this, you may wish to look at your current life for answers, rather than the past.

5. The fifth card is the card of karma. It should tell you what type of specific past-life situation actually contributed to your current difficulty.

6. The sixth card reveals anyone involved in your present problem who was also a part of your past-life difficulty. If the problem directly concerns family, friends, or romantic relationships, there is usually someone the querient can easily recognize. If the card does not represent another person to you, look for it to speak of what consequences your actions, right or wrong, might have had on others in that past life.

7. The seventh card attempts to tie cards four, five, and six together by presenting you with a broad overview of the past root of the problem now at hand.

8. The eighth card is the card of rectification. It should provide clues enabling you to overcome your problem and escape from a destructive cycle.

9. The ninth card is the clarifier, the final outcome of the action suggested to you by the eighth card.

10. The tenth card is optional. It should only be turned over if the ninth card is too vague to interpret. Do not try to use this card to better an unwanted outcome or you will only cheat yourself out of the knowledge you seek. Use it only to help sharpen the focus of the reading if needed.

Only you can interpret the correct meaning of this spread. Not only should you use whatever Tarot guidebook you work with to assist you, but you should also examine your intuitive feelings and gut reactions to each of the cards and the symbols on them. After all, it is your life (lives?), your problem, and only you can make the final decision about it. Remember that one of the basic tenets of Paganism is self-responsibility. The Tarot is simply one tool for helping you to make wise, informed decisions.

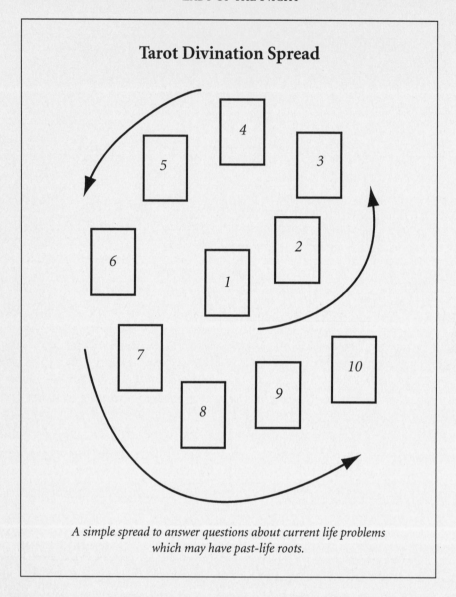

Tarot Divination Spread

A simple spread to answer questions about current life problems which may have past-life roots.

Before you take up the spread, be sure to record it in your Book of Shadows or other magickal/Pagan diary, and thank the crone Goddess for her help.

In order to wholly experience all things Pagan, and to gain the fullest measure of your personal power as a Witch, you must learn to work and worship within all the moon's phases. Practice with waning moon ritual and magick, get to know and love the crone. Her time is not one of evil and it never has been. She is your own loving grandmother, waiting patiently for you to return to her.

A Waning Moon Ritual

They waved until she was clean out of sight
... and then they cried.
— Laura McKenna, from *Old Granny's Visit*

The following ritual to honor the waning moon and the crone Goddess is intended for solitaries. Few, if any, covens regularly meet on the waning moon. For those who do, this ritual can be adapted for group use by assigning roles and writing out spoken dialogue for the mental speeches, gestures, and/or alignments used by the solitary.

You will need to gather your tools and set up your altar in your regular working spot. Of course, working outdoors is nice if you can assure yourself of quiet and privacy, but there is nothing wrong with working indoors.

When you have your tools and any other chosen items ready, you may cast your circle in your usual manner and begin the main body of the ritual. (Refer to Chapter 2 for ideas on ritual tools, directional associations, circle-casting, calling quarters, etc.)

Waning Moon Solitary Ritual

Stand in front of your altar with arms spread and eyes looking heavenward. Breathe deeply and feel yourself aligning with the waning lunar forces. Either mentally or out loud call upon the crone, stating your love for her and the purpose of your ritual. You can call her by any crone-Goddess name you like. I prefer to call on the Irish crone Badb. If you don't have a preference or haven't yet found the crone image you feel most in tune with, just call her by the loving term "Grandmother."

Blessed Be, Grandmother. I, (state mundane or Craft name), stand here
in your dimming light this eve that your deep mysteries might be revealed
to me and that you might bless my magick.

Raise a glass of wine, water, or juice and offer her a toast of honor:

> *Blessed Be, Grandmother, on this night when you rule the hearts and lives of your children. Blessed Be your narrowing silver crescent riding low in the night sky, and Blessed Be me, your loving child, whose earth-bound feet seek to follow your ways.*

It is accepted practice in many traditions to light a candle in her honor. Black is the traditional color of the crone in Celtic Paganism; the Dianic Tradition uses gold. The choice is yours to make.

You may wish to recite seasonal or ritual poetry which has meaning to your working, or to sing a song in the crone's honor. Praise what she stands for and ask her to help impart those values into your life:

> *Grandmother, as I stand here under your waning light, help me to understand that there is as much value in slowing down as in moving quickly, as much to be gained from introspection as from outer-analysis, as much good in goings as in comings, as much to look forward to in the past as in the future, and as much to be valued in the old as in the new. Help me to know that this moment is but a small part of a larger whole, the never-ending cycle of time which is taking me swiftly back to where I was and will propel me forward again. Help me to see the worth of this moment now. So Mote It Be!*

You might want to use an even more traditional elemental blessing, one which utilizes all four of the elements (or five if you count the element of spirit). This blessing should come from your heart and be tailored to your current needs, goals, and level of spiritual development. Plan ahead how each element's attributes can be taught or enhanced by the crone's powers of wisdom and hindsight.

Take whatever tool you use to represent an element on your altar and walk with it to the direction which you, or your tradition, deems to correspond to that element. Move clockwise around your circle starting at any point you like.

For the element of air, associated with communication and intellect, you might use words such as the following:

> *May your sharp thinking be present in my conclusions, my reasoning, and all my communications.*

For fire, linked to life, passion, and transformation, you might offer this:

> *May your vast experience and knowledge guide the steps of my life, taking me where I need to be both spiritually and physically.*

The element of water, concerned with emotions, fertility, and purification, could be worded thus:

> *May your divine presence purify my heart so that it will be always open to love when offered.*

The element of earth is the realm of home, family, and prosperity:

> *May your rich hindsight imbue me with the ability to make sound financial decisions. Bless my home with your grandmotherly love.*

If you wish to honor the element of spirit, raise your arms high and say something like:

> *May your crone wisdom be in my heart and in my soul, carrying me through each moment of time in peace and transcendent understanding.*

End the blessing with words that express your wishes for the crone:

> *May your wisdom be the ever-flowing fount of strength from which your loving children may always drink deeply, both in this life and when we return to you at its end to drink from the cauldron of regeneration. So Mote It Be!*

If you follow a tradition which honors each of the thirteen moons of the year as having a specific energy, now is the time to honor that aspect. (See the Waxing Moon Ritual in Chapter 4 for a full explanation).

After this, turn your attention back to the waning moon. Spend some time attuning your inner-mind to its energies, or invoke her if you prefer, using the method presented in the full moon ritual for Drawing Down the Moon.

If you are new to exploring the dark phases of the moon and do not yet feel comfortable invoking the crone into yourself, you can still use this circle as a place to meet with her and learn. Using visual imagery similar to that of a guided meditation, you can create an inner-plane space in which to meet her. To begin, breathe slowly and steadily, slowing your mind and allowing your thoughts to flow so far inward that you begin to feel separate from the thinking part of yourself. When you reach this point, embark on your inner-journey. Allow it to go something like this:

> *You find yourself on the shore of a great ocean just as the last of the red-orange sun sets beneath the far western horizon. Very shortly it is dark and you see a large, waning crescent moon directly overhead, throwing a subtle light over the desolate countryside. It is winter. A light crust of snow crunches underfoot and the nearby trees are bare of foliage, their black spikey branches barely visible against the night sky.*
>
> *Somewhere far off in the night you hear the flapping of wings, like the sound of a giant bird coming closer and closer to you. Then you see it, flying smoothly above*

the dark sea. It is a huge, oil-black raven which sweeps gracefully down and lands beside you. Surprisingly you have no fear of this creature. The bird intimates that you should get on its back. Sensing that the animal has only your best interest at heart, you do as it asks, and it flies into the air again, carrying you over the night-blackened sea, far, far from the snow-covered shore.

The raven lands on a dark, fog-shrouded island where you dismount. While looking around and deciding what to do next you notice a thin firelight coming from deep within the nearby woods. You follow the light until it leads to a clearing where you find the most intriguing old woman you've ever seen standing over a large boiling cauldron. The image is anything but sinister; several small animals are gathered near her, animals usually timid of humans. If they show no fear or hesitation you realize you shouldn't either.

The old woman looks up at you without expression as if waiting for you to make the first move. You step into the clearing and approach her with a smile, which she returns. You catch the jolly twinkle in her sharp old eyes and see the ages of wisdom stored therein.

Greet the crone with the traditional words "Merry Meet" and allow your inner-senses to finish dictating the direction of the meditation. Allow the crone to teach you either by showing or telling you something you need to know. Or simply stand near her, getting comfortable with her presence. When it is time to go, thank the crone for her wisdom and assistance in any way you feel is appropriate. Then head back out of the woods to where the raven waits to take you back to the shore. After you are there you can return to your normal consciousness by any means you choose.

You can now begin any spellwork you are interested in performing. Keep in mind that most spells can be tailored to fit the moon cycle. Spellwork can be done with or without any invoked energy (i.e.; Drawing Down the Moon).

After the spellwork is done you should build and release the pent-up energy through dance, or by some other method (see Chapter 2 for suggestions).

On the waning moon, dances and other movements are usually made in a counter-clockwise direction (also referred to as widdershins, tuathail, left-walking, reverse, or against the sun). This is done not only to honor the diminishing lunar forces, but also because most magick made on the wane is done to eliminate or banish something and it is traditional to move counter-clockwise when banishment is needed. This is also called destructive magick, but don't be misled by this label. In this case the term destructive means to dismantle something unwanted, not to cause harm. Just because the movement is counter-clockwise does not make it a negative act. It is merely a tool for raising power. Magick, both good and bad, can be performed by moving in either direction. Only the intent of the spellcaster for good or evil can determine the outcome of the spell.

While the Ceremony of Cakes and Ale is generally not a part of waning moon rituals, you should still offer some sort of sustenance to the beings you have called forth to your circle. This is especially true if you follow one of the Celtic traditions. Offer a libation to the animals, too. If you are inside, this portion can be set aside to be taken outdoors later.

You can then release any invoked energy you may have inside you, and/or dismiss any beings called to your circle. Thank the crone for her presence and assistance:

> I thank you, Grandmother, for your wise and loving presence, for your gentle teaching light which will guide my steps homeward and bless my dreams. Until next time, Merry Part. And may Merry we Meet Again. The rite is closed. Blessed Be!

Close the circle in your usual manner.

Waning Moon Ritual Ideas for Covens

Since virtually no covens regularly meet on the waning moon, the coven who wants to experiment with the energies of the wane has lots of freedom to interpret without running up against the inevitable arguments about what is "always done" that crop up when planning major festival rites.

The following is a list of possibilities you might wish to incorporate in a waning moon ritual for groups. Hopefully these will provide you with a firm base for beginning your new venture and stimulate your own creative inspiration.

- Work in darkness as much as possible in order to align yourselves more fully with the energies of the darkness, the natural culmination of every moon cycle. You can begin your rite with well-lighted space if you wish, but extinguish your lights one by one as the ritual continues to symbolize the movement of the waning phase.

- Allow members of the group to speak to the crone Goddess in their own words, voicing their feelings about her and the darkness. Surprising revelations may be forthcoming.

- Ask members to tell a story about their relationships with the darkness. Most will likely begin with fears rooted in childhood and how these have changed or begun to change since they were initiated as Witches.

- Group guided-meditation can be a powerful experience among people who work well together, and bring a greater sense of cohesion to your coven by uniting your group mind in ways you may never have thought possible. You can adapt the meditation given in the solitary ritual in this chapter, or write your own. At the conclusion of the meditation, compare notes to see just how many of your members experienced similar visualizations and feelings. It is not uncommon for long-time group members to have startlingly analogous experiences.

- There is no rule which says that only the full moon can be Drawn Down. Honor the eldest member of your group with being the crone Goddess, or begin experimenting with offering that honor to a man in your group. Men age too, you know!

- If you do not wish to Draw Down the waning moon, you can still allow one person to portray the crone Goddess. Allow him or her to offer blessings to the group, and allow the group to express their feelings towards the crone in this safe environment. Remember that to many she still conjures up unsettling images of death and endings with which they are not yet comfortable. Let each person have time to work out his or her own difficulties.

- You may want to pick a specific crone Goddess and honor her. For instance, in autumn you might choose to pay homage to Hecate, the Greek Goddess of the waning moon who is so deeply linked with our modern Halloween Witch image. Or you might select Badb, the Irish crone who presides over the cauldron of life, death, and rebirth.

- Group past-life exploration is another practice which has an affinity to the waning moon. Often groups whose members share a common outlook and instant attraction for one another will find they have a common past. You can explore your past through any means you prefer: Tarot, Runes, group-meditation, etc. Select one person to lead the session, portraying the crone Goddess who will one day lead us all to the Land of the Dead to await rebirth.

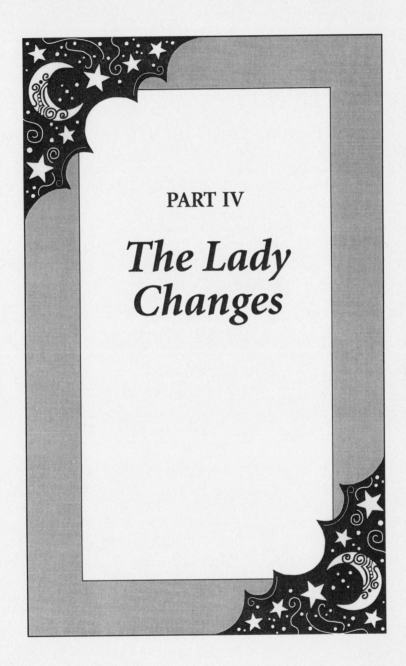

PART IV

The Lady
Changes

Moonrise, Moonset, and
From Dark to New

Her shape arises,
She is less guarded than ever,
yet more guarded than ever,
...nothing is conceal'd from her,
...She is the best belov'd,
...She is silent —

— Walt Whitman

Moonrise, moonset, and the dark and new moons are all times usually overlooked by Pagans. Yet these moments hold a subtle energy all their own, a unique spirit that can be harnessed for many magickal and ritual endeavors.

Moonrise and Moonset

Moonrise and moonset go almost unnoticed by humanity, even within the Pagan community, whose members are unusually well-attuned to subtle psychic changes in the atmosphere. Certainly the moon's appearance and departure each night or day is less dramatic than that of the sun, and is so brief as to be seemingly unimportant. Yet these points in time mark the appearance of the most potent known symbol of the Goddess, the coming of the energies of the night, and a visible reminder that one of her eternal faces is always smiling upon us.

To complicate matters, the times of her coming and going do not necessarily correspond to the arrival of twilight and dawn. They are dependent upon the tilt of the earth, the season of the year and the phase of the moon itself. Moonrise and moonset can occur at anytime during the twenty-four hours of our solar-standard day. For example, during the first few days of the new moon, she rises and sets just behind the sun, impossible to see in the glare of its brighter light, becoming visible only after the sun has dropped behind the horizon, leaving her thin crescent alone in the western sky. Near the time of the last quarter she peeks over the horizon around midnight (approximately eighteen hours, or three-quarters of a day, after the sun rose), and at her dark phases, when she cannot be seen by the naked eye, she is still rising and setting, but in tandem with the sun. As she approaches fullness she rises during the hour or two before or after sunset. During part of the year you can go outdoors and see the sun resting at the western horizon while the full moon hovers over the eastern one. (By the way, this is a perfect time to work spells or rituals whose goal is the attaining of balance, stability, wholeness, or peace. It is also an efficacious moment for couple's magick, since the symbols of both the masculine and feminine energies share the heavens.)

The archetype of moonrise is linked to the awakening of Goddess energy, the time when she arises from her daily slumber to seek out her children, and is hoping to find them seeking her in return. Rituals designed for greeting the rising moon can be very meaningful, even if they are done in daylight.

The only unusual item you will need for this ritual is a crown of some kind. It can be made of cardboard, metal, aluminum foil, or any other item you find convenient. Or you may wish to purchase one at a toy store or costume shop. Size is also unimportant. It may be made large enough to set upon your head, or it can be small, like a doll's accessory, to be used to crown one of the moon's symbols on your altar.

With an ephemeris or some other astronomical guide, pinpoint the time of the moonrise on a night when you have the time to ritually greet her. If you live in a location where tall buildings, trees, or hillsides will block your view, you may wish to postpone the ritual for an hour or two in order to allow the moon to rise above these obstacles and be visible to you.

About half an hour before the appointed time of her appearance, set up your altar and your working tools. Orient them as much as possible to the point on the horizon where you expect to first view the moonrise.

Cast your circle and call your quarters, do any other preparatory formalities you usually observe, and then turn to face the horizon point where you expect to see the moon rise. Begin a slow and steady chant in her honor. Approach this like an act of sympathetic magick designed to woo the Lady back from her absence. (Those wishing to honor a lunar God at moonrise should feel free to altar the words to reflect a masculine gender.) For this you might wish to choose one of the following:

Mystic Lady of the Night,
Silver glow, and shimmer bright.

Horns (or disk) of pale shine,
Rise now in the sky of thine.

Silver Lady shining bright,
Rise and shed on me your light.

Keep the mantra simple, so that its steady rhythm can take your mind into a slower, ritual level of consciousness that will help prepare you for the rite to come. Even if it is daylight, phrase your words as if it were completely dark. The moon is still the potent archetypal symbol of the night and should always be approached in this manner, in order to feel the full impact of her presence.

When you finally see the moon, either in whole or in part, stop your chant. Raise your arms or a favorite ritual tool and welcome her:

> *Greetings to you,* (insert here the name of a moon Goddess, or God if you prefer, or use terms like Gentle Maiden, Loving Mother, or Grandmother, depending upon the moon's phase at the time of the ritual). *Welcome back from your day's slumber.* (Again, this is merely a metaphor to help us to attune to her energies. She is really present all the time, whether or not our side of the planet is facing her.) *Bright Lady, who flees the sun, the night and all its creatures are yours.*

Take the crown from your altar and hold it up to the moon saying:

> *Queen of the Heavens, blessed be your return to your nightly throne.*

Place the crown on your head as a symbolic gesture of the moon's sovereignty over the night, or place it on or around some moon symbol on your altar. If you have no specific moon symbol available, positioning the crown either on or around your chalice is an excellent choice.

Spend time meditating on the moon's rise. Take the opportunity to leisurely watch her slow ascent, taking her higher and higher into the sky. If it is twilight, focus on the sun receding behind you as if abandoning the heavens, symbolically bowing down in favor of his Queen. With practice you should be able to sense the change in the atmosphere when the moon becomes visible on the horizon, the moment when her faint light and influence spill over the earth below her, whether or not the sun is yet out of sight. Many Pagans prefer to do moon-centered magick only when she is visible to the eye. Knowing when this takes place can help you in planning spells.

You may wish to check what astrological sign she is rising in so that you may tailor your welcome, and your magick, accordingly. For example, if she is rising in Pisces you might want to focus on her psychic or emotional aspects; if she is in Libra you might honor her as a beacon of balance and justice.

By contrast, moonset is the archetype of retreating to slumber, of hibernation and repose, of vitality being stored and rebuilt. It is the time when the Lady abandons her throne in the heavens to make way for the coming of the sun deity.

While her disappearance is not a time that inspires many of us to lunar magick, it is a time when we can ritually bid her farewell and wish her a good day's sleep, attuning with yet another aspect of her energy

As in the ritual for her welcome, you should pinpoint the moment when she will disappear over your visible horizon. Again, be sure to take into account any buildings, trees, hillsides, or other obstacles that will hasten her departure from you.

About half an hour before you expect her to disappear, set up your altar and open your circle in your usual manner. When you are ready to begin the ritual, call out a greeting to her and thank her for her benevolent energy which has seen you through the night. Regardless of the time of day, phrase your sentences as if dawn is imminent:

> *Greetings* (insert a name or title here as you did in the moonrise ritual). *Blessed Be your light, which has graced the sky this night. Blessed be your many divine names, cherished and unforgotten by your loving children even though you slumber away from us. Sleep well, my Lady. May your dreams create a magickal new world for all the creatures of the earth. So Mote It Be!*

Allow yourself time to watch the moon sink below the horizon. You might choose to use this time to allow yourself to sense the energy of the departing moon, or you might wish to do a divination that will reveal what the day ahead holds in store. Or you might choose to follow an old Polynesian custom which demands that, in order to ensure the safe return of a departing loved one, a farewell song be sung until he or she is completely out of sight. No matter how involved you are in this ritual, or if you are deep within a closed-eyed altered state, with practice you will find that you can sense when the moon's light no longer falls upon your corner of the world.

When the moon is gone from your range of vision you may close the circle.

It would be nice if you were able to pick one entire month during which you could greet the moon at both her rising and setting. This would allow you to feel and attune more completely with the full range of her subtle changes as she comes and goes through all her phases. This could be of immeasurable help in virtually all areas of your spiritual and psychic development. Sadly, in modern lives tied to the punch of the time clock, this is almost an impossibility.

The Dark and New Moons

The Lady of the night is not visible to the naked eye when she approaches the moment of total darkness. The dark lasts for only a second then, ever-turning, she starts her ancient cycle once more. Yet we can know when this time occurs by consulting astronomical calendars, and we as Pagans can learn to make the most of this transitional energy.

Whereas popular culture refers to the moment of darkness as the new moon, I prefer a more accurate reference and call the dark time the "dark moon" and reserve the term "new" to refer the first whole day on which her cycle toward fullness begins again.

The new moon has always been seen as a time of fresh starts and new beginnings. Many cultures that still adhere to a lunar calendar honor the new moon with religious rites or festivals, or with divinations, offerings, and symbolic magick to ensure prosperity in the month ahead. They welcome her as a sign that all in the universe is good and well and that, at least for another month, life will go happily onward.

The most evident example of lunar worship at the new moon in the west has been carried on monthly for over five thousand years by the Jews. Before the Roman occupation of their homeland, on the day of the new moon (known as Rosh Hodesh), Jews brought free-will offerings and sin offerings into the Temple as a way of saying they wished to attain atonement for past wrongs and to seek the blessing of the deity. They also made sacrifices that included wine and flour, similar to the libation offered at the end of the Ceremony of Cakes and Ale. Early in Jewish history Rosh Hodesh was considered a woman's holiday and it was the women of the community who made the offerings and prayers to the Shekinah, the feminine half of the creator.

Jews still use a lunar calendar and continue the practice of holding special worship at the new moon. The focus of their worship is now on the male Judeo-Christian God, and in many synagogues women are forbidden to participate in any of the rituals. However, the remnants of one of the old prayers of greeting to her retains the flavor of one honoring a mother rather than a father figure. The following is an English translation of an old Hebrew prayer still used today to honor the appearance of the new moon. The sentiments are not only very old, but quite beautiful. You may wish to incorporate them into your own lunar rituals:

> *We thank You for the miracles which daily attend us, for Your wonders and favors morning, noon and night. You are beneficent and boundless in mercy and love. From old we have always placed our hope in You.*

By contrast, the dark of the moon has not always been seen as a time of positive power, but as one of negativity, during which the dark (read "evil") forces of the night can roam free. That attitude has unfortunately tainted not only popular thinking, but Paganism as well. The dark moon is indeed linked to things hidden and unseen, and fear of the unknown is a potent force, but seeing negative attributes in the hidden or unknown is the creation of a collective mindset uninterested in exploring beyond surface impressions, and controlled by those who had much to gain by fanning the flames of fear.

When women were beginning to be subjugated to the patriarchy, the dark moon was seen as an accursed time because it was associated with the bleeding phase of the menstrual cycle. Though this relationship is often dismissed today as a foolish notion, the moon may indeed have helped correlate women's cycles. Experiments have repeatedly shown that ovulation can be induced by limiting and lengthening light exposure under controlled conditions. Similar techniques are used today to control the laying cycles of hens (an animal deeply associated with the moon). Instead of viewing the bleeding of women as a positive sign, one linked to the continuation of life itself, it was an occurrence condemned by churchmen and associated with the dark forces, of which the moon was the primary symbol.

Many Witches who concede to working magick on the waning moon will absolutely not work on the dark moon. They feel this dark time will pose some danger to them. Be assured there is nothing to fear in darkness; it is merely another aspect of the light and of the Triple Goddess whom we worship. To deny ourselves access to the powers of the darkness because of medieval notions about evil forces and Halloween witches with wart-covered noses and pointy hats, is to give up a part of our Goddess-given heritage. If you buy into this "avoid the dark" thinking, keep in mind that the same medievalists who taught us to fear the dark also told us that it was dangerous to expose one's self to the light of the full moon, for they believed it would induce madness.

If you're still not convinced that magick on the dark moon is safe, I suggest you spend some time in study and introspection to discover exactly why it is you feel this way. Then, if you still feel opposed to dark moon magick, fine. At least you will have made an informed decision.

There are many magickal and ritual uses for the night during which the moon turns dark and then begins its journey to fullness once more. Many of the rituals surrounding this time are quite ancient. For example, some cultures who rely solely on lunar calendars sit vigils for the moon on this night, in much the same way as modern western Pagans will sit up on Midwinter's Eve lighting candles and performing other acts of sympathetic magick to lure back the waning sun.

Pagans can take advantage of the power in this interval by using an intense visualization which acts as a magick spell for complete banishment or transformation and renewal.

The first thing you will need to do is find the night on which the moon will go completely dark. Remember that this precise moment only lasts a second and, although we cannot see it taking place, the moon will immediately begin waxing again.

Plan your visualization session to cover the hour during which the moon will go dark. Start about half an hour beforehand and plan to end about a half hour later

Like waning moon spells, the tail end of the waning phase lends its energy to banishment work, and the totality of darkness is symbolic of that which consumes all unwanted energy in its black void. But unlike the waning phase, the quick turn to waxing that the dark moon makes lends its energy to positive self-transformation.

When you are in a place where you can be undisturbed for the hour this exercise takes, place yourself into an altered state of consciousness. There are many methods for slowing the mind, and many Witches have one or two of which they are fond. If you have no such preference, you can simply try using deep, rhythmic breathing while focusing on the change you wish to make in your life. After a few minutes of sustained concentration your mind will automatically slow and take you into its inner-realms, into the world of the sub- and superconscious that connects you to all the knowledge of the universe. Don't become upset if, when you are first learning to do this, your mind wants to wander. Like a child, the mind must be disciplined to develop in the way you want it to grow. If it wanders, simply treat it like an errant toddler and bring it gently back to where it is supposed to be.

When you are in the altered state, begin to form a clear picture of the aspect of your life you wish to banish. This can be anything from a bad financial situation to a bad habit or illness, or anything else from which you wish to totally disengage yourself.

In the last few minutes of the waning phase, begin to mentally chip away at the visual image. You can do this by seeing it fade away, be chopped off in chunks, or be buried; or you can actively participate in the destruction of the problem by visualizing yourself vigorously dismantling that which is unwanted. Use your hands, a sledge hammer, a shovel, or any other implement that seems right to you at the moment.

You should attempt to time the complete destruction of the mental image to coincide with the exact moment of darkness. In the beginning this will not be easy since, unless you are exceptionally gifted in altered-state work, you will be unable to be a clockwatcher. In either case, with practice you can begin to get a sense of when this change takes place.

When the dark phase passes and changes to the new, rebuild the image in your mind to what you want it to be. For instance, visualize your bank balance growing, your carefree life without your former bad habit, or your joy in having your complete health returned to you. Stay focused on the fulfillment image of this transformation for about thirty minutes.

Other spellwork involving transformation can also be done at this time. Experiment with combining banishment and attraction spells to cover this point in time. Chapters 8 through 12 can provide you with a firm basis for beginning your experimentation.

Attuning Yourself to the New Month

If you belong to a tradition that gives names or special attributes to its lunar months, you can pick a night just after the new moon to attune yourself to the shift in energy. Experiencing the change will come most easily for those who have been a part of specific traditions for a long time, but novices can easily train themselves to tune in to the attributes of each new month.

Though the full power of the particular month is felt most strongly at the full moon, and is usually formally celebrated at that time, all lunar calendars start counting the new month from the time of the new moon.

In a quiet, private place, get comfortable and begin to slow your mind. Mentally reach out to the thin silver thread in the heavens and form a psychic link with her. Some people like to visualize this as a beam of purple or silver light going from their brow straight up to the moon. Others prefer to see the link as a busy highway of energy, with lanes flowing both to and from the moon's surface.

Recalling the name of the new month, focus on those qualities as you perceive them or as your tradition teaches them to you. For example, if you follow a Celtic tradition and this is your Oak Moon, concentrate on the attributes of the oak tree in Celtic mythology. Think of the the quality of strength, masculine power, or of the Oak King, the divine ruler of the waxing year. Feel the subtle change in the moon's energy from that of the previous month, which in the Celtic lunar calendar would have been the Hawthorn Moon, a decidedly more feminine symbol.

Taking time to make such an attunement each month can be deeply satisfying, even if you belong to a coven which whom you will later meet to celebrate the full moon together. It can be a time for regaining your balance and realigning yourself with the forces of nature so important to Paganism. It can also be a time of introspection, when personal issues for the month ahead are decided.

If you or your tradition have no names or special attributes for your lunar months, you may wish to consult Chapter 1 for some you may wish to adopt in your own practice, as well as for suggestions for creating your own lunar calendar.

PART V

Moon Magic

The Physics and Ethics of Magick

*What we truly and earnestly aspire to be, that in some
sense, we are. The mere aspiration, by changing the
frame of mind, for the moment realizes itself*
— Anna Jameson

Magick has always been part of Witchcraft. From the dawn of humanity it has
been a tool used to help alter the forces which shape our lives. Today's Pagans
have reclaimed this viewpoint; we are not merely helpless masses of flesh, void
of any personal power, groveling at the mercy of the fates.

The precise content of our spells has changed over the centuries, but not the methods, and certainly not human need. It is interesting to note that the magickal desires
found in weathered grimoires are the same desires we have today, principally: love, security, health, and fertility.

What Magick Is and How It Works

Our detractors try to tell us, and anyone else who will listen, that magick is inherently
evil; that it utilizes "unnatural" or evil forces in order to work. They believe that mere
humans cannot naturally possess any power of their own; therefore it must be obtained
from some supernatural source and, they illogically rationalize, any force that would aid
human desire must therefore be wicked and ask a perverse allegiance in return. This
source was personified as (need I say it?) their Satan*, or anti-God.

It is this inherent power, one with which we are all born, that is the force behind
successful magick. Often we may combine this personal energy with that of nature (by

---

*The word Satan is taken from a word in the Hebrew Bible, *ha-satan*, meaning "an adversary." In context,
the word never referred to any actual being, nor was it intended as a personification of an anti-God. This
appellation did not begin to be used until the early years of the Christian Church in Rome, and was then
employed primarily as a scare tactic to convert Europe's Pagan population. The appearance of Satan was
always adapted to correspond to the general beliefs about the primary Pagan God in whichever land the
church was proselytizing at the time.

using herbs, stones, etc., as our catalyst and focal point), or with that of the elemental world (by aligning our inherent power with that of faeries, elementals, or of the elements themselves), or by working in tandem with the creative power of Gods and Goddesses. But no matter how many of these combinations we try, we, the practicing magickians, are the ultimate source of magickal power.

Belief in magick as part of religious practice was an accepted part of everyday ancient Pagan life, and flourished for many, many centuries before Satan became an accepted theological construct of Christianity nearly two thousand years ago. For the old Witches, magick was not viewed as an operation of supernatural forces since, logically, nothing supernatural could exist. Whether one believed the universe was created by a sentient deity, or wished to believe that it exploded into existence of its own accord, the fact remained that certain natural laws operated from which no deviation could occur. Cats don't sprout antlers overnight, autumn does not suddenly appear to follow winter, and a maple tree doesn't become an elm at will. Everything has its place in the time/space continuum — including magick.

Magick has long been understood by its practitioners to be no more than the manipulation of natural forces not yet understood by either science or psychology. To create a spell we teach ourselves to sense and "see" these energies, and invest them with our own energies in order to bend them to our will. On the physical plane we can see this same concept used in the martial art known as Judo. Through Judo one is taught to take advantage of the natural energy and momentum of one's opponent, making it possible for a ninety-pound woman to toss a two hundred-pound man over her head. The natural energy that makes this feat possible is there, waiting to be harnessed and directed to release itself to the desired outcome.

Look around you. Right now. Put down this book and note all the items in the place you are in at this moment. Note all those modern miracles of technology you take for granted that would have gotten you hanged for being in league with the Devil only two hundred years ago: your car, your television, your CD player, radios, electric lights, even a simple ballpoint pen. All of these things would have been seen as manifestations of magick by virtually everyone, and as a sign of the presence of evil by more than just a few. But for those who understand — or pretend to understand — the factual scientific principles on which these items work, they are not "magickal" at all. They are simply things which operate through natural scientific principles.

It is highly likely that the magick of today will be the science of tomorrow, that eventually we will discover what it is about the energy of the trained magickal mind that can manifest wishes and desires. As scientists and psychologists continue to study the evolving human mind, they may unlock the secrets of creation from a single directed thought. This conceptual hinge upon which all magick is hung may be seen as being overly simplified, but it is the basis of all spellwork. Everything that exists — everything — had to first begin as a single thought, and somehow those thoughts had to be directed, both on the mental and on the physical planes, in order to manifest as reality. (Even Judeo-Christian mysticism teaches that we are merely thought-forms in the mind of God and, when he ceases to think about us, we will perish.)

Five basic ingredients are needed for any successful spell.

1. The desire or need for something
2. An emotional investment in the outcome of the spell
3. The knowledge to work the spell
4. The belief that it exists on the mental/astral planes
5. The ability to keep silent

Without desire and need there can be no spark of the imagination that fires the emotions to drive the spells. Without magickal knowledge a Witch has no idea of what to do to make the magick. Without belief that focused thoughts create a reality that can be brought into the physical world, there is no magick at all.

Keeping silent about magickal work is another very old belief. It may have stemmed partly from fear of discovery by the Witch hunters. On another level there is an old adage that energy divided is energy lost. In other words, the more you speak to others of your work, the more energy you lose, energy which could otherwise be channeled into your desired outcome. You may also find yourself talking to someone who does not believe in the power of magick, or has some vested interest in your failure, perhaps jealousy or a need to "prove" the unworkability of magick. Such people can do great damage to your magick by their counter-energy. Never mind that they do not believe in what you are doing. We all have the power to project energy, and their mental output can work against you.

Those who do not understand the principles of magic fear the mysterious source of the manifestation more than the manifestation itself. If we look again to the natural laws of the universe for answers, we find there is really no mystery. All of us were taught the basic law of physics in junior high science which states:

MATTER CAN BE NEITHER CREATED NOR DESTROYED,
IT CAN ONLY CHANGE FORM.

Unlike television Witches, such as the ever-popular Samantha Stephens, we cannot wiggle our noses and create something from nothing. In order to manifest a house on a vacant lot we do not — and cannot — create matter. Rather, we set up energy patterns that draw the desired energy to us and shape it into the form we want to see. This would involve consorting with a good contractor rather than with demons.

The language that has evolved around magick over the centuries also tells us that it is not an instantaneous event, but a process of building piece-by-piece. Various mythologies tell of Goddesses of magick who are spinners and weavers, creating their reality step-by-step as a seamstress embroiders a tapestry. With her patience and persistence a rich picture is born, and it is no accident that we have adopted the words spinning, weaving, casting, working, crafting, and creating to describe our spellwork.

There is no rule anywhere in Paganism to tell us how much or how little magick we must weave, or even that we have to make magick at all. If you are not sure about its working principles, or feel that you are not ready for magick in your life, then don't do it. If you continue to follow a Pagan path the time will eventually come when you will find yourself casting a spell as easily as you call upon your deities.

Once you decide to create a spell to meet a need, begin constructing it by following these twenty-four steps:

1. Clearly understand and define your magickal goal. Write it down or state it out loud to help form it solidly in your mind. By doing this you begin to invest the spell and the desired outcome with your emotions and energy. If you have more than one need, you may wish to spread them out. You can work more than one spell at a "session," but doing so will dissipate and scatter your energies, leaving less for each spell. If you feel you must do multiple spells, limit them to three and try to relate them in some way, so that the energy you raise remains as focused as possible.

2. Be sure of the ethics of your hoped-for outcome. Approach the spell from all angles to satisfy yourself that you are not violating anyone else's free will or being manipulative. Many Witches like to do a divination first, to be doubly sure that their spell will not have any unforeseen ramifications. If the results of the divination are negative, try rethinking your intent to see if you can circumvent the problem. Then do another divination and see what comes up.

3. If you wish to use a specific element as a focus for your magick, decide which one is most appropriate and collect items to represent that energy.

4. Plan how you will visualize your goal and believe in what you see.

The powers of the mind are only just now beginning to be explored by science. We have all heard stories of terminal patients who have healed themselves, and of faith healers who use belief to manifest miracle cures. Visualization uses that power to form mental pictures that are invested with personal energy and emotion. It is the soul that breathes life into all magick, and the soul that is the most important element in its outcome. The moment you start visualizing the resolution of a magickal need is the moment you begin to create the changes in your deep mind necessary for the magick to manifest.

5. If you are working with advanced natural magick (discussed in full in Chapter 12) you will need to prepare a long-range plan in accordance with the above guidelines. This will entail checking moon phases, laying in enough supplies for the duration of the spell, and planning how the energy can be sustained through each day.

6. Gather candles, stones, or whatever else you intend to use as a catalyst for your focus or to direct the energy you will raise. Empower those items with your personal energy by projecting into them the energy of your goal.

Keep in mind that these tools, including your cherished ritual tools, have no power in and of themselves. The power is not in the tools, but inside the Witch trained to use them. Without you, they are useless. They merely provide a way to focus your energy and a means for directing it towards its goal.

7. Decide upon your "words of power," the words or chants you will use to help focus and raise energy. You may write them out, or simply remember key phrases you wish to use as you improvise. Some Witches like to create simple poems so they will be easier to remember.

8. If you wish to use a special deity or mythic figure in your magick, decide on which one or ones, and on how you will evoke, invoke, and/or honor them. You may wish to write out special prayers or blessings and memorize them.

9. Decide when you want to do the spell. This can be any time you personally need the magick, at the time when your coven regularly meets, or you may wish to take into consideration moon phases and/or other astrological influences. If your life is as busy as most people's today, you may have to choose the only night when you will be free and alone. The timing is much less important than the energy you bring to the spell.

10. At the appropriate time, gather what you will be using and go to the place where you will perform the spell. This can be at your altar, indoors or outdoors, at your coven meeting site, or anywhere else that feels appropriate, comfortable, and private.

11. Cast your circle and, if you like, call the quarters, or do as you would when opening any other ritual. If you are using advanced magickal techniques you will definitely need to employ these visualizations to be effective.

12. Your magick is now beginning in earnest. Invite whatever elementals, faeries, spirits, or deities you wish to have present as you work. They should always be welcome, but they are not necessary for spellwork.

13. Clear your mind and begin visualizing your goal. This is probably the most important step in the spell-casting process and you should invest the mental image with as much energy as you can muster. Recall your need and make your emotional connection with it as deep as you can, on as many levels as possible.

14. Raise energy within yourself and pour it into the magickal object(s) in whatever way feels right to you. This can be done as a mental projection, through dance or song, or intense visualization.

15. Do whatever physical actions your spell requires. Some need no special actions, but many require some basic movement, even if it is only lighting a candle. Use your words of power, light your candles, bury your herbs, mentally charge your stones, and/or raise your cone of power.

16. Take advantage of natural phenomena that can help you raise energy. A storm, for instance, is an excellent source of energy that any Witch can draw upon to help feed a spell. Allow yourself to become part of the storm and feel yourself psychically drawing on its vast stores of energy as you seek to raise your own energies or cone of power.

17. When you feel you have put as much energy into the spell as you possibly can, send the energy out to do your will. You can visualize this as a cone of power being sent out, or use any other mental image you like. Body language helps, too. Relax, throw up your arms, raise a tool, kneel, send out a cone of power, or do whatever else makes you feel the energy go forth. Be sure to direct it out from you visually as well.

18. You should finish your spell with words such as the traditional "So Mote It Be." Mote is an obsolete word for "must". The phrase is synonymous with "Amen," "So It Is," and "It is Done". It is a statement of completion and an affirmation that you know your magick is successful. All magick is worked from the point of view that the desired goal is already manifest — it will not come to be, but IT IS. Always phrase your magickal desires in the present tense; for example, "I have love in my life now," or, "My bills are now paid in full." Talking of magick happening in the future will keep it forever in the future, always just out of reach.

19. Meditate briefly on your goal. Again, visualize it as already manifest. Smile, breathe a sigh of relief, and know the magick is already at work for you.

20. Thank and dismiss all faeries, spirits, and deities who have come to witness or aid in your magick.

21. Ground your excess energy into the earth and open your circle. Excess energy, raised during your spell work but not fully sent away from you when you sent it to do its job, lingers on and around you. The best way to ground this excess is to place your hands palms down on the earth, into a bowl of soil, or on the floor of your home. Physically and psychically feel the excess energy draining out of you. Know that it is being absorbed and dispersed into mother earth.

22. If you have ritualized your spell, dismiss your quarters or do whatever other endings your rituals traditionally require. If you are working your magick with a coven this is standard practice.

23. Record your spell in your Magickal Diary or Book of Shadows with the date, time, weather conditions, and any astrological data you wish to include. This will be useful later when you have done enough spells to look for patterns. For example, you may see that your most efficacious spells were done on Sundays or when it was cloudy or snowing, or when you had faeries present, worked with a particular deity, burned green candles, or when the moon was full. Everyone has different affinities. These patterns will help you pick the best times for your spell work.

24. Back up your desire on the physical plane. This is a must. For example, if you have done a spell for healing don't avoid seeing your doctor. You will need all the help at your disposal to overcome your illness, and magick and medical science make great partners.

Until you achieve your magickal goal you should spend some time each day focusing on it by clearly visualizing it as a *fait accompli*. These added boosts of daily energy can often mean the difference between success and failure.

Magickal Ethics

Paganism has few rules, but because it is a spiritual system, it does have laws governing ethics to which virtually all Witches adhere. The first of these is commonly called the Pagan or Wiccan Rede —

AS YE HARM NONE, DO WHAT YE WILL.

Acceptance of this law prohibits a Witch from doing anything that might harm any other living being and, most significantly, prohibits us from violating any living being's free will. Some argue that this law also applies to the self, and that you have an obligation to keep yourself from harm.

If one deliberately chooses to do anything magickal that might cause harm, the second law deals with retribution —

THE THREEFOLD LAW.

Witches believe that any energy sent out by them, either positive or negative, deliberate or unconscious, will be revisited on the sender three times over. Like the popular principle of karma, the Threefold Law means that we will be held accountable for our actions. This law is not intended to be a scare tactic like the Christian Hell, but a simple reminder that we will ultimately have to assume responsibility for all that we do, think, and say.

Love magick is especially vulnerable to this law. For instance, when one chooses to work a love spell there is a great temptation to design it to draw a specific person into a romantic situation, whether they are interested in you or not. Nothing could be more against the Pagan Rede, or more likely to invoke the more dangerous aspects of the Threefold Law. As tempting as it may be, don't risk manipulating another person through magick; the consequences are too great. If you want to draw love into your life, make a charm or construct a ritual that draws "the right person for me now" or "the person who seeks me as I seek him (or her)".

Many Witches will add a line to their incantations, such as "as it harms none" or "as all will it freely" or some similar sentence to insure that they are not violating the Rede. The inclusion of this line may negate certain aspects of the spell's success, but it will keep you free from unpleasant karmic entanglements.

Because of these beliefs in free will and balance, Witches generally do not accept the labels white, black, and gray when referring to magick. In popular belief, as well as in many non-Pagan magickal traditions, these distinctions are made, just as many people divide all things into good, evil, and maybe. For Pagans, magickal energy is merely there for us to use. We must have the integrity to decide what is right and what is wrong and, if we overstep those ethical boundaries, we will have to atone for the injury done.

Another way to decide whether or not a spell is harmful is to do a divination prior to its working. My personal preference for pre-spell divination is the Tarot cards. The many cards of any Tarot deck cover a wide range of possibilities, and their picture symbols offer deep insights into every nuance of both the outcome and of each individual influence involved in its manifestation.

The following is my preferred layout for the cards before the working of a spell (see page 110). It covers virtually all the possible influences and results, giving the clearest picture possible of the outcome. The reading should not be done until after the spell has been completely constructed so that all possible occurrences that may stem from it can be analyzed.

Interpret the positions in the following manner by using the meaning of the cards in relationship to these influences.

1   **The Need** — This card defines the need or desire on which the spell is based. It may be expected and straightforward in its interpretation, or it may offer you a new insight into your desires.

2. **The Underlying Need(s)** — Card 2 provides a look at the root of the desire, the real reason you want the object or situation to manifest or be banished. Again, it may be readily recognizable, or it may offer a new twist for you to think about further.

3. **Hidden Influences** — This card looks at energies working on the spell of which you may not be aware. These can be karmic (related to a past life or action) or the input of some other random energy that may inadvertently block your spell. The card can also be an indication of how your true inner-self feels about the spell. We do not always really want all the things we think we do, and this card may show you what it is you do want.

   If this card turns out to be one from the Major Arcana, it is an indication that much of what you want for yourself is currently beyond your control. This should not prevent you from working the spell, but keep in mind that it may take more than one working of the spell, and more concentrated physical effort to manifest the desire.

4. **The Influence of Others** — Usually our friends and family want only the best for us and sincerely hope we achieve all our heart desires. Whether or not anyone but you is aware of your spell and its intention, the persons closest to you can influence you in ways of which you may not be aware.

   For example, one friend may have hidden designs on the job you are working the spell to get. Another may hope you get it because s/he would be genuinely proud of your accomplishment. Your mother may want the position for you for the prestige, but deep down resent that it would force you to move away. This card will reveal the sum of those combined intentions.

5.   **The Spell's Weaknesses** — This card may indicate what aspects of your spell are in need of attention so that it can be altered and made into the most effective tool for change possible.

   My experience has shown that if the card makes no sense at all in relationship to the issue at hand, then the spell has no tangible weakness. If the card clearly indicates a flaw, you are not obligated to change it, but the addition or subtraction of the suggested item, concept, etc., can help push it along. However, if such a suggestion is implied, it would be worth your while to at least give it some thoughtful consideration.

   Those new to magick would do well to heed the indications of this card. We old timers have discovered, usually to our chagrin, that fledgling efforts at magick tend to be poorly thought out. Ask anyone who has been practicing magick for a while and they will have at least one story of the spell that went awry, from the one for the blue car that yielded a toy, to the visualization of companionship that resulted in a pet dog.

6.   **The Spell's Strengths** — Card 6 tells you what you are doing right in the spell you have constructed. Use this card as a gauge to measure your progress in the magickal arts. I have found that if the card makes no sense in relation to the issue then the spell is fine as is, but that it has no outstandingly brilliant qualities.

7.   **Inner-World Outcome** — There is an old magickal adage that "thought is action on the astral plane." Like a nurturing womb, the astral world is the realm in which all magick must be conceived, grow, and form, and from which it is born. And like a womb, it will always bear the scars, both good and bad, of the child it carried. This card indicates what changes your spell will create on the inner or astral plane because of the visual/mental energy you are creating there.

8.   **Outer-World Outcome** — This card indicates changes in the physical world that will be brought about by your spell. This is not a complete view of the actual outcome, but a direct indication of the mundane results. For instance, perhaps you really need a new car to get back and forth to work or else you will lose your job. This card may indicate safe travel or employment, tangible physical outcomes of the spell that are a physical byproduct of the actual goal.

9.   **The Final Outcome** — The ninth card will tell you the probable culmination of your actions. Between this card and Cards 7 and 8, you will be able to tell if your spell will be beneficial to all concerned, if it will bring harm to anyone, and/or if it will yield what you desire.

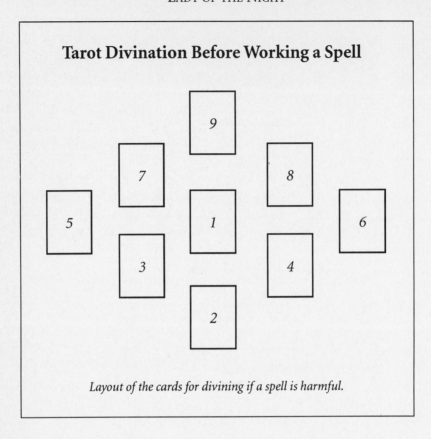

Tarot Divination Before Working a Spell

Layout of the cards for divining if a spell is harmful.

Breaking a Spell

To break a spell means to end it, to stop the flow of energy that is working on your behalf, and to ground the excess. The majority of spells need not be "broken" because, without your sustained input, they naturally fade and die. Only when other "beings" are directly called upon for assistance, or are created by your own projected thoughtforms, does a spell need to be formally recalled.* For most spells the breaking is done simply when thanks are given for its success or when your interest in the outcome is lost.

If you wish to break and ground a spell, simply visualize the energy you have projected into it ceasing activity. Create a firm mental image of all things being just as they are with no change, or no further change, in your current reality.

Spread your arms wide and feel any of your excess energy which may still be out there returning to you. Allow it to enter and collect in the palms of your hands. When you sense that it has all been reabsorbed, place your hands flat on mother earth, or on the floor of your home, and allow it to be safely diffused in her.

---

*The techniques for creating thoughtform elementals are somewhat complex and lie outside the scope of this work. They are discussed in full in the alchemical writings of sixteenth century physician and magician Parcelsus, and in my own A *Witches Guide to Faery Folk.*

Realistic Magick

Not every spell was successful thousands of years ago, and not every spell will be successful today. Our detractors take great glee from this fact, even though their own prayers for assistance go unheeded just as often as our spells fail. The difference is that when a spell is not successful the Pagan does not blame the Gods or the fates, but looks within for the fault and, if the need and desire are still there, prepares a new plan of attack. Magick can enhance anyone's life, and is a valuable, wholly natural tool for achieving our dreams and goals.

Magick can and will assist you in any crisis, but is not a panacea for all your woes, and it would be dangerous to use it as such. If you are sick, magick cannot be a surrogate for a skilled physician. If you are in legal trouble, it cannot substitute for a good lawyer. And if you are emotionally distraught, or are a victim or an addict, it will not replace solid professional counseling.

The best way to ensure success in spellcraft is to keep in mind these three common sense reminders:

1. Make sure your desires conform to the physical laws of the universe. Realize that no magick will make you grow taller, restore a lost limb, or allow you to grow wings or sprout gills. However, it can help you overcome self-consciousness about your physical appearance, give you the strength to adapt to life with a missing limb, or open up opportunities to experience hang gliding and scuba diving.

2. An old Witches' charm tells us, "As ye bind, so are ye bound." This is to remind us that any time we indulge in manipulative magick, put magickal restrictions on ourselves or others, or tie ourselves to worn out, impossible desires, we will be tied up with them, bound and immobile, unable to move on spiritually. Not only will these spells not work, the restrictive energy pattern that has been established may hinder all future spellwork.

3. Work toward your goal with the same effort and intensity with which you dream it. Even in the Judeo-Christian tradition in which many of us grew up, a popular cliche says, "God helps those who help themselves." No magickal work, even if done with the aid of a deity, will work without some assistance on your part.

All About Moon Magick

I speak the pass-word primeval ...
— Walt Whitman

The term "moon magick" is loosely used to refer to any spell that, one, has lunar associations, and/or two, uses the energy of the moon to enhance the spell. Spells with lunar associations share an affinity, or compatible energy, with the moon. These spells are sometimes said to be "governed" by the moon or by its element, water. Listed below are some of the spells and magickal/occult practices that share this affinity.

- Astral projection
- Contact with water elementals
- Divination
- Dream work/magick
- Empathic development and skills
- Fertility spells
- Love spells (shared with Venus)
- Magick for or with cats
- Magick for or with nocturnal creatures
- Past-life regression
- Peace spells
- Psychic development and skills
- Safe childbirth spells/Pregnancy spells
- Sleep spells
- Spirit contact

Spells that utilize lunar symbols and moon-governed herbs also fall within this category. Among the most prevalent moon-linked items used as catalysts in spellwork are apples, jasmine, eggs, camellia, magnolia, Irish Moss, and sandalwood.

Any spell, regardless of the planet which governs its realm, can be enhanced by the energy of the moon. This is usually accomplished by aligning the need with one of the moon's two principal phases. For example, if you wish to gain or increase something, you would work that spell on the waxing moon; if you wish to banish, lose, or decrease something, you would work on the wane. These alignments are not absolutely necessary for successful spellwork, but they can help. Since many Pagans are highly sensitive to the moon's phases we generally prefer to coordinate our magick accordingly whenever possible.

Harnessing Lunar Energy

By directing the energy of the waxing, full, and waning phases of the moon into knotted cords, the energy can be harnessed and preserved until it is needed. Cord magick is a very old practice. Several cultures claim its invention, particularly the Celts, who were fond of knotwork as ornamentation. In Celtic magick, cords represent the unifying force of the fifth element of spirit and, properly used, have the ability to draw together all the elements into manifestation.

Cords as an archetype have long been thought to "tie up" things and "hold" their power. Cords with knots have been used in binding spells (preventative magick), handfasting rites, to measure circles, and have even been considered dangerous to have around. Lots of extant folklore reflects these old beliefs. For instance, it was once common to make sure no knots were to be found in the household of a pregnant woman until after she had given birth, for fear that the sympathetic magick of the knots would tie the umbilical cord around the infant's neck and suffocate it. Circles were often drawn with the aid of a cord to measure its radius, and high priests and priestesses were bound together with them for fertility rituals. Handfastings use garlands as cords to symbolize the union of marriage, and cords have been used to symbolically tie up negativity, and to bind an object to its owner to prevent loss.

Moon cords should not be confused with the larger cords sometimes referred to as one's "measure." These large cords are cut either to the length of one's height, or in the traditional nine-foot length. They are worn around the waist as vestments of power, stretched to measure personal circles, and sometimes used to store the power of various deities. Moon cords are thinner and much shorter. They are, by tradition, three feet long when completed, but keep in mind that measurements of "feet" and "inches" date back only a few hundred years, to the time of Henry VIII, and it is impossible for us to know exactly what type of measurement various ancient peoples might have chosen for their magickal instruments.

By using a ritual technique similar to that of Drawing Down the Moon, we can capture the essence of the moon phases in the knots of the cord; this power can be released at a later time, as needed. Think of the cord as a source of emergency reserve power for those times when your need is immediate, but time available for a lengthy ritual is not.

Material for your cords can be found at any craft store. Ask for craft or macrame cord, no more than a quarter- to half-inch in diameter. Such cord may not be made from all-natural fibers but is still effective, since its power comes from drawing the moon into it, not from the plant material from which it was woven.

Many Pagans feel that organic material is more conducive to natural magick and prefer cords made from nature's fabrics. They feel that if an item does not come from nature, it cannot function in magick. Certainly ours is an earth religion, and the bounty of mother earth can symbolically provide us with a deep connection to the magickal items we create. We should use natural objects whenever possible, but we should not allow ourselves to become enslaved to them. Remember that we use many things in the Craft that are not "natural," yet still effectively hold power and direct energy. The black handle of an athame is one example; it is rarely organic in origin. Nor are many of our candle holders, or some types of stones used in stone magick. On the other hand, most modern synthetics are made from fossil fuels which once were living material (read organic). Feathers, fur, and wood are also organic and aesthetically appealing, but using them raises ethical questions for those of us who worship through nature.

If you feel strongly about using natural materials for your cords, and are ambitious, you can weave your own by taking long strips of wool, silk, or cotton fabric, and braiding three separate strands into one long piece. As with any magickal tool, the more you handle the cords, the more you will empower them with your own energy and intent. If you do not weave your own cords, spend an hour or so (the time can be divided over several nights) holding each cord, getting the feel of it and making it truly your own.

Various traditions attribute different colors to the three lunar aspects. White, red, and black are the Celtic version and probably the most popular choice of today's Witches, but the ultimate choice will have to be yours. We all have different affinities; one person's gentle blue virgin may be another's cold blue crone. Below is a chart of other common choices for cord colors.

Cord Colors	Aspect	Moon Phase
White, Yellow, Blue	Maiden Goddess	Waxing
Red, Silver, Green	Mother/Father God/dess	Full
Black, Gray, Gold	Crone Goddess	Waning

When you have decided upon your colors, and have purchased or made your lengths of cord, cut the raw material in lengths of four-and-a-half feet. This allows room to tie them and reach a finished length of three feet.

At this point it is a good idea to bless and purify the raw cords. Traditionally this is done either with salt water or with water containing a touch of lemon juice. You can also use a drop or two of jasmine or sandalwood oil, both herbs with strong lunar associations. As you touch the purifying liquid to the raw cords, visualize all the past energy they might have absorbed dissipating, falling away, leaving the cord pure and free from any energies save your own. You might wish to offer a verbal affirmation of this such as:

Strand of (insert name of cord material), *pure and clear,*
Free you are from all past tears.
Purged you are of needless blame,
A fitting vessel for a holy name.

While the rhyme scheme leaves a lot to be desired, the chant has worked well for me, and it can be changed or adapted to fit your individual needs.

Next, you will have to charge the cords, one by one, under the moon during the appropriate phase. The process is similar to that of Drawing Down the Moon, except that you transfer the energy into an object rather a person.

On the night you choose to capture the moon energy you need a clear sky and a place to work from which you can see the moon and stand beneath her with no visual obstructions between you. This does not rule out standing by windows, or even sitting safely alone in your car somewhere, but this evocation process works best if the moon is in sight.

Cast a circle and begin drawing moon energy into your cord by presenting it like an offering to the lunar light. Hold it up so that the cord is in your field of vision, directly in front of the moon. Call on the name of the proper aspect of the moon deity: maiden, mother/father, or crone. You may also call on a particular moon deity who is connected with the phase you are working with if you deeply associate the two. If you were consecrating your full moon cord your words might sound something like this:

> *Blessed be, Mother Moon, riding high in the night heavens. From your silver throne I feel your benevolent face shining lovingly on me and this magickal cord. Your spirit is ever with me, and in me. Let it also be in this cord, a tangible vessel for your power which I will carry, cherish, and use again when you are hidden from me. Enter this cord that I may take with me a part of your eternal love and power as I leave this sacred space.*

Hold the cord in front of you so that it is silhouetted against the full face of the moon and sense the fusion that is occurring. Feel the lunar energy begin to flow into the cord and tingle on your palms. Chanting can help the process along. You might try one of the following couplets:

> *Mother Moon, enter here,*
> *Your loving child holds you dear.*

> *Lady, Lady, shining bright,*
> *Enter in my cord this night.*

> *Father strong, and Father bright,*
> *Enter in my cord this night.*

> *Full moon draws down, in here to store,*
> *Locked inside this tool e'er more.*

> (Name of deity), *God/dess of old,*
> *Into this cord send your powers untold.*

While still holding the cord in front of the moon, begin tying the first eight knots, each an equal distance from the last. As you are doing this, try to line up the cord so that you are viewing the moon through the loop in which each knot is being tied. This visual image will, more than any words could, get the message through to your deep mind that you really have captured lunar energy within the cord. You must know — not believe, but *know* — that with each knot you make a part of that moon phase's energy is held within the tied knot for it to be effective.

When you make your ninth knot, the power will be sealed in the cord, like the completion of a closed circuit. You may tie it so that the two ends of the cord are fused together, or you may leave them loose. Consider how you will be using the cords when you make this decision. If you want to loop them around magickal objects, then a circular form is usually the best choice, but if you wish to untie the individual knots with each spell, or tie magical objects with them, then leaving the ends loose is probably best.

Tie the last knot with as much ceremony and feeling as possible, thanking the God/dess, or the moon phase you have called upon, reaffirming the success of the rite:

Blessed Mother Moon, we are always one. By my will and by the bounty of your love I hold a part of you in my hands. May this cord be used only for good and kindly purposes. Thank you, bright Lady. So Mote It Be!

A finished moon cord hangs over a smiling crescent candle holder. In the background is the cord's protective corduroy pouch.

Once made and charged, the cords can be utilized in all future spell work. For example, if you need to quickly banish a negative influence and don't want to work your spell while the moon is waxing, use your waning moon cord to lend banishing energy to your magick.

To use the energy of the cord you can hold it, wear it around your neck, encircle a candle or stone with it, drape it across your spell items, tie up your magickal catalysts, or use it to charge herbs by encircling them with the cord. Just having the cord present imparts the lunar influences you seek, and you can use visualization to help further the transfer of the cord's energy toward the object of your magick.

By contrast, some Witches like to use what I call the "untying" method of cord magick. This theory reflects a belief that each knot represents moon energy; to release it, the knot must be untied during the spell. If this symbolism appeals to you, you would need to untie a knot to transfer the moon magick into the spell, rather than mentally or tactilely moving it from the cord.

Both the mental transfer and the untying methods work equally well. I have used both and find that I prefer the mental transfer, although I have had good success with the other. Experiment for yourself to see which works best for you.

Many Witches new to cord magick are afraid that the power in the cord can seep away. If the cords are used regularly and treated with the same respect you give to all your magickal tools, then rest assured that the energy is in the cord to stay. However, if you wish to "boost" the cord's power reserves, or if you subscribe to the "untying" theory of their use, you will need to renew the evocation every few months to keep the cord properly charged to its maximum potential.

Remember that these cords are not like the larger ones you would wear openly for all festivals and rites. They should be kept for moon and night work only. When not in use, your cords are best stored in a dark place where they will remain untouched by sunlight. I keep mine in hand-stitched pouches sewn from black cotton corduroy. Corduroy is almost always made from one hundred percent durable cotton, and is sturdy enough to protect the cords while still being easy to tuck into a pocket for transport to your ritual site.

These pouches are easy to make and require no machine stitching. All you will need are three rectangles of black corduroy, approximately six inches wide by ten inches long, black thread, and a needle.

Start by turning in the raw edges of the fabric approximately one quarter inch all around to make a hem. Stitch this in place so that the pouch will not unravel.

Next, fold up four inches of the bottom of the cloth with the two RIGHT SIDES of the fabric facing inward. This is the nice part of the fabric, the side that you will eventually want facing outward. Stitch up the two adjoining sides, then turn the fabric inside out. You should now have a small, five-and-a-half- by four-inch pouch, with a two-inch flap that can be folded over and tucked in to protect the cord when not in use.

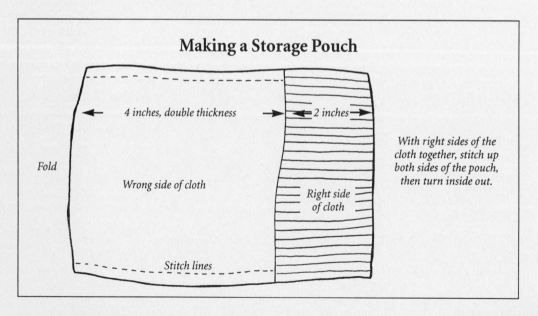

Making a Storage Pouch

4 inches, double thickness

2 inches

Fold

Wrong side of cloth

Right side of cloth

With right sides of the cloth together, stitch up both sides of the pouch, then turn inside out.

Stitch lines

Moon Astrology in Magick

While all magick should be worked when it is most needed, considering the various lunar influences can give an added boost to any spell.

Monday is the day of the week governed by the moon, the twenty-four hour period during which her powers are at their peak. In general, all the days of the week and their corresponding planets exert a strong influence on spellcraft, but since the moon is only assigned one day, it would be virtually impossible to arrange the casting of a moon-oriented spell for a time when the Lady is traversing a good sign, has favorable aspects, and which also happens to fall on Monday. So just keep Monday in the back of your mind and, if you have to pick only one astrological influence to work with, this one is the best.

Other influences exist and, while they should not cause you to postpone magick you really need, they can add their own slant to the outcome of your spell. These include not only checking to see if the Lady is in her waxing, full, or waning phase, but also looking in a good ephemeris or astrological calendar to see what sign she is in.*

The twelve signs of the zodiac all have specific influences, which they impart into the atmosphere around us. While these are not as strongly felt as the rulership of the days of the week, their subtle energies can give new and unexpected twists to our magick. Remember that none of these will harm your spells, but they have their own spheres of influence which can color or boost them.

Moon in Aries — Aries (a masculine fire sign) is a barren sign, not known for being conducive to inner-plane endeavors such as pathworking, dream work, or astral projection, although it is an excellent time to work magick for new ventures, particularly if they are financial, medical, or related to construction. Because Aries is a fire sign it is energetic, good for working magick for personal strength and stamina. On the negative side it is also connected with impatience and dominance. Arian Correspondences: the ram, thorns, iron, diamonds, honeysuckle, Tuesday, the head.

Moon in Taurus — The moon in Taurus (a feminine earth sign) makes us protective and stubborn, and brings out our artistic natures. It is a good time for magick where issues of trust and loyalty are at stake, and it can give a boost of determination to see you through to the end of any endeavor. Astrologists say that the moon is "exalted" in Taurus, in this case meaning that it stabilizes and hones the emotional influences of the moon. Passions can run high during this transit and spells to increase one's sensual nature are at their best. One warning, however: spells begun with the moon in stubborn Taurus may be hard to shut down once they are under way. Taurean Correspondences: bulls and cattle, emeralds, copper, poppies, pastels, Friday, the neck.

---

*I recommend using either the *Daily Planetary Guide* or *Llewellyn's Astrological Calendar*, both published annually by Llewellyn Worldwide. They contain all the information about moon phases, zodiac transits, and aspects that any Witch could ever need.

Moon in Gemini — Gemini (a masculine air sign) is the most eclectic of all the signs, but also the most mercurial and fickle. Because the sign is ruled by Mercury, it is an excellent time for any type of spells concerning communication, writing, mass media, or for ferreting out one's hidden enemies. Moon in Gemini can make the superficial appear stable; you should not jump to conclusions about the success of your spells at this time. Healing spells also work very well during moon in Gemini. Geminian Correspondences: mercury, nuts, winged creatures, the arms, hands and lungs, Wednesday.

Moon in Cancer — Cancer (a feminine water sign) is the home of the moon and is the most fertile sign in the zodiac. Virtually any venture undertaken during this time will grow favorably, especially psychic and inner-plane endeavors. This is also the best sign for dealing with matters relating to the home, fertility, pregnancy, children, or the emotions. Planting and growing are also under the influence of Cancer, and magick for any type of growth or increase will quickly take root. Moon in Cancer also brings out our protective natures and lets the imagination flourish. Cancerian Correspondences: silver, willow, moonstone, jasmine, purple, the number nine, the crab, the breasts and upper digestive tract, Monday.

Moon in Leo — In contrast to fertile Cancer, Leo (a masculine fire sign) is the most barren sign in the zodiac, one seemingly desolate and unfit for magick. On the other hand, Leo is governed by the vibrant power of the sun, which rules prosperity, leadership, celebration, and celebrity. Moon in Leo brings out our magnanimous natures and can be a good time for working magick on behalf of others. On the negative side, it can make us self-indulgent, a time when the temptation to do negative or manipulative magick is strongest. This is also a fine transit for working spells for leaders, for the sane use of power, and for binding spells. Leonine Correspondences: heliotrope, sunstone, citrus trees, all felines, gold, the heart and back, Sunday.

Moon in Virgo — Virgo (a feminine earth sign) is the fastidious intellectual of the zodiac. When the moon is in Virgo it is a good time to work with matters pertaining to education, volunteerism, and health. It is also a prime time for casting spells requiring great attention to detail, as this is also the province of Virgo. Spells worked for mental prowess, stability, and conscientiousness take deep roots in Virgo. Keep in mind that Mercury, the planet which rules Virgo, is cerebral, whereas the moon is emotional; this can be a source of either conflict or harmony for your spells, depending upon the desired outcome. Virgoan Correspondences: nuts, mercury, writing tools, domestic dogs, the lower digestive tract, Wednesday.

Moon in Libra — While the moon is in Libra (a masculine air sign) our minds turn to aesthetics and to balance. It is a good time for couple's magick, and for all spells for peace and balance, or for the promotion of fairness and justice. Venus rules romance and this is a propitious transit for love magick. Spells requiring, or aligned with, diplomacy and adaptability also work well. Libran Correspondences: copper, cypress, pink, reptiles, kidneys and bladder, Friday.

Moon in Scorpio — Scorpio (a feminine water sign) is the keeper of secrets, and a good time to try and unlock occult wisdom through divination and ritual. It is also a very fertile sign and a good time to work on fertility and sex magic. Matters pertaining to deceit, trustworthiness, and things hidden are best dealt with now. Scorpio is the sign of ambition, and spells for personal promotion work well at this time. Ruled by Pluto, the sign is linked to the world of the dead, and conditions for solid magick for the spirit world are optimal. This transit is very compatible with almost all lunar spellwork. Scorpion Correspondences: plutonium, thorns, red, the scorpion, poisonous animals, insects, sexual organs, Tuesday.

Moon in Sagittarius — Moon in Sagittarius (a masculine fire sign) makes us all philosophers and places us in a frame of mind to deal with issues of humanity, peace, and the right way of the universe. Sagittarius is the sign of the non-conformist, an excellent time to experiment with new spells and ritual methods. Because of its optimistic nature, challenges are often accepted during this transit, making it a good time to work magick for the more elusive things in your life. Sagittarian Correspondences: horses, tin and aluminum, holly and all berry trees, the liver, hips and upper legs, Wednesday.

Moon in Capricorn — While the moon is in stable Capricorn (a feminine earth sign) is the time for dealing with material concerns, such as magick for obtaining that much-needed new car. It is also a transit when pessimism and despondency tend to come to the fore. If you are prone to depression, avoid divination during this transit and, instead, work spells for a better mental attitude. This is a time of stability, when grounding rituals and centering spells work especially well. The influence of Capricorn's ruling planet, Saturn, can assist in uncovering past-lives and overcoming past negative influences. Capricornian Correspondences: lead, evergreens and ivy, cloven hoofed animals, the bones and joints, garnets, Saturday.

Moon in Aquarius — There has been a lot of New Age hype about the sterling qualities of Aquarius (a masculine air sign) but, like all the signs, it has its negative aspects. These include a tendency to selfishness, air-headedness, thought without action, and generally allowing one's mind to wander aimlessly in some vast pseudo-intellectual wilderness. However, it is also a time when people as a whole tend to be inspired with inventiveness, ponder deeply, and become more acutely connected with their higher consciousness. Because of this, the Aquarian transit is a good time for troubled covens to meet. Magick for world peace and understanding are best undertaken during this sign. Warning: because this sign is now outwardly fighting for its identity in this New Age, anything can happen in your Aquarian/moon magick. Aquarian Correspondences: uranium, fruit trees, amethysts, large birds, sky deities, the lower legs and circulatory system, Wednesday.

Moon in Pisces — Because of the dualistic character of the Piscean Age, Pisces (a feminine water sign) has gotten a bad reputation as a two-faced character. This is anything but true. Ruled by watery Neptune, Pisces is a highly psychic sign and is a good time to try that divination method which has always eluded you. The two fish which symbolize the sign point not merely in two different directions, but to the upper and lower worlds, and the inner and outer realms, offering us a bridge between them. It is a time when emotions can become clouded and melancholy; you should avoid protection spells unless you are sure you will not be tempted to cross the line of manipulation. Moon in Pisces brings out our compassionate natures and can aid in making magick for others. It is also a good time for dream work, astral projection, guided meditations, and is highly compatible with all lunar spellwork. Second only to Cancer, Pisces is the most fertile of all the signs. Piscean Correspondences: aquamarine, platinum, figs, poppies, water plants, fish, the feet, Friday or Monday.

Even if you cannot work your magick during the sign you prefer, keep in mind the special influences of the moon when evaluating the outcome of any spell. (I keep this information in all my magical records, and can attest to its usefulness.) For example, a spell worked for romance in Virgo may turn out to have a very intellectual bent because of the Mercurian influence. This is neither bad nor good, but an interesting byproduct of magickal astrology.

Less important than the moon's zodiac transit are lunar aspects, the relationships between the moon and other planets at the time the spell is worked. Aspects are calculated by the degree of relationship between any two planets at any given moment, as drawn on an earth-centered horoscope chart of the heavens. While these aspects should never prevent you from working a spell at any given time, they do exert some minor influence over your magick, and should always be recorded in your Book of Shadows. You may find over time that specific aspects are subtly more or less efficacious for you, and you will wish to tailor your magick accordingly.

Several dozen aspects have been cataloged and are used by professional astrologers, but only eight have an influence strong enough to be felt at all in magick. The influence of major aspects can be felt for about a half hour to either side of the precise moment when the aspect occurs.

Conjunction — A conjunction, considered to be the most potent of the aspects, occurs when the moon is within 12 degrees of another planet. This causes the energy of the two planets involved to merge. This is neither inherently good or bad, but can add to or detract from the minor prospects of your spell. For example, the moon in conjunction with Venus would blend the psychic aspects of the moon with the sensual aspects of Venus, resulting in a good time during which to work magick or divination aimed at providing new insights into romantic relationships. Conjunction with Mercury would add a cerebral quality to the otherwise emotional outlook of the moon.

Opposition — Two planets are in opposition when they are within 9 degrees of being 180 degrees apart. This produces disharmony between the opposing planets, which manifests in our lives as a challenge or choice. An example would be the moon in opposition to Mercury, during which the intuitive and intellectual nature are at war. An opposing aspect enhances this disharmony. Likewise, it lessens the harmony of two compatible planets.

Quincunx — This is not a powerful aspect; many astrologers still debate its precise influence. A quincunx occurs when two planets are within 2 degrees of 150 degrees of each other. The standard interpretation is that the two planets involved will be in a state of minor disharmony which cannot be overcome until the transit ends. This should not stop your spellwork, but be aware that this aspect is occurring.

Semi-Sextile — This is another minor aspect, occurring when two planets are within 2 degrees of 30 degrees of each other. During this time the two planets involved are in harmony with each other, but their combined energy has little lasting effect on our spells. Planets normally compatible, such as the moon and Venus, will be slightly enhanced, and disharmonious combinations, such as the moon and Mercury, will be negated.

Semi-Square — A semi-square aspect occurs when two planets are within 2 degrees to either side of 45 degrees of each other. This aspect carries the same sense of disharmony as the square aspect, but in less severe proportions. In general, if the energies of the two planets are normally compatible, such as the moon and Neptune, their mutually beneficial qualities are enhanced. If they are not easily compatible, such as the moon and Mercury, they cancel each other out.

Sextile — Two planets are sextile if they are within 5 degrees of 60 degrees of each other. This is considered a minor aspect on the whole, but a favorable time for magick. During this transit two planets are in inner-harmony with each other, each of their energies bringing out the best in the other. Some astrologers feel this can be a time of new opportunity which, if not realized, may be lost.

Square — Two planets are squared if they are within 9 degrees of 90 degrees of each other. This is one of the major aspects during which the influences of each planet are in direct conflict with each other. This does not mean it is a negative time for magick, but that the magician must take into consideration the influences of the planet which is square with the moon. For example, if you want to harness the fertile, gentle energy of the full moon in Cancer, it can work to your advantage to have it at war with the barren, aggressive aspects of Mars.

Trine — A potent aspect, during which two planets work in harmony to the point that we can become complacent or overly-confident. A trine occurs when two planets are within 8 degrees of 12 degrees of each other. In terms of magick, this aspect can provide the added boost of helping you truly believe in your outcome.

When the moon has moved out of its last major aspect with another planet before moving into another astrological sign, it is considered **Void of Course.** Astrological studies have shown that events begun and spells undertaken during these hours tend to travel a bumpy road and are difficult, if not impossible, to manifest; when they do come to pass, they rarely pan out as expected.

Full Moon Magick

The old moon laughed and sang a song...
"Where are you going and what do you wish?"
The old moon asked the three...
— Eugene Field, *Wynken, Blynken, and Nod*

From the earliest days of humanity, when the moon was first linked to the powers of the divine, magick has been crafted under the gentle glow of her full face. This brief period, when lunar power is at its peak, is an excellent time for almost any kind of spellwork. This chapter presents spells and exercises for this special phase.

Moon Bathing and Purification Rites

In many spiritual traditions it is prerequisite to purify oneself in some manner before performing religious rites, touching sacred objects, or approaching the deities. Paganism shares this history, and today still has many advocates of purification rites, usually performed prior to Esbat and Sabbat observances and before any magick or inner-world explorations.

Purification has the dual effect of not only cleaning away any negativity that may be clinging to you, but also, like any ritual preparation, alerting your deep mind to the fact that some profound change is about to take place.

Pagan purification rites often utilize water charged under the full moon as a cleansing source. To gather your own full moon water you will need a cup, bowl, or chalice of silver, or else a piece of silver coinage or jewelry to toss in the bottom of a non-silver vessel. If you use a non-silver container, glass is the best substitute, as iron and aluminum are not thought to be conducive to moon magick. On the night of the full moon set the chalice outside, or in a window, where it can absorb the lunar rays. After a few hours of exposure, it should be well-charged and ready to use.

Before taking the water to your ritual site, hold it securely in your non-dominant hand while placing the other hand over the top. Visualize your hands as two poles of an energy field sending your own personal power through the water. Finish empowering the liquid with words such as:

> *By the silver light of Lady Moon,*
> *By my hand and will so sure,*
> *By all that's holy, true, and strong,*
> *I bid you cleanse me pure.*

There are two ways to purify yourself with the water.

1. By anointing your body at selected spots
2. By taking a moon bath

For the former, you will need to decide ahead of time just where on your body you wish to anoint yourself. All traditions teach varying configurations. In central Asia and India these places are usually the seven chakra points (energy centers). In the Celtic traditions, purification points most often involve the forehead, lower stomach, and feet (also called the Threefold Blessing). In the Saxon and many of the Gardnerian paths purification is done through the two feet, the hands, and the forehead (or sometimes between the breasts) so that the points roughly resemble a pentagram. All of these traditions allow for solitary rites of purification.

Traditions with roots in far eastern Asia usually sponge-bathe the entire body with holy water, and those from Africa and the Middle East wash only the hands and feet in purification rites. In these cultures, the rite is usually administered by a priest or priestess.

Regardless of which points they choose, many modern, eclectic Pagans like to take a sip of the water afterward to fulfill the imagery of having the purifying energy become one with themselves. The choice is yours to make; none will be wrong, even if you decide to mix several of these ideas or create your own.

Once you have decided upon the purification points and are safely inside your circle you are ready to begin your ritual/magickal work.

Dip the fingers of either hand in the water and state your intention to purify yourself. Then, with your fingers still wet, place them on the first part of your body you are purifying. Many traditions ask that you progress from the lowest point upwards when performing these rites, in order to take advantage of the sympathetic action of "raising" one's consciousness to the divine world. However, if you would rather work from the top down, focus on the image of your impurities falling away from you and being grounded safely in Mother Earth. As you do this, consecrate the act with simple, meaningful words. For example, if you are anointing your feet you might say:

> *Silver Mother of the night,*
> *Bless my feet that they may always*
> *Walk securely on your sacred path.*

Traditional Anointing Points on the Body

**Chakras of
the Human Body**

Crown (Just Above the Head)
Third Eye (Between and Just Above the Eyes)
Throat (Center of the Hollow of the Throat)
Heart Center (Middle of the Breast Bone)
Solar Plexus (At the Center of the Solar Plexus)
Navel (Just Below the Navel)
Root (At the Base of the Tailbone)

**Anointing Points for
the Celtic Threefold
Purification Blessing**

**Anointing Points for
the Pentagram
Purification Blessing**

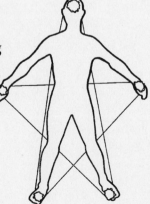

If you are anointing your forehead, you might wish to tie this action in with your spiritual intuition or sacred thoughts:

> *Mother of all life, be in my spirit, my magick, and my visualization.*
> *Fill me with your creative energy, and cleanse me from thoughts unworthy*
> *of your child.*

There are as many possibilities for words of consecration as there are Pagans. The best way to choose them is to think back on why you selected this particular spot on your body as a site for purification. Your heart area may speak to you as being a center for love and compassion, and your genital area may feel like one of creation. Use these associations to help form your words.

When you have anointed all the spots you wish, thank the moon God/dess, then continue with your Esbat ritual and/or magickal work. You may also want to take a sip of the water to seal the act. [Note: If you do not use all the lunar water, it can be kept and used until the new moon appears, at which time it should be discarded into mother earth. However, if you will be keeping it unrefrigerated for more than a day it is best not to drink it, since bacteria and algae will start to form. It is also unwise to drink water into which you have placed essential oils unless you are a highly skilled herbalist. Many of these oils are toxic, and even the non-toxic ones can wreak havoc on delicate digestive tract tissues.]

If you would rather bathe to purify yourself you will need to do this before you move to your circle area. You might wish to dim the lights and bathe by candlelight, burn a little incense, or add a drop of purifying essential oil to the water. Incenses and oils with strong lunar and purification affinities are sandalwood, myrrh, camphor, vervain, and wintergreen.

Take the vessel of moon-charged water to your tub and, before pouring it in, state your intention of purification. You will want to include as much of the imagery in this evocation as you would if you were using the anointing method. The following is an example of what you might say:

> *By the silver light of Lady Moon,*
> *By my hands and will so sure,*
> *By all that's holy, true, and strong,*
> *I bid you now to cleanse me pure.*
> *May both my hands the good works do,*
> *My feet walk firm the path,*
> *My head and heart stay free from harm,*
> *As I take this sacred bath.*

While you are bathing in the lunar water you can also visualize any moon magick for which you are preparing. This will give the magick an added boost because you will be more deeply aligning yourself with the energy needed for it to succeed.

You may remain in the tub as long as you like, but when your mind starts to wander from your goal(s) it is best to prepare to get out. Allow all the water to drain before you

Water-filled chalices of silver and blue glass easily absorb the energy of the full moon.

leave the tub. As it is draining, visualize all the negativity and mundane influences that may have had an adverse effect on you being sucked away. When the last drop of the water leaves the tub, get out and towel off, still thinking about removing the contaminated water with the towel. When you are dry you can end this rite with the words:

> *I am free from all unworthy influences, fit to meet, greet, and be the*
> *God/dess. As I was in the beginning of time, I am now, and always will be.*
> *So Mote It Be!*

Psychic Dream Teas

Look inside any spellbook and you will inevitably find at least one "sure-fire" method for inducing dreams that prophesy the future, reveal past-lives, or offer the perfect solution to a perplexing problem. The common flaw in most of them is that they attempt to make the magick easy. They tell you what herbs to sew up into a pretty, lace-covered pillow, and ask only that you sleep on them and all will be revealed.

The truth is that special pillows, incenses burning in the bedroom, and oils on the temples can help push the magick along, but they will not do it all for you. Magick isn't that easy. If it was, we'd all be rich, beautiful, healthy, and constantly adored by all. If you really want to make dream magick you will have to put some effort into it...even while you're asleep.

I have found that herbal teas, coupled with visualization and use of a dream diary — all employed assiduously — produce excellent and consistent results within a few months. For the most auspicious start, begin your dream work on the night of the full moon.

Teas have been used in many cultures to induce a light, altered state of mind conducive to both sleep and psychic receptivity. The imagery of a relaxing hot drink before bedtime is almost irresistible to the harried, modern mind and, since magick works through symbols, making a special tea is much more likely to trigger results than a smokey room of incense, which generally conjures up thoughts of ancient temple rites.

A psychic dreaming tea can easily be made from jasmine, an herb that shares affinities with dreams, the moon, and all astral world experiences. You may wish to add a bit of catnip to the jasmine to help you relax. Both of these popular herbs are staples in many health food stores or herbal shops, and can be found already ground for use in tea balls.

You can further align your tea with the particular type of psychic dream you seek by adding to it another herb known to be conducive to that end. If you desire dreams of the future, try adding a bit of hibiscus, dandelion, sage, cinquefoil, rose, or saffron. If you seek revelations of past-lives, use a pinch of vervain, buchu, anise, yarrow, or sunflower. If you wish to attempt conscious astral projection while you sleep, experiment with mugwort, chicory, or poplar bark. If you want to find the solution to a problem, try adding rosemary, spearmint, or dill, and if nightmares are a problem for you, perhaps agrimony, valerian, chamomile, or gotu kola can help suppress them.

To prepare the psychic dream brew, begin by handling the herbs as much as possible to infuse them with your own energy. Then, as the water boils, keep your visualization fixed firmly on your goal. Use a tea ball (look in grocery stores for these) to put the herbs into the hot water. As they steep, you should see the steam rising from the cup as the beginning of your magick, the power you have put into the herbs being released on your behalf. Drinking the herbs without a sweetener is best but, if you must sweeten, use a bit of honey or rice syrup. Avoid sugar, which can be overly stimulating and at cross-purposes with your goal.

When the tea is ready, sit down somewhere quiet and comfortable. A comfy arm chair or rocker is perfect. Before you take that first sip, begin the chant which you will later repeat as you start to fall asleep. Try one of the following or create your own:

> *Open wide ye doors of all worlds tonight,*
> *Come and bless me with second sight.*

> *Swirling, misting, foggy veil,*
> *Lift this night without fail.*

Dream of past and future be,
Tonight and always remembered by me.

Take the first sip. As you do, feel the herb charging your entire being with psychic energy.

Go to bed as soon as possible after you have finished the tea, and repeat the chant to yourself as you fall asleep.

Next to your bed have ready a pen and notebook or a small tape player so that you can immediately record any dream or snatches of dreams upon awakening. This is the overlooked step which most often causes failure of psychic dream spells. It is imperative that you record any dreams, feelings, or impressions you have as soon as you awaken. Dreams are like mist in the sunshine and will quickly evaporate if not captured. I have kept dream diaries at various intervals throughout my life. They have been very useful, and are great fun to look back on. After all, not every dream is prophetic in nature, and some of the images are very amusing in hindsight.

The general experience of those who keep these diaries is that after several weeks the dream memories begin to come rapidly, and there are very few nights when at least one dream is not remembered — frequently there are more. After a few months the diarist is awakened sometimes five or six times a night with vivid dreams to record. For those who are looking for strictly psychic insights, these results show up in bits and pieces early on, and usually become consistent within six months.

Unfortunately, those of us who must work for a living (that's most of us, right?) find it more annoying than enlightening to be awakened by intriguing dreams a half-dozen times a night. The temptation is to become selective about which dreams are recorded, or to feel that one has become proficient enough to remember all of them until dawn (trust me, that never happens!). So instead of following through, the now-former diarist wants only to heave a contented sigh, roll over, pull up the covers, and return to la-la land. I have been through this scenario many times myself and, each time, I swear it will not happen again. There is one gentle hand of comfort in all of this — once you have become used to keeping a dream diary, it takes less time to get the flow going again when each new one is started.

I repeat: if you are serious about dream work you must keep a complete, consistent diary. So what is the best way to keep yours? Scribbling out sentences as you squint in the half-darkness is no fun, and leads quickly to frustration. It is also laboriously slow and makes it easy for important details to escape your mind as you write. However, if you take shorthand, or are adept at jotting down clear, memory-jogging notes, writing may be the best way to go. Tape recorders save midnight writer's cramp, but on the whole they work better only if you are coherent enough not to mumble. Many were the times I sat down to transcribe my dreams and was sickened to find I had nothing more than ten minutes of unintelligible murmurings on the tape. Taping also does not work well if you share a bedroom with a light sleeper who does not wish to hear the lurid details of your latest night adventure while he or she is trying to sleep. Experiment with what works best for you, and enables you to capture the most memories with the least time and effort.

Moon Mirror Magick

Mirrors and magick have been linked together since the first human looked out over a night-shrouded lake and was mesmerized by the silvery play of the full moon reflecting off the water's surface. Since that momentous point in history humans have strived to produce a mirror that would offer a perfectly reproduced reflection, an act considered to be highly magickal in itself.

Throughout recorded history, writings suggest the high regard in which mirrors were held. The Old Testament mentions brass mirrors, and old papyri talk of polished silver being used in ancient Egypt. Medieval grimoires make vague hints at the uses of mirrors in astral projection, spirit conjuring, and other spellwork. In many European countries, the mere possession of a mirror by a non-member of the nobility was cause for the death sentence, either by charges of Witchcraft or for the crime of attempting to rise above one's appointed station in life.

Despite this limited access to one's own reflection, early scientists sought to enhance the quality of mirrors. By the late Middle Ages a process using pressed tin treated with mercury and silver nitrate greatly improved quality, but also escalated the price out of the range of common folk.

Mirrors as we know them today were developed in Vienna in the late seventeenth century. They were quite costly and highly prized, so much so that France's Louis IV, who loathed all things Austrian, ordered Viennese mirrors for the famous hall of mirrors at his Versailles palace. The folk superstition which tells us that breaking a mirror equals seven years bad luck probably began in the servants' quarters of European palaces, where poor domestics lived in horror of breaking these costly decorations.

As court Ceremonial Magicians came into vogue in Europe, the idea of the magick mirror was revived. With the coming of the Industrial Revolution, mirrors could be mass-produced at prices that made them accessible to most of the population. Pagans began to reclaim mirrors as a source of magick and, since reflective surfaces were long linked to the powers of the moon, mirrors were used extensively in divination and other psychic work.

Many magickal books on the market offer elaborate and sometimes high-priced methods for making moon mirrors. Since so much time and money is invested in their creation, they no doubt work well, but you can achieve the same results with much less fuss and a fraction of the expense.

In the health and beauty department of most discount and drug stores you can find small mirrors in a variety of sizes. Look until you find a round one. It need not have a fancy border. Mine is a simple, round piece of glass that has served me well for more than ten years. Select a mirror which you feel will fit easily in your hands and not clutter your altar. Mine is six inches across and has proved to be the right size for every magickal need.

You will need to consecrate the mirror under the light of the full moon. This can be done through a window if you like, but for this procedure you will need the actual light of the moon reflecting off the mirror's surface. You will also need a lunar-related oil such as sandalwood, jasmine, lotus, myrrh, camellia, gardenia, eucalyptus, camphor, or lemon. A non-water-soluble paint in silver, white, or purple, and a thin-tipped paint-brush are optional accessories.

Before you begin, surround yourself with as much darkness as possible, draw your circle snugly around you, and hold the mirror in front of you so that you can see the moon reflected there. Visualize the lunar energy being absorbed by the mirror and know with all your heart that this is happening. You can do anything else you like to help you feel this occurrence.

As you watch the play of light on the mirror, call to the Lady of the night (or the Lord of the night, if you prefer), asking her blessing on your effort. You may call on a moon deity by name if you feel moved to do so, or simply address the moon as mother or father:

> *Bright Lady of the Night Heavens, shine your countenance on this magick-*
> *al tool. Let it hold your mysterious energy within itself to guide, instruct,*
> *and teach me as I need.*

Begin rotating the mirror slowly clockwise, but do not move it so much that you lose sight of the moon in the surface. Gaze at it, allowing the motion to take your mind into a deeply receptive state. All the while, clearly visualize the lunar energy continuing to be captured there. Chanting softly can further this process. Try any one of these couplets, or create your own:

> *Silver orb so shiny bright,*
> *Captured is your lunar light.*

> *Lady moon* (or Father moon) *high in the sky,*
> *I now draw down your all-seeing eye.*

> *Mother, Lady, Father white,*
> *Enter in my mirror this night.*

> *Eternal mother, crone, and maid,*
> *Mystic, ancient, here to stay.*

When you feel that the mirror has absorbed all the energy it can hold, take the oil you have chosen and dip the forefinger of your power hand into it. With the oil, trace the astrological glyph for the moon [☽] on the back, saying:

> *Crescent silver, full moon white,*
> *Sealed you are in here this night.*
> *Ever vigilant, eternal power,*
> *Blessed and kept here from this hour.*

If you have chosen to use paints, you should paint over the oil tracing with the paint-brush. You may also add any other designs on the back that, to you, symbolize the moon and her associated powers. These can include pentagrams, the alchemical water symbol, wings, or any other sigil that catches your fancy.

When you are finished, hold it up to the moon again and reaffirm its powers:

> *By the Lady (or Lord) and by my will,*
> *I hold up here the sacred wheel.*
> *By all that's blessed and all that's good,*
> *Within this tool the power I seal.*
> *So Mote It Be!*

Your finished moon mirror can be used in any spell requiring a mirror, so long as you avoid exposing it to sunlight. (Examples of spells using mirrors are the Prosperity Spell and the Returning Unwanted Energy Spell found in Chapter 11.) Other common uses for the moon mirror are the divination process known as scrying, and some methods of past-life exploration.

Scrying With the Moon Mirror

Probably the most common use for a lunar mirror is scrying, an operation that works best at night. Scrying is the art of gazing softly into a reflective surface until the mind slows and prophetic visions appear. In this way the mirror is similar to the crystal ball of popular mythology.

The technique for scrying is simple, but it takes practice to become successful. Light one single candle, or use the light of the full moon as your only illumination. Allow that single light to fall over the surface of the mirror. Relax and clear your mind of all but the issue you wish to have clarified, and begin gazing into the mirror. Don't strain or stare. Blinking is encouraged. Merely soften your focus and gaze gently. You may need to move the mirror around sightly as you gaze so that the candle flame or the moon image becomes blurred. This unformed likeness can help trigger visions.

Your visions can appear either as completely played-out dramas or as simple symbol pictures which only you can interpret. You must trust yourself to interpret your own symbols; they are projections of your subconscious and only you can fully know the symbology of its darkest realms. With steady practice the visions will come more quickly and clearly.

Viewing Past-Lives

Many persons who have difficulty using eyes-closed methods to view past-lives, such as dreamwork or guided meditations, often find success with the eyes-open method using the moon mirror. Like scrying, this exercise works best at night.

Find a dark place where you have only enough light to make out your reflection on the mirror's surface. Close your eyes for a moment and allow your mind to relax. Concentrate on the past and focus on seeing what and who you were/are. If you have a particular issue you wish to understand (i.e.; why you are afraid of cats), or problem to solve (ie; ending your compulsive gambling), or if you want to see if you shared a past with someone from your present, you can also focus on that to see if it has roots in a past-life.

Close your eyes, and allow your mind to begin to slow and detach itself from your everyday reality. Then begin softly chanting about your goal. As you do this, feel yourself slipping backwards through time with each rhythmic beat. Try one of the following couplets, or create your own:

> *Mirror's face in dark of night,*
> *Open the past bringing knowledge to light.*

> *Darkened misty hidden past,*
> *Open your secrets to me at last.*

> *Across the veil of time and space,*
> *Show me myself in another place.*

When you feel sufficiently in the right frame of mind, open your eyes and gaze gently into the dark surface of the mirror. Don't try to force images — wait for them to come to you. Some people see only the face of who they once were; a few will see entire dramas from their past playing as if on a movie screen. Most experiences fall somewhere between these extremes. As with any occult endeavor, the more you practice, the better you will become.

I have tried this exercise with another person when both of us felt there was a past link binding us, and have found the process works equally well with two persons participating. Before you do this, you will need to charge a moon mirror large enough for the two of you to see into without bumping heads and, if you are regular working partners, you should both have a hand in its creation. You should then save it exclusively for all magickal work the two of you wish to do together which requires a mirror.

Care of Your Moon Mirror

Unlike any other magickal mirrors you may have, moon mirrors should be stored away from the sun. I keep mine in my magickal cabinet encased in the same type of black corduroy pouch in which I keep my moon cords (see Chapter 9 for instructions on making these). I have been fortunate in that my mirror has not been broken nor has it seen the sun since I made it more than ten

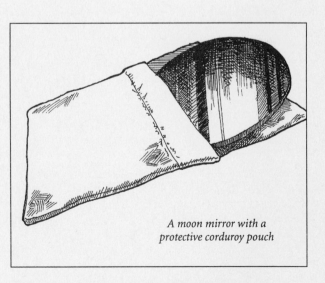

A moon mirror with a protective corduroy pouch

years ago. If sunlight touches its surface you will need to recharge and bless it under another full moon. If it breaks, don't panic. No permanent harm is done, you will just have to reinvest in the creation of another. Many Witches advocate allowing the mirror to keep working for you by sweeping the shards into a glass jar and placing them somewhere in your home where they can reflect negativity and harm away from you and your dwelling. However, if yours is a home with curious children or pets, it is best to dispose of the broken glass altogether.

A lunar mirror, cradled in the boughs of a young tree, recharging under the full moon's light and the watchful gaze of the Witch's familar.

If your mirror needs to be cleaned you should use an old and simple formula of warm water in which the herb mugwort has been boiled. Mugwort shares affinities with the moon and the earth and has been used for centuries as a psychic enhancement and purifier. Wipe the surface of the mirror gently with the mixture, using a clean cloth. As you do this visualize all things unclean — both the seen and unseen — being removed. It is not necessary to reconsecrate the mirror under the moon after a cleaning, but many of us feel better if we give it a recharge every now and again. I do this just by setting mine outdoors under the full moon and leaving it for several hours, but there is no rule which says you cannot have a full-blown ritual to reconsecrate the tool.

Fertility Magick

The full moon's image as mother, and its propensity for marking the fertile time of women, makes it a natural focus for fertility magick of all types.

Fertility of crops, animals, and people was of great concern to our Pagan ancestors, and many old grimoires and folktales contain references to fertility rites and spells. We still acknowledge this ancient magick whenever we put stalks of wheat in bridal bouquets, toss rice at a newly-married couple, or decorate our homes with grains in autumn. With today's falling birthrate (hard to believe with over five billion people on the planet!), fertility has once again become a concern and, when all else has failed, even the most modern, mainstream couples find themselves looking to the old ways for assistance.

It is not necessary to work fertility magick directly under the full moon's light, but you should perform your spell under its influence whether you are indoors or out. In many Pagan traditions, this time is considered to extend from about three days before until three days after the exact moment of fullness.

Fertility spells have been designed almost exclusively for the use of women, but since they are most effective when worked as a couple, this one will be presented with two people in mind. If you are a woman working the spell alone, simply perform all of the actions yourself.

For this spell you will need:

- One small raw potato, peeled
- A sharp knife (not your athame)
- A glass of moon-charged water (see Purification Rite earlier in this chapter), approximately eight ounces
- A large, clean glass jar with tight lid
- A wooden spoon with a bowl small enough to fit into the mouth of the jar
- Any combination of essential oils and/or dried herbs related to the moon and fertility such as mugwort, bistort, vervain, olive, pine, rice, wheat, carrot, almond, corn, lotus, or wintergreen

Begin this spell with full ritual opening: cast your circle, call your quarters, etc. You might also be wise to call upon a mother Goddess, or a divine couple, to lend support to the spell. After this, make your statement of intent. You may wish to write out lines for each of you to speak in turn, or you might prefer to say what you have to in unison. Both ways are fine, but in either case all wording should be carefully planned out and agreed upon beforehand. When my husband and I tried spontaneous fertility spells, we inevitably found that one of us didn't care for the other's choice of words. We also saw the flaws in the each other's visualizations, and sometimes in our own which, while they sought the same end, initially seemed to be in conflict. Needless to say, these unhappy feelings detracted from the spell and made it less effective. If, when the main body of the spell is completed, you wish to offer each other words of love, commitment, and support inside the sacred space of your circle, these can be as spontaneous as you like.

You may charge the lunar water now if you have not already done so. Use your combined energies, intense visualization, and skin contact to speed up the charging process.

While the water is charging, hold onto the potato, a symbol of mother earth and fertility, and pour your combined energy into it while clearly visualizing your end goal. Then begin to take turns carving the likeness of a baby in the raw potato. Don't expect it to be a work of art. The important thing is to connect its energy with your own and with your desired goal. Select a chant to say slowly together as you work in order to help keep you focused. Try one of the following or create one of your own:

Moon and earth and love-light bright,
Create we here new life this night.

Shaping life from shapeless form,
Grant us, Lady, a new life born.

Across gentle veil to earth plane wild,
Shaping, loving, birthing a child.

When you have decided the potato carving is finished, set it aside and take the oils and herbs you have chosen and, one by one, begin to place them in the lidded jar. As you pick up each item, hold between your hands (both of you should do this at the same time) and charge it with your combined energy. After this, put it into the jar with words such as:

Oil of olive (or name of other item), carry my wishes to the four winds.
Blessed of the moon, earth, and the Eternal Mother, be this night the per-
fect bridge between the seen and unseen worlds.

When all of the items have been added, stir them clockwise with the wooden spoon. Use the spoon like a wand, a tool to focus and project your energy further into the spell.

Add the moon water on top of this mixture. As you do this say words such as:

Water blessed by the mother's love,
Symbol of the mother's blood,
Flood the herbs from womb of earth,
Fill my womb and give us birth.

When this is done, cap the jar and hold it together between your hands in a final blessing, combining your energies as you envision combining your bodies to create a new life.

Because of the sexual nature of this magick, a loving couple should feel free to engage in love-making to seal the spell. Remember, sex is the most basic physical act with which a fertility spell can be enhanced. No spell — no matter how good it is — can induce immaculate conception!

The magickal water you have created should be used to anoint the womb area nightly until conception occurs. Both partners should be involved in this part of the ritual and, as it is done, restate together your purpose, making it a mini-re-enactment of the spell.

Repeat the spell nightly as necessary.

Give yourselves six months to a year for success. After that time, use the spell in tandem with the advice of a reputable reproductive endocrinologist. What they are capable of doing for infertile couples today is almost like magick.

Assisting in Childbirth

Your full moon cord (instructions given in Chapter 9) can be used to facilitate a smooth, safe childbirth. As with any health-related magick, this technique is not meant to replace the care of a doctor or midwife, but can assist both mother and baby in the separation transition.

For this spell you will need only your full moon cord with all nine knots tied and charged with lunar energy. If you are able to charge the cord with the specific birth in mind, all the better.

You do not have to be with the birth mother in order for this spell to work, although it is considered ethical to get her permission before working the magick.

As the labor pains intensify, hold the cord in both hands, mentally linking it to the birth process, creating a flow of positive energy which will help the cord to work on her behalf. Remember that it was made under the light of the full mother moon, and deeply shares her affinities. As the birth progresses, begin to untie each knot, visualizing the mother energy being released to aid the mother and child. Do this slowly, pouring as much feeling into the act as possible.

For a long labor, you may want to untie a single knot every hour or so, spending fifteen to twenty minutes on each session with the cord. Create a mini-ritual for each knot, including intense visualization, charging words, and pleas of assistance to a mother Goddess.

If you are the mother, or are in the birthing room during delivery, you will be better able to time the untying of your knots. This is also an excellent way to help the mother focus on something other than the pain during natural childbirth, and is an excellent task to assign to the birth/labor coach. When in the room, try to time the untying of the last knot to occur just minutes before a safe delivery.

The cord can also be retied to provide magickal assistance in the event of birth distress such as hemorrhaging. In this case you would want to bind the cord in as tight a knot as you can while visualizing the runaway blood vessels being clamped shut. The cord can also be used as a tool of sympathetic magick if the umbilical cord appears to be wrapped around the baby's neck. This is a dangerous situation which can cause brain damage or strangulation. If this occurs, physically twist the cord around to mimic it unwinding from the infant's throat as the doctor or midwife takes whatever steps he or she feels is necessary to save the baby.

Astral Projection and the Making of Flying Ointments

Astral projection is the ancient art of sending out one's consciousness at will to a location away from one's physical body. While in this state you are free to travel through the barriers of time and space, and return with full knowledge of your explorations.

Opinions have been divided for centuries on what exactly takes place during astral projection. Some persons believe that you have a subtle, or astral, body that actually leaves your physical being during this practice. They even claim to see it linked to the physical body by a silver cord that keeps the body alive. Others, myself included, have never seen this cord, and believe it to be an illusion the mind uses like a security blanket during a practice that can be frightening the first few times it is done. According to this theory, it is only your deep mind that projects its consciousness into other places or realms, very much as it does when you are dreaming. However, don't allow yourself to be confused by the word "dream." Astral projections of any kind are very real. Never make the mistake of thinking that because they take place "only" in your mind that they are not part of reality. After all, it is inside your mind that magick takes place, and from which you project it into the manifest world.

Many metaphysical books attempt to teach astral projection, and beginners should explore all of these to find the one — or a combination of several — which works best.* I and three very good friends have all learned to project, and none of us learned the same way. Many of the published methods have been gleaned from ancient texts, and some techniques are claimed to have been passed down through secret orders. For instance, the Celtic Druids were said to be skilled in the art of "becoming invisible," which is another way of saying they could astral project with ease. Their method was said to include a dead raven, a crossroads, and baneful herbs in proportions lost to us. The magi of the Middle East called upon spirits to assist them, and European mystics often used divination symbols, such as the Tarot or a crystal, on which to focus as they projected outward.

A helpful tip — one that I know works, from personal experience — is to begin projecting on the full or waxing moon. The sympathetic pull of the lunar energy seems to stimulate compatible energies to assist the process. During one of these phases, begin meditating for extended periods while concentrating on moving your consciousness out from yourself. You may sit or lie down, as long as you are completely comfortable and in a position in which you can easily remain for an extended period.

Don't try for big leaps in time and space at first. Stay within the room where you are working. Gently force your inner-self to go to a point a few feet away from your body. If you keep imagining your consciousness at this single point, after a while your mind will become so bored with the exercise it will automatically go elsewhere in search of more lively entertainment.

Other methods include projecting your consciousness into another vehicle or object. This solid imagery, as opposed to simply focusing outward "somewhere," is sometimes an easier one onto which to latch. You can mentally create an astral vehicle, standing nearby waiting for your consciousness to come to it, or you can project yourself into an object such as your ceiling fixture.

Some methods involve using elemental symbols or divination cards like the Tarot as passageways to the astral world. This technique involves gazing into the symbol or card until you can mentally project its detailed image in your mind, then step through.

You can also use a system that requires pushing the astral body "out" through one of the chakra points, or any other point on your body which feels natural. I have a friend who insists that the back of the neck was her first exit point, and it is the one she has used since. To do this, concentrate your astral energy on gathering at this point inside the body. Then, when you feel it cannot be contained any longer, push it out, either on its own or into a waiting vessel.

---

*In my opinion the two best books available to teach astral projection in detail are *Astral Projection* (Llewellyn) by Melita Denning and Osborne Phillips, and *Astral Doorways* (Aquarian Press) by J. H. Brennen. These books cover numerous projection methods and present two different points of view on the practice for you to consider.

Another solid method for learning astral projection is the persistent use of guided meditation. After repeated workings you will be stunned to find that your perception of the events has changed and that you are on your own, no longer following the words of the guide. The solitary rituals in Chapters 2, 4, and 6 contain short guided meditations with which you can begin your experiments.

At first you will probably not get any further with your projections than stepping out into your own room. For months I was frustrated by the sensation of snapping back into myself as soon as I realized my consciousness was out, looking down upon the room and my prone body. I would get too excited, start craning around to see everything from this new perspective, and end up right back at my starting point. Only persistent practice will allow you to gain control over your projections. Eventually you will find you can move more and more easily across time and space.

Don't become discouraged if you do not have success immediately. This is one of the hardest occult practices to learn, and some pick it up faster than others. The November-January 1993-1994 issue of *Llewellyn's New Worlds of Mind and Spirit* published a survey on astral projection taken from among their readers. Sixty-three percent of the respondents said they had learned to successfully project, though for some it took as long as five years!

Even after years of success, almost no one is as adept at consciously controlled astral projection as they would like to be, and there will always be times of failure. People who claim otherwise are lying or kidding themselves. Becoming proficient even to the point of 80 percent success takes much effort, more than most people are willing to give.

Learning astral projection can be aided by the use of flying ointments, herbal concoctions contained in a lard base, that help induce a deep altered state of consciousness allowing for easier projection. For centuries Witches and magicians have guarded the secret ingredients of their flying ointments. Some of the old concoctions were outright dangerous and used toxic hallucinogenics to assist the process, many of which had an odious smell that was believed to aid in the detachment of mind from body (probably in self-defense!)

The term "flying ointment" comes from the sensation of buoyant weightlessness, or feeling of flight, that accompanies astral projection. That sensation, coupled with the fact that Witches once practiced this art while lying in front of fireplaces, is responsible for the popular idea that Witches rode up through chimneys on their broomsticks, an item always kept by the hearth for practical reasons during the centuries when the ever-burning fireplace was the center for heating and cooking in every home.

Today, flying ointments are still made by Pagans and students of the occult to facilitate the astral state, minus the baneful ingredients.

All the formulas for flying ointments given in this text are non-toxic, although you should patch test in advance for allergic reactions that can affect you like a toxic substance. Gently rub some of the oil or crushed herbs you will be using onto your bare skin. Two days later repeat the process. The waiting is important because allergens take time to react in your body and it is rare that you will react with your first exposure. If you are allergic to a particular substance, a red rash or hive will appear at the application site any time from half an hour to two days after the second application. If this happens, discard the offending item.

For your ointment, select whichever oils and dried herbs appeal to you. Mix these together and then crush them to as fine a powder as possible using a mortar and pestle. Then either stir them into a lard base like the old Witches did, or use a less messy method by mixing them in a non-scented body lotion easily found in drug stores. I prefer the lotion myself. It is easier to wash off, more ecological, and is a bit easier to launder out of sheets or clothing.

Following are nine different recipes for flying ointments. Use about two cups of lard or lotion for each recipe. Be sure to visualize and project your energy into the ointment as you make it.

1. ½ teaspoon lavender
    1 teaspoon mugwort
    ¼ teaspoon sage

2. ¼ teaspoon valerian
    3 drops lilac oil
    1 drop benzoin oil
    1 drop cinquefoil oil

3. 1 teaspoon catnip
    6 drops carnation oil
    1 teaspoon orris root
    pinch of chicory

4. 9 drops jasmine oil
    1 teaspoon orris root
    (easy to find powdered)
    ⅛ teaspoon damiana

5. 1 teaspoon lemongrass
    ¼ teaspoon valerian
    1 drop jasmine oil
    1 drop lilac oil
    pinch of saffron
    (very pricey!)

6. ½ poplar bark
    4 drops cinquefoil oil
    (or ½ teaspoon of the herb)
    6 drops sandalwood oil
    (a bit expensive, but worth it)
    ¼ teaspoon yarrow
    pinch sage

7. 3 drops honeysuckle oil
    ½ teaspoon eyebright

8. 1 drop jasmine oil
    1 drop lilac oil
    2 drops sandalwood oil
    1 drop rosemary oil
    (or ½ teaspoon of the herb)

9. ¼ teaspoon damiana
    2 drops yarrow oil
    (or a ¼ teaspoon of the herb)
    pinch parsley
    ½ teaspoon Irish Moss
    1 drop rosemary oil
    4 drops sandalwood oil

Feel free to create your own ointments by mixing your favorite ingredients from any of these formulas in proportions you find pleasing. There are no right or wrong measurements, there is only what works best for you.

You can add to your working environment any other items that you feel will help you. A friend of mind burns jasmine incense before he projects and claims it assists him very well. I have found that tea made from valerian root is an excellent psychic enhancement for any magickal endeavor, astral projection included, but it does have two drawbacks. One, it can make you sleepy, and two, it smells pretty bad. You can cut the strong odor of the herb by adding a bit of peppermint.

After the ointment is made, it should be consecrated and charged under the influence of the full moon, the planet that governs psychic activity and the astral realm. To do this, take the ointment out under the moon, or as near as you can get in your circumstances, and cast your circle. Present the jar to the moon. You will not have to spend lots of time aligning the two. This has already been done in the preparation process. Simply call upon the lunar energies, and/or any moon deity with whom you feel an affinity, and charge and bless the ointment:

> *By the Lord and Lady and all that's holy,*
> *This ointment I charge with the power of the light,*
> *By the gentle beings of the inner-worlds,*
> *I bid you bless me on my journeys in the night.*
> *So Mote It Be!*

Allow your own energy to flow through the ointment once more, adding your personal touch to the lunar charging.

The traditional method of using the ointment is to slather it over the entire surface of the naked body before settling down to work. Nudity in this case not only helps you project by giving you a feeling of freedom from constrictions, but is also sensible, since the oils and grease can stain clothing. Or you may want to lie on an old blanket or wear a loose, inexpensive robe kept just for astral projection work.

Another reason for covering the entire body was that the lard helped contain warmth. The inert physical body tends to get cold during astral projection, just as it does in sleep. This is the primary reason why the Witches of old traditionally practiced this art while lying in front of their fireplaces.

You can modify the traditions somewhat by covering only key energy points, such as the feet, hands, temples, and chakras, without losing the efficacy of the ointment, although you must still guard against stains and chills, the latter of which can be very distracting to your efforts.

As you apply the ointment, be sure to visualize or state aloud your intent. Inhale the concoction, feel its vibration on your hands, sense the change it is bringing to both your physical and psychic selves.

When this is completed, you may begin your astral projection work. The ointment should be washed off as soon as you have finished.

Besom Construction and Consecration

Besoms, or round-shaped brooms, are deeply linked to Witches and their magick, both in popular fantasy and in actual practice. Today, Witches all over the world are reclaiming nearly-forgotten broom lore and are again making it a part of the Craft.

Brooms were one of the "safe" tools of Witchcraft, meaning they were a necessary household object that could not be held up as evidence of Witchcraft in the clerical courts. This convenient fact naturally elevated their prominence as magickal tools. Brooms are used as wands to focus and direct magickal energy, to sweep areas clean of negativity, to ground a finished circle, and to protect hearths and kitchen magick. Two crossed brooms were used in medieval Ireland to prevent negativity from entering homes through the fireplace or front door.

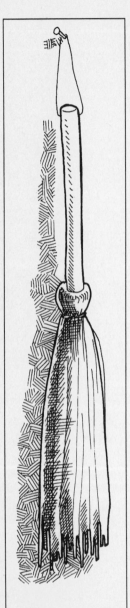

A handmade magickal broom can hang on the Witch's kitchen wall, spreading its goodly influence throughout the house.

Popular folklore says that unpleasant consequences will result if an old broom is taken into a new home, used while walking backwards, or stored with the bristles up. It should never accidentally brush across the feet of a single girl or else she is doomed to spinsterhood.

Ashes, which contain protective energies, were collected from fireplaces by magickal brooms so that their beneficial energies would remain undisturbed. Throughout Europe and Africa, Pagan women rode broomsticks over newly-planted fields in spring, and later at the harvest, to encourage growth and continued prosperity. It is from this image that the popular idea of the Halloween witch riding around the moon mounted on a broomstick was born.

Brooms are strongly featured in folktales, usually associated with a female figure. In the faery tale *Cinderella* we read that one of the heroine's primary tasks was sweeping the hearths clean. Cinderella's Scottish counterpart Rashincoatie wears clothing made of broomcorn. In a popular nursery rhyme we read of the woman who in her hand "carries a broom" and flies "seventeen times as high as the moon" in order to sweep the cobwebs from its face.

The broom itself is symbolic of those things Pagans cherish. Scott Cunningham and David Harrington in their last collaboration, *Spell Crafts,* discuss this potent imagery, saying, "... brooms are emblematic of the moon and of its energies, as well as of women, water, and the Earth itself ... evocative of past times, when magic was an accepted part of life and when the broom was a tool of this ancient art." Their physical shape, representing the God's sacred phallus uniting sexually with the Goddess, makes them ideal tools for fertility magick, hence the popular custom of "jumping the broom" at the conclusion of a Pagan wedding ceremony.

There are two types of magickal brooms you can make. Both will require a stick or dowel rod (available at hardware or craft stores) and either some twigs and herbs, or broomcorn or straw (also found in craft stores). My magickal broom is made from broomcorn and is attached to a three-foot dowel painted an earthy brown. This is short enough to allow me to use it as a wand without it being clumsy and cumbersome, and long enough for me to make magickal sweeping motions without having to bend myself into a backache.

Witches sometimes hesitate to make a broom from herbs and twigs because it doesn't actually "sweep," and usually decomposes rapidly and must be remade. Keep in mind that this is a magickal broom; it isn't supposed to be used for mundane cleaning tasks, nor should the energy of living herbs be expected to be endless. Although temporary in nature, tying dried herbs or twigs that have affinities with your magickal intention to the end of your broom can work very well. Let's say you wish to use the image of the broom sweeping away evil in a protection spell. A broom made with with protective twigs (like oak, elder, or ash) and/or protective herbs (such as blackberry roots, burdock, or rosemary) would accomplish your goal.

An herb and twig besom

To make a more traditional Witch's round broom you will need the following:

- A dowel or stick, about one inch thick and three to four feet long
- Broomcorn or straw
- Craft glue
- Twine and scissors, or craft wire and pliers to fasten the straws to the stick
- Paints and brushes are optional to decorate the broomstick

Begin by laying the straw upward along the bottom of the shaft, keeping the tops of the straw even with the bottom of the stick. Make your first tie approximately two to three inches above this end. Use either twine or craft wire tightened with pliers to secure the straw. Of course, you should keep visualizing the magickal intention of the broom as you are doing this.

After you have made this first tie you may want to apply a little glue to the loose straws at the bottom to further secure them to the stick.

Carefully bend the straws back over the top of the tie so that they extend below the shaft like those of a normal broom. Just below the end of the stick, make another tie.

You may decorate the shaft any way you see fit. You can paint symbols on it, or Runes, your magick name, or anything else that has meaning for you. Many Witches leave their broom natural, or paint it an earthy color like brown or green, or a lunar color like white or silver.

The broom is now finished and needs only to be consecrated to your magickal needs. Naturally, this should take place during the duration of the full moon's power.

Take your broom to your circle. After you have called your quarters and any deities with whom you wish to work, present the broom to the moon. Allow its light to wash over the broom, infusing it with lunar power. If you cannot be outdoors or someplace else where you can see the moon, do this mentally, remembering that the moon's magickal influence can penetrate the thickest roof.

Making a Traditional Round Besom with a dowel, broomcorn or straw, and twine or wire

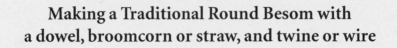

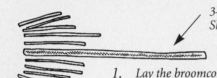

3–4 foot wooden dowel, 1 inch in diameter.
Shaft can be painted or decorated to taste.

1. Lay the broomcorn or straw up against the bottom shaft of the dowel. Cut straw approximately 4–6 inches longer than desired finished length.

(Areas for optional glue)

2. Approximately 2 inches above the end, tie twine tightly or twist on craft wire with the aid of pliers. You may wish to apply some craft glue to the lower 2 inches to help secure loose straw ends.

3. Bend the straws backwards over the tie. Secure more twine or wire just where the dowel ends.

As you offer your broom to the moon you might say:

> *Hail, Moon Mother, bless this broom of magick, tool of my ancestors, that I might use it successfully in all my rites.*

Take the broom and, moving clockwise around the circle, present it to each of the quarters, asking the corresponding element to lend blessings to the broom. These words should come from the heart and reflect what you feel about each element. Use the following as a guideline.

Water:

> *Powers of water and the shiny deep,*
> *Realm of psychic secrets keep,*
> *Bless this broom with spring-like showers,*
> *Bless by hidden, watery powers.*

Earth:

Powers of earth, womb-dark and cool,
Bless this broom, this magick tool,
Bless this broom which I hold here,
Bless the magick I hold dear.

Air:

Powers of air, of whispering wind,
Blessing upon this broom do send,
Sweeping out the bane and harm,
Sweeping in the blessed charm.

Fire:

Powers of fire, of heat and light,
Blessings burn on my broom this night,
May it always and only good works do,
Until all my desired ends come true.

Lastly, move back to the center of the circle, and hold the broom upwards, the bristles reaching for the moon. Feel the power of this object you have created. Know that it is part of you and of the moon, a tangible link between you and the vast powers that move the universe. Laugh along with the old ones who are smiling down upon you, and say:

This is my will. So Mote It Be!

You may wish to sprinkle some moon-charged water or saltwater onto the broom when you are done. This is another old method of cleansing and blessing any magickal tool. The broom is now ready to use. Let its first act of magick be to sweep your circle closed.

A Talisman for Overcoming Fear of the Dark

The full moon was the world's first nightlight, and its soft, comforting glow makes it a perfect symbol under which to craft a talisman for a child to use to help overcome fear of the dark. You can make this charm for a child you know or, if it is appropriate, assist the child in creating it for him or herself.

For this talisman you will need:

- A cardboard cut-out of some object the child will view as protective a pentagram, athame, etc.
- Colored paints and brushes
- A protective essential oil such as cinnamon, frankincense, clove, or garlic

Create the talisman on the night of the full moon and, if you are assisting a child through the process, it is best to actually go outside — even if for only a second — to actually expose the talisman to the light of the moon. For children, who do not readily grasp abstractions, the light, representing security in the darkness, will be very important to the success of their spell.

When the cardboard has been cut, it should be handled while visualizing the end goal. If you are helping a child, get him or her talking about why there is a fear of the dark, and let him go off on a fantasy of how the talisman he is making will work on his behalf. This image of frenetic action is how kids visualize, and it works very well for them since they have the enviable ability to project themselves wholly into their daydreams.

The next step is to paint protective symbols on the cardboard. These can include X's, pentagrams, favorite super heroes, or even gaping, tooth-filled mouths that can gobble up the monsters of the night. These images, which we may find silly, are those with which children can readily identify. Certainly allow the child to do the painting if he or she is capable. Again, in order to keep his mind focused, get him talking about the images he is painting and let him express how they will work for him in any way he sees fit.

The last step will be "sealing" the magick into the talisman. This is the point at which the young one will want the light of the full moon falling over the item. Take a small bit of the oil you have chosen and rub it onto the talisman with words such as:

> *Guardian protector of the full moon's light,*
> *Chase away all harm in the night.*
> *From dream to dream my safety keep,*
> *And bless the room wherein I sleep.*
> *Monsters be gone! So Mote It Be!*

Another good choice for your charging words is the old Scottish charm:

> *From ghoulies and ghosties,*
> *And long-legged beasties,*
> *And things that go bump in the night,*
> *Blessed Lady deliver me. So Mote It Be!*

If the child for whom the talisman is intended did not have a hand in its making, you should explain exactly how it was made. Be sure to emphasize the image of the moon as a nightlight, and feel free to use whatever embellishments are necessary to make the child believe in the magick. Children often choose their own talismans to which this new one can be added. For instance, if the child uses a stuffed animal as a protector, allow it to hold the talisman during the night. If his purple dinosaur looks funny to you wielding a giant cardboard athame, then so be it. The child will understand and accept this image.

The Wishing Moons

I first came across the idea of "Wishing Moons" in 1986 when I read Marion Weinstein's newly revised and beautiful Book of Shadows, *Earth Magic*. In her Dianic tradition, these are called "List Moons" and they occur every third full moon. These nights are used for making lists of wishes, hopes, and aspirations which, over the next three months, should begin to manifest.

Since that time I have come across numerous Pagans from many different traditions who follow this custom, although they have never read Marion's books and call the practice by different names. What I found most curious was that they all used the same dates, and I was at a loss to understand how these were being determined. When I asked about the origin, no one could explain it to me. "It's just a tradition," was the usual response. To me, the moons seemed very arbitrary, senseless in the larger picture, and I couldn't fathom their popularity.

Several years later, I decided to chart out these moons for my own use, using the reckoning that had been given to me over and over again. After charting out only a few years of moons I quickly discovered that they worked out to be the full moons nearest to the four major Celtic Sabbats of Samhain (October 31), Imbolg (February 1 or 2), Bealtaine (May 1), and Lughnasadh (August 1 or 2). When I discovered this correlation I felt an immediate kinship to them, adopted the name "Wishing Moons," and developed my own little wish-making ritual around each one.

I follow Marion's advice and write out my wish list, usually after all other Esbat ritual work is done. Then I add a single drop of sandalwood oil to the paper. This is an oil that not only has strong lunar associations, but has also been used successfully for centuries in wish magick. (I also happen to be crazy about the scent!) Other oils that share these properties are dogwood, jasmine, willow, and camphor.

After the oil is added, I slip the list in my Book of Shadows with the words:

> *If wishes were horses then beggars would ride,*
> *Over land, sea, and air on the wings of their pride.*
> *With never a doubt and never a dare,*
> *Never lose sight of the dreams in my care.*

After I put my Book of Shadows away, I remove a moonstone from my magickal cabinet and take it out under the light of the full moon, where I project into it my need for the wishes I have made. I keep the stone on my person until the moon grows dark, then store it safely in my cabinet for the next Wishing Moon.

The Wishing Moons for the rest of this century are:

March 5, 1996	August 8, 1998
June 1, 1996	November 4, 1998
August 28, 1996	January 31, 1999
November 25, 1996	April 30, 1999
February 27, 1997	July 28, 1999
May 22, 1997	October 24, 1999
August 18, 1997	January 21, 2000
November 14, 1997	April 18, 2000
February 11, 1998	July 16, 2000
May 11, 1998	October 13, 2000

A good twenty-first century ephemeris, many of which should start to appear on the market in the next few years, will guide you past this date. Remember to count the actual full moons and not just the months of the year, which can contain more than one full moon.

Waxing and Waning Moon Magick

Nothing that is can pause or stay;
The moon will wax, the moon will wane,
The mist and cloud will turn to rain,
The rain to mist and cloud again,
Tomorrow be today.
— Henry Wadsworth Longfellow

Waxing and waning moon magick may seem at first to involve two totally separate operations, but in truth they are closely related. Only the mind of the Witch casting the spell, and the spin he or she gives the working, makes it more or less compatible with one phase or another.

All of the spells presented in this chapter are designed with either the waxing or waning phase of the moon in mind. Immediately following the spell are instructions for adapting it to harmonize with the opposite lunar phase. The skills for reorienting your spells will come naturally after a little practice; there should be virtually no spell that cannot be adapted.

A Prosperity Spell For the Waxing Moon

This spell uses the energy of the waxing moon to enhance general prosperity. Prosperity means more than just monetary security; it is also indicative of an overall quality of life. When deciding to work a prosperity spell you should have firmly in mind exactly which areas of your life you wish to enhance in order to better focus your visualizations.

For this spell you will need:

- A small chalice or cup of water
- A mirror (it doesn't have to be your moon mirror)
- Three tall taper candles (silver or green in color)
- Three coins (preferably of silver)

Altar Lay-out for Waxing Moon Prosperity Spell

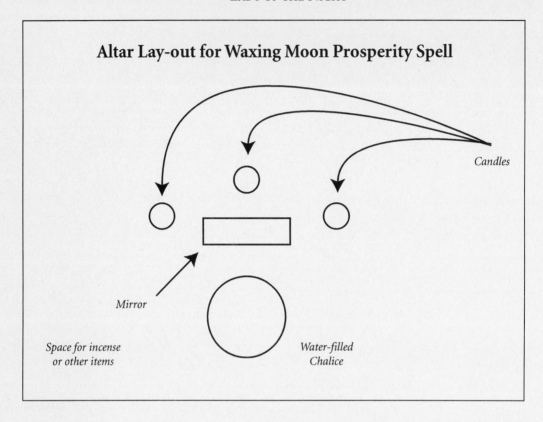

Candles

Mirror

*Space for incense
or other items*

*Water-filled
Chalice*

On any night during the waxing moon, set up your altar so that the three candles are in a row farthest from you, the chalice is nearest you, and the mirror is between so that you can see your face and the top of the chalice.

You may also wish to have on the altar any personal symbols of prosperity, herbs, oils, and/or incense that share its affinity. Examples of such items are currency, pine needles, jewelry and other luxury pieces, family photos, patchouli oil, or wooden pentagrams.

When you have cast your circle and are ready to begin, light the center candle, saying:

*Blessed Be the light of prosperity,
Glowing and growing for mine and me.*

Grasp the silver coins — long-revered symbols of good fortune — in your hands and stand before the altar. Allow the warm glow of the single candle to slow your mind and help you focus on your goal of a prosperous life. Feel your energies merging with those of the coins and begin to visualize your fulfilling life with the special sort of prosperity you need. See the coins as a tangible presence of the fulfillment that has so far eluded you, and the chalice as the great womb of the mother Goddess from which flows all creation.

When you are ready, drop one single coin into the chalice of water. Visualize the coin merging with the great cosmic flow which is now being manifested in your life. As you drop the coin say the words that follow:

By silver moon and silver light,
All I desire is mine tonight.
Money, happiness, prosperity,
All these things are part of me.

Keep your visualization going strong; feel confident of your success. Already the spell is working for you, and you should be able to begin to sense the waxing prosperity which is yours. Make it real in your mind and heart and it will be real in your life.

Drop the second coin and repeat the above quatrain.

After you speak, take the lighted center candle and light the one to your left. The flames represent the proverbial "light at the end of the tunnel" which is now growing brighter as you approach your goal.

Repeat your visualizations.

When ready, drop in the last coin and repeat the quatrain again. Then, taking the candle on the left, light the candle on the right, and repeat an affirmation of your success:

By the coin and by the light,
Dark world vanish, now all is right.

Now gaze into the mirror and smile smugly. See your pleased reflection in the glow of the candlelight enhanced by the glossy water. Know this is the light of success shining on you; see how the light and the silver-charged water bathes you, has become a part of you.

Spend as much time in your circle as you like, raising the energy of your success. When you feel you have done all you can, release the energy and say:

As by my will, I am Prosperity incarnate. The light of success shines on me.
The rite is done. So Mote It Be!

Altering for the Waning Moon

To rework this spell for the waning moon simply reverse its processes. Keep the coins in your hand, but begin with all the candles lit and allow them to represent your lack of prosperity, burning up all your money and happiness. Alter the visualization so that you see all the obstacles in your life which prevent prosperity being drained away with the waning moon. As you toss each coin in the water, extinguish a candle while making an affirmation such as:

As prosperity enters my reality, my difficulties vanish like a flame in the wind.

Take a sip of the water, then remove the coins. Pour the water into mother earth and pocket the money so that the coins can act as talismans of sympathetic magick, drawing prosperity to you.

A Love Spell for the Waning Moon

Rather than focusing on drawing love into your life, this spell focuses on removing the lonely longing we have all experienced when we are not part of a special twosome.

For this simple magick you will need:

- Three glasses or chalices
- A small picture of two happy people
- A love-associated oil such as rose, apple blossom, or vanilla (vanilla extract from your kitchen is an excellent substitute for the oil)
- A candle in pink, red, or silver

The picture you choose does not have to be anything special; in fact, it works better if it is something you cut from a magazine that can be viewed as an overall concept of your goal, rather than as a concrete image.

Fill two of the chalices about half-full with water and set them on opposite ends of your altar. These will represent yourself and the person who will soon come into your life as being apart, each feeling like only "half" of something you have yet to discover. Set the empty chalice in the center of the altar. Put the oil, picture, etc., wherever it is convenient for you to place them.

Perfuming the air with your oil by using it to anoint a working candle (one lit to offer you light to see by) can also add to the atmosphere. If you choose to do this, make sure you visualize your goal and project it into the candle as you work. Light it as soon as you have cast your circle, so that it can function as your working light.

Candle red (or silver or pink) *as lovelight bright,*
Carry my prayers to the Gods tonight.

Begin, as always, by slowing your mind and focusing inward until the visualization of loneliness ending comes clearly to you. Form a picture of yourself as you are now ... alone ... and allow yourself to build up a complete hatred and intolerance for this state of being. Pour all of that deeply-felt emotion into the mental image and then, with a burst of will, force that image far, far away from you. See it flying out into the vast darkness of the universe, exploding, and being harmlessly absorbed in the endless vacuum of space.

Now focus your attention on the center chalice, which is empty. See it as unused potential waiting to be filled by you. Invest the empty cup with all of your hopes and dreams of romance, companionship, love, and loyalty.

If you are female, the chalice on the left will represent you; if you are male, the one on the right is yours. These are the traditional directional attributes of the feminine and the masculine in many, many cultures. Lift the chalice that represents you, and then the other, holding them both out to your sides as far away from each other as possible. Feel your need pouring into yours, and the need of someone yet unknown to you filling the other.

Look into the depths of the empty chalice and feel the aching loneliness inside you melting away as the cup fills with loving potential, representing unity and wholeness, aching to be used.

While still focusing on the empty vessel, bring the two cups to your breast and sense the energy you've invested in them straining to come together. Many old creation legends tell that, in the beginning of time, the divine creative power split itself into male and female halves who are always striving to be rejoined. Pour as much energy as you can into this image and then, when you feel the time is right, pour the contents of the two chalices into the empty center one. Sense the happiness and relief of the two halves of the whole which are now united.

Seal the magickal union with a single drop of the oil you have chosen. As it mingles with the energy of the joined waters, intone words that affirm the success of your spell:

> *Separated at birth, full circle come,*
> *Two halves of wholeness are joined as one.*
> *With harm to none, leaving all choice free,*
> *By my will, So Mote It Be!*

Lastly, take the picture and hold it over the chalice, allowing the joyful energy within to be transferred to the picture. Project your likeness, and that of the one you have drawn into your life, onto the image. When you have invested it with as much energy as you can, place a single drop of the water, and another of the oil, on the picture, fold it tightly, and carry it with with you until the moon phase changes. At that point it should be burned. If you feel the need, repeat the spell on the next waning moon.

Altering for the Waxing Moon

To weave a spell of romance on the waxing moon, adjust your visualization to encompass the gaining of companionship and the merging of two lonely lives into one big happy one. The imagery of pouring the water together and carrying a talisman until the moon changes its phase works equally well here.

Healing Magick For the Waxing Moon

Almost every day you can hear someone in the media, your workplace, or even your own home, recite the old doggerel: "If you have your health, you have everything." Many of us begrudge this cliche, thinking it sounds fine up to a point, then dream lustfully of all the things that would make having our health so much more enjoyable. Of course, all this cynicism vanishes the moment we start feeling the least bit ill; then we are willing to do almost anything to feel on top of life again.

For this healing spell you will need:

- A purple candle (a color linked to healing and to the moon)
- An essential oil with healing affinities, such as rosemary, garlic, or vervain
- Some purple body paint

Body paints can be found in novelty and gift shops, costume stores, or in shops specializing in erotic paraphernalia. A very good paint substitute is purple-toned lipstick. The texture of lipstick makes drawing on your body simpler and far less messy, and it scrubs off fairly easily. You can also make your own body paints using liquid soap thickened with a little cornstarch or flour, and purple food coloring (made from equal parts of blue and red). However, this mixture does have a drawback: it does not compliantly wash off of the skin. The plus is that you can invest it with the energy of your goal as you make it. Either way, spend some time before your spell projecting your need into the paint you choose so that it will be better aligned with your energies.

Because you will be using the body paints to mark on your body, you will want to be as undressed as you feel comfortable with for this spell. You will definitely need easy access to any part of your body in need of special healing attention. If you are indoors you might also want to consider working over newspapers or on some other type of dropcloth to avoid staining your carpet.

When you are safely inside the confines of your circle, anoint the candle with the healing oil while pouring your desire for increased health into the action.

Set the candle down UNLIT in the center of the altar, in a sturdy candle holder. Stand before your altar and affirm the candle's empowerment with a chant such as:

> *Candle rich as the fruit of wine,*
> *Healing, health, and wholeness mine.*

Begin to visualize a purple aura growing brighter and stronger around your body, sending life-affirming energy pulsating through you. Next, form a mental link with the healing powers you have invested in the candle, which in this spell represents the healing energy of fire. Visualize a purple flame rising in you, a protective light that you wear like a talisman to safeguard your health. Feel the candle representing yourself, and your internal flame. Then light the candle while empathizing with the rising blaze:

> *Candle rich as the blush of wine,*
> *Healing, health, and wholeness mine,*
> *Flaming brightly ever more,*
> *Healing power in me I store.*

Take the purple body paint and mark healing symbols over the parts of your body you feel need special healing attention. You might draw invoking pentagrams (see Chapter 2) or clockwise spirals, which are also linked to healing and manifestation magick, or one of the runes associated with healing properties such as Uruz, Kenaz, or Berkano (see Chapter 3). Even little smiley faces work well if they conjure up the right mental images for you. As you make these markings, visualize the purple color of the paints sending an extra boost of healing to these troubled spots.

Spend as much time in your circle as you can, focusing on the waxing healing energy, but don't strain beyond the time you can easily hold the image. At this point you should close your circle, but you can leave the candle burning for as long as you like.

Spiral Markings

A spiral for manifesting, to be used on the waxing moon. Start at the center and go outward, moving clockwise.

A spiral for banishing, to be used on the waning moon. Start at the center and go outward, moving counterclockwise.

[Warning: Don't ever be tempted to leave any candle burning when you are not present! Candles can fall over, be accidentally toppled by curious pets, and sparks can and do occasionally fly away and land on highly flammable materials — such as a box of tissues — with disastrous results.]

You may wash the body paint off whenever you are ready, and the spell can be repeated as needed.

Altering for the Waning Moon

To alter this spell for the waning moon you will need to focus on banishing illness rather than on gaining health. Use a black candle instead of a purple one. Contrary to popular opinion, black is not a color of evil. Black is merely the absence of all color, a void in which all light is lost. Because of this property, it has the unique ability to absorb unwanted energies.

In this spell the candle represents your inner-flame which burns away illness.

While you are meditating after the spell is done, see the illness in you being consumed like the candle shaft. When it has burned down as far as you can let it go, treat it as if it actually contains the sickness you wish to be rid of, and bury it somewhere.

You will also need body paints in black which you will visualize as drawing the illness out of your trouble spots, or blocking the progress of a disease. Black lipstick (yes, they do make it) is the most washable, but you can make your own following the aforementioned formula and substituting a few drops of water-soluble children's paint for the food coloring. Make banishing pentagrams, counterclockwise spirals, or X's over your trouble points.

A Finding-Employment Spell for the Waxing Moon

Like death and taxes, periodic unemployment is a fact of modern life. You can increase your chances of finding a job, or landing a better one, by using magick.

This spell falls in what we usually term the "Kitchen Witch" category of magick; it uses a normal cooking project as a focal point for raising energy.

For this spell you will need:

- Some small, non-melting, non-flammable symbols of good fortune, such as a gold piece or a golden ring. These can be drugstore reproductions and do not have to be real; they are only a mental image upon which to focus your goal, not the goal itself.

- You will also need two prepared bread pans, a floured cutting board, and some bread dough. Bread is an ancient symbol of plenty with a long and successful history in prosperity spells. It will be used as the catalyst for your gaining a job, or for finding one that pays you more and/or makes you happier.

The following is my favorite bread recipe. It is very simple to make, almost impossible to ruin, and can probably be made with items you already have on hand in your kitchen. The magickal directions are written into the recipe since, with Kitchen Witchery, the cooking and the spell are woven together as one single operation.

White Yeast Bread Employment Spell

After you have assured yourself that you have all of the necessary items on hand, purge the mundane energies of your kitchen by spreading around some basil, rosemary, or garlic, or by burning some protective incenses such as cinnamon or frankincense. Using a magickal broom is also an excellent image for cleaning a kitchen working space.

Since drawing a circle around an entire room can be difficult, you will need to mentally project your circle into place. Because you will be moving around your work area you might want to mentally encase yourself in a protective egg of white or golden light, both colors of protection. Gold also shares a strong affinity with monetary prosperity.

Begin visualizing your goal. Clearly and undeniably see yourself gainfully employed and happy in your work. You may chant about it, sing, or gaze at a pictorial representation. Keep this up all through the cooking process.

Pre-heat your oven to 325° and grease two standard-size loaf pans. Glass works better than aluminum and is generally thought to be more conducive to magickal cooking.

Mix the following in a pan:

¼ cup sugar	1½ cups lukewarm water
2 packages yeast	

As you mix, visualize yourself happily, gainfully employed.

Allow the mix to sit undisturbed for twenty minutes. During this time raise more energy by humming, chanting, singing, and meditating on the desired outcome, and by continuing with the next step.

In a large bowl combine:

¼	cup powdered milk		2	well beaten eggs
⅛	pound vegetable shortening		⅛	rounded cup instant
⅔	teaspoon salt			mashed potato flakes

To this combination, add the first mixture. Then begin stirring in the flour one cup at a time until the mix is heavy and doughy. This will take approximately four to six cups, but don't hesitate to use more or less if you feel you should. Begin learning to develop your magickal instincts.

Use your hands to work the ingredients together. Lots of hands-on work is the trademark of Kitchen Witchery. Knead the dough with feeling, pouring your need into the mix. Feel your desire grow in your heart. Channel this energy down through your arms and into your hands; from your hands pour it into the dough. Remember that for thousands of years breads have represented abundance.

After the mixture is well kneaded, cover it with a cloth and let it stand undisturbed for twenty minutes. Use this time to raise personal energy as you did while waiting for the yeast to activate. You might also want to mentally align the rising dough with the image of the waxing moon.

After twenty minutes return to the dough and, with ceremony and feeling, drop in the golden symbols you have chosen. These will be baked into the loaves.

Begin kneading again and repeat the rising process.

Divide the dough into halves and place into the loaf pans, pushing it down evenly.

Bake at 325° for 30–40 minutes. Baking time will vary depending upon your oven calibration. Use the old folk method of determining doneness — when you tap on the loaf it sounds vaguely hollow. Be careful not to overbake.

While the loaves are baking, keep up the mental activity that is feeding your spell. Wash the dishes in rhythm to a chant, read the classified ads or a book on winning interviews, or do a mediation or a guided meditation on your goal.

As you eat the loaves, keep in mind that, like the Cakes and Ale Ceremony (see Chapter 1), Pagans believe that the magick they consume becomes a part of them. Visualize the bread filling you with job-winning energy, and when you find the golden prize in your slice say, "So Mote It Be!" and pocket the item as a talisman of success.

Remember that you will need to follow up this spell with physical effort. Don't let up on that job search, but go after it with a renewed tenacity born of your new self-confidence.

Altering for the Waning Moon

To alter this job-finding spell for the waning phase you will need to switch your visualization from one of gaining employment to one of losing your unemployed status. The twist is a subtle one, but this simple alteration makes the very same spell more compatible with the energies of the waning moon.

A Returning-Unwanted-Energy Spell for the Waning Moon

Whether intentional or not, all of us from time to time experience the fallout of someone else's negativity. Witches who sense this happening will take decisive steps to deflect it.

Deciding just how to deal with unwanted negative energy is a sticky point in magickal ethics, hotly debated by Pagans from all traditions. Some will claim the only sane action is to collect and ground the energy, and others say that it should be deliberately returned threefold. My point of view falls somewhere in between these two extremes. While I don't advocate malicious retaliation, I do feel that if someone sends ill-will your way you should not feel obligated to play the victim and accept this action, any more than you would accept someone sending you unsolicited items through the mail and asking you to pay for them. Don't think of this spell as bestowing a whammy on the head of an enemy, but as politely refusing a "gift" with a firm "thanks, but no thanks." I believe this is your right and I do not feel that anyone, including the original sender, will suffer any added harm as a result of your action.

The following spell is designed so that the negative energy will be returned to the sender, and ONLY to the sender. It does not magnify the force by three as we Pagans believe will eventually happen, but just gently gives it back and lets the natural laws of the universe take care of it from there.

For this spell you will need:

- A round mirror, easily and cheaply found at any drugstore (don't use your moon mirror if you will be performing this exercise during the day)
- Four black candles and holders
- A protective oil such as cinnamon, frankincense, thyme, or clove
- A lemon
- A sharp cutting knife
- Four nails, each at least an inch and a half long

Orient your altar to any direction, but do try to square it with the compass points as much as you can. The idea behind this is that you will send back the unwanted, negative energy to the four corners of the universe where, somewhere, it will surely find its rightful owner. On the altar, place your mirror in the center with the black candles at the directional points.

After you have cast your circle and called your quarters, the first step is to make a statement of your intent, being sure to include your wish that no one be unduly harmed. Use as much time as you need to say everything you intend. Don't allow any detail to escape you, or you may not achieve your "harm none" end. Say this aloud and with feeling, as a commitment to yourself, your ethics, and your deities:

> *Blessed Be to the four winds, the four corners of the universe, and the Gods and Goddesses who rule there. I, (state your name), have the right to live free from the negative will of those who, by intent or innocence, wish me harm. Tonight I return that energy to my hidden enemy. (Avoid using a*

name or visualizing a face or you may accidentally send harm to someone who doesn't deserve it. After all, you could be wrong. Allow the
spell to seek out the enemy for you.) *By all that I hold sacred, I will that
no energy sent from me this night will originate from me. I only return to
the sender what harmful intent has been given. I make no effort to invoke
the Threefold Law, that will be for the laws of time and the universe to
give. Tonight I free myself from all harm and, for the good of all concerned,
I will that no harm will be given to anyone else. By all that I hold scared,
this is my will.*

Slice the lemon in quarters, all the while focusing on it representing your enemy. As your
knife cuts, think of the fruit as representing the sourness of your enemy's actions, and
see yourself dividing it up, lessening its power. Place each lemon quarter on the outside
edge of the candles.

Beginning with any direction you like, light one of the candles with the chant:

> *Candle black and burning bright,*
> *Absorbing, burning harm this night.*
> *By the moon, and by the flame,*
> *End for all this baneful game.*

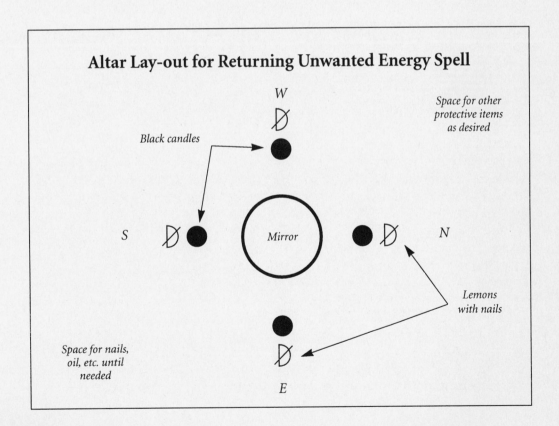

Altar Lay-out for Returning Unwanted Energy Spell

Allow yourself to spend a moment visualizing the black candle already absorbing the negativity that has been sent your way, consuming it as the candle is consumed by the blaze. This is pure sympathetic magick, a process by which a physical act of magick causes a similar reaction on the inner-plane.

Pick up one of the nails and place the tip of it into the candle's flame. Hold it there for only a second or two. Metal is a superb conductor of heat and if you wait too long you'll burn your fingers. Remove the hot nail and push it purposefully into the lemon quarter next to the candle. Visualize the heat "sterilizing" the enemy, rendering his or her power against you "impotent."

Continue this process, moving counterclockwise around the circle, until all of the candles are lit and all of the lemon quarters pierced.

When you have finished, spend time "gathering" the negative energy that is all around you and, with a huge push from your solar plexus (the area just above your navel), send away any of this lingering negativity. Spend some quiet time visualizing yourself free from this influence. Then you can shut the spell down with a "So Mote It Be!" and close the circle.

If you will be where you can keep an eye on the candles, let them burn down. They will serve as vacuums that continue to clear the area around you. When the candles are extinguished, bury the stumps.

Altering for the Waxing Moon

There is little you can do to specifically alter this spell to another moon phase, other than add to its focus. In addition to negativity being returned, visualize your protective defenses against future attacks increasing with the waxing moon. You may want to use white candles as well as black, to symbolize growing protective energy replacing the negative.

Because of the secretive nature of psychic attack, this spell also works very well when the Lady of the night shows her dark face.

Advanced Natural Magick

"What would you have me give you which you do
not already possess?" asked the Old One.
"What can you not give me?" the seeker cried.
"I can give you anything you desire so long as
it is that which you already own."
— Laura McKenry Stevenson

Witches often ask about so-called "advanced" spellcraft, but when pressed, few are sure exactly what they mean by the term, or even if such a thing exists. Indeed there is such a thing as advanced natural (Pagan/earth-centered) magick, although it bears no resemblance to the advanced techniques used in Ceremonial/ Kaballistic Magick, which relies on compelling more and more powerful spirits to do one's bidding and/or adding more elaborate accouterments to the rites. These are the glamorous, mysterious, and wholly distorted images that, thanks to the fantasy novel industry, haunt our minds.

The advanced magick of Witchcraft is much easier to learn, but more difficult to master. It is intimately linked to the phases of the moon in that it uses the rise and fall and rise of lunar power to boost visualizations for as long as it takes for the spell to manifest. It also requires a deep emotional involvement and prolonged commitment to the goal which most of us — myself included — cannot keep up for long, no matter how badly we feel we want something. This is unfortunate, because advanced magick can be a very powerful tool for change.

With all of the advanced work I have done I have always achieved some gratifying measure of success, but I will admit that very few of the advanced workings I start have been seen through to their conclusion, no matter how obsessive I was about my desire in the beginning. Advanced magick sucks up a lot of personal energy and, in our busy lives, is a tough mouth to feed.

The overriding advantage is that advanced magick can often bring success where one or two workings of a regular spell will not. Unlike an average spell, an advanced spell uses everything and anything that touches our lives to help us raise and send energy out to work on our behalf, and it demands that we use these tools on a daily basis.

Below are listed the basic steps involved in advanced natural magick.

1. An initial spell, well thought out and done in strict ritualization

2. A deep, prolonged, emotional involvement, and the acceptance that no matter when in your life your difficulty began, it can be overcome using these techniques

3. Continual supportive reworkings of the original spell, coordinated with the waxing and waning phases of the moon, usually performed on a daily basis

4. Long-term involvement in, and commitment to, the outcome on both the mental and physical planes

5. Sustained intensity using everyday events and items to channel power

6. Persistent use of creative visualization between bouts of spell workings and intensity exercises

7. Song and/or story spells to stimulate the mind and help connect the conscious and unconscious thought processes toward the goal

8. Use of supportive dream work and/or organized guided meditation as provoked by the story and song spells

Advanced Visualization

Unlike Ceremonial Magick, anyone, including the novice Witch, can perform advanced natural magick without having to worry about being physically or psychically harmed. However, if you read between the lines of the steps involved, you will notice that two skills are prerequisite which many novices do not possess. The process requires the Witch to have the ability to work in a focused, prolonged, altered state of consciousness, and — for some spells — to have a well-developed sense of non-linear time, so that spells can be worked backwards or forwards throughout the time/space continuum.

These skills must be learned with regular practice, and cannot be acquired overnight. The exercises in this chapter will help the novice develop these essential talents, and will strengthen the existing skills of the adept.

Exercises to Help Develop Your Concentration

Many books and tapes that teach meditation techniques are on the market. This deliberate slowing of the mind and focusing of thoughts is what altering your consciousness is all about. Every writer and teacher has their own variation on the process, but they all reach the same end.

Anyone who wishes to perform any type of psychic work, including magick, must first learn to sustain a single thought for increasingly long periods of time, until deep concentration can be achieved at will. Because of the ups and down of living, and the current state of development of — and repression of — the human mind, you will probably not achieve perfection of this art in this incarnation, unless you are studying daily with a Zen Master. But you can train your mind to respond to your wishes with surprising ease if you just practice. You make this shift in perception every night when you go to sleep and again in the morning when you awaken. You alter your consciousness when watching television, daydreaming, even while you're involved in reading this book. It is perfectly natural, but the trick is learning to control the response.

Exercise 1 — Find a quiet place to work where you will be undisturbed for at least half an hour. Get comfortable; choose a position in which your arms and legs are not crossed in any way that puts stress on the joints or impedes circulation. Meditation has been described as physical sleep combined with total mental awareness. Hence, you will be maintaining physical stillness for a prolonged period and will grow rapidly uncomfortable if you don't plan ahead. Either sitting or lying down is fine, but make sure if you choose the latter that you can remain awake.

Relax your body and take a few deep breaths. Release all the tensions in your body and feel them flowing away from you. All of your problems and concerns will still be waiting for you when you finish, so for now put them out of your mind.

Allow your eyes to settle on some object in the room, the simpler the better. Pick something you like because you will be working with it for several months, in this exercise and in Exercises 2 and 3.

Begin to focus your concentration on the object, to the exclusion of all else. Let your eyes become heavy and relaxed, but don't close them. You don't need to stare. Just gaze. Success in any psychic endeavor has been described as using a "will-less will," the use of effort but not force.

Contemplate the object's texture, recall what it feels like to touch it, try to imagine all the hands that have held it over time. Focus on its shape, its size, its meaning for you. Note the color and how it makes you feel. Contemplate it from all angles; nothing is off limits as long as it is related directly to the object.

If your mind wanders — and it will at first — don't stop or get frustrated, just bring your attention gently back to the exercise.

Keep practicing, daily if possible, with the same object until you can maintain your concentration for five to ten minutes without fail.

Exercise 2 — For this exercise you will need to go to the same quiet spot in which you have been working and get comfortable in the same way, but this time close your eyes. Take a few deep breaths and allow yourself to feel your mind slowing, moving inward and reaching outward.

When you are fully relaxed, form a mental picture of the object you worked with in Exercise 1. Make this as real as possible. At first you will find that the object will want to appear to you in the context in which you saw it in the room. Try to peel away the background so that the object stands alone in your mind.

Again, allow yourself to feel and see the texture, shape, and size of the object, only this time do it with the power of your mind.

Keep practicing until you can do this, without your mind wandering, for five to ten minutes. Then select other objects, perhaps some that are more complex in their shape or coloring. Keep practicing until you can conjure up in your mind clear images of any single item you choose.

Exercise 3A — This exercise is an extension of Exercise 2. Instead of visualizing just the object you were initially working with, you will be visualizing it in its normal setting. To the best of your capabilities, mentally reconstruct the area surrounding the object just as if you were gazing at it with your eyes open. Mentally see and feel the surface on which it rests, the items nearby, and what remains in the background or at the edge of your vision.

Don't skimp on this exercise if you are new to the process of visualizing because it is some of the best training you can get. When it comes to magick, the more sustained detail you can pour into your visualization, the more solid your magick will become.

Exercise 3B — With your eyes still closed, mentally take the object out of its normal setting and project it into another habitat. This can be a place with which you are familiar, or it can be a fantasy setting. Practice using both until you find it easy to slip into a state of consciousness where you can intellectually paint any scene you desire in your imagination and give it as much detail as if it were "reality."

Exercise 4 — This exercise involves controlled daydreaming, the making of inner-world dramas of your own choosing. You will be in charge of the action and should not permit it to take on a life of its own. This self-determined action will be needed for learning practices such as astral projection or deep, guided meditation, but for now your goal with these exercises is to learn sustained, focused concentration.

You will need to go to your private place again, get comfortable, and close your eyes. Start your daydreaming exercise by seeing yourself moving step by step through something you do everyday, an action you know intimately but rarely think about consciously. An example of this would be going to work. Chances are you could do this in your sleep. Mentally go through each step you make from waking to arriving at your workplace. Mentally recall the ugly feeling of hearing the alarm blare its unappreciated message, see yourself rising from bed, pad to the shower, fix your breakfast, etc. Make every step as complete and clear as possible. Repeat the exercise until you can get through an entire cycle without your mind wandering.

Next, select more complex, less reflexive actions, and begin to work step by step through them. Add smells, sounds, and words to complete the picture. Again, do this until you can get through the entire cycle without wavering from the visualization.

Lastly, move on to images of things you want to have happen — pleasant fantasies, goals, dreams — and work with them. Such visualizations are the seed from which all magick grows. The better you are at doing this, the better your magick will work for you.

Don't get discouraged if you feel you are not progressing with altered state work as quickly as you would like. Chances are you are doing much better than you think. This type of inner-plane work is subtle and many do not realize that they are in an altered state. On the inner-plane, time has no meaning. A good indication of success is finishing your exercise, looking at the clock, and realizing to your surprise that much more or less time has passed than you thought possible.

Learning to Think in Non-Linear Time

Pagan people of long ago saw little difference between the mysterious places called the past, the present, and the future. It was accepted that the shamans, the psychically-gifted spiritual leaders of the tribe or clan, could move backward and forward through time, shifting their physical forms and altering current events. Today, the modern science of physics supports the old belief that all time exists in one great omnipresent now, one which we only perceive as being linear in nature.

When casting a spell, Witches have always seen their visualizations as current events and construct all statements of desire in the present tense. The idea behind this is to project our desire into the existing future, then draw it "back" to us to manifest in the perceived here and now. Making statements of magickal intent in the future tense is likely to keep them always in the future, always just out of reach of our perceptions.

We can also work backward in perceived time by altering "past" events to reshape our current lives. For example, imagine you were in an accident and suffered a broken leg which refused to set properly, leaving you with a pronounced limp. You can work magick to reshape the past — which still exists somewhere out of our normal consciousness — to attempt to eliminate the problem, by reliving the moment of the accident and seeing yourself avoiding it. While you probably do not have the power to erase the accident from your past altogether, you can certainly lessen the severity of its effect in your present.

As a historian, I have always wanted to visit the past, to peek through the murky veil that separates human consciousness from the active existence of "other" times. If we can believe some of the skilled magi in history, it is quite possible. One must accept the fact that humanity could not exist with a perception of all time in their consciousness, but we can learn to accept the idea that all time is now. This wisdom is the first step in working with time.

The next three exercises (with a fourth one optional) will help you to gain that wisdom and acceptance and perhaps, in the process, give you a tantalizing glimpse of life beyond the constraints of your own time frame.

Exercise 1 — Watch films and read books and articles about time perceptions and time travel ideas. The non-fiction versions will enrich your mind by making you think about time in new ways, and will introduce you to all the theoretical possibilities. The fiction versions will stimulate your sub-conscious, the brain's fantasy realm, and show you how time has been perceived and described by different creative people.

Time travel has proved such a universally fascinating subject that, in recent years, an entire genre has been built up around it in the lucrative romance novel industry. Leisure Books has been one of the leaders in this movement, with Silhouette/Harlequin and Berkeley following closely with their own presentations. Ask in any bookstore and someone can point you in the direction of the most current paperbacks.

Articles on time theories and time travel can be found in popular science and science fiction magazines such as *Omni, Discover,* or *Analog.* Movies and television shows covering the subject can easily be borrowed from your local video rental store. Again, just ask someone for what you want.

The following is a brief list of some of the many books and films which cover the subject of time from a variety of angles, from the deeply scientific to the fantastically fictional.

- Piers Anthony, *Bearing an Hourglass* (novel from the Incarnations of Immortality series)
- Barbara Britton, *The Red Balloon* (novel)
- *City on the Edge of Forever* ("Star Trek" TV series' episode written by popular sci-fi author Harlan Ellison)
- Peter David, *Imzadi* (novel from "Star Trek: The Next Generation" series)
- Philip Jose Farmer, *Time's Last Gift* (novel)
- *Final Countdown* (movie)
- Jack Finney, *Time and Again* (novel)
- Barbara Hambly, *Ishmael* ("Star Trek" series' novel)
- Stephen Hawking, *A Brief History of Time* (non-fiction)
- *Just Over the Hill* ("Twilight Zone" TV series' episode written by the creator of "The Waltons" Earl Hamner, Jr.)
- Richard Matheson, *Bid Time Return* (novel) which was made into the movie *Somewhere in Time*
- John W. Macvey, *Time Travel* (non-fiction)
- "Quantum Leap" (TV series developed by Donald Bellisario) which has, as of this writing, been novelized eight times by Ashley McConnell and others
- *Running Against Time* (tele-film)
- *Star Trek IV: The Voyage Home* (movie)
- *Time After Time* (movie)
- *Time Bandits* (movie)
- *Time Flyer* (movie)
- "Time Tunnel" (TV series)
- *The Two Lives of Jenny Logan* (tele-film)
- H. G. Wells, *The Time Machine* (novel and movie)
- Robert Anton Wilson, *The New Inquisition* (non-fiction)
- *Yesterday's Enterprise* ("Star Trek: The Next Generation" TV series episode)

Exercise 2 — Linear time is a delusion of the human mind, and every now and then some lucky — and frightened — person gets an unexpected peek behind the veil and is actually allowed to see people or events thought long-vanished (incidentally, this is one explanation for the existence of ghosts).

My oldest friend is one such lucky person. We have known each other since we were seven years old and I have never known her to be particularly fanciful. Several years ago she moved with her family into a home built on the old road that connects her city with an adjoining suburb. Though today there is no differentiation between the two towns, a hundred years ago they were several miles apart.

On one occasion when she happened to be staring absent-mindedly out her front window, she was surprised to see people in turn-of-the-century dress standing down at the edge of her yard near the street. She tried to blink them away, but they remained where they were.

My friend stood there in silent awe for several minutes, until the images slowly vanished. She mentioned the experience to her husband who, though he believed her completely, could not explain it away any more than she could. Several times over the next few weeks she tried unsuccessfully to summon the vision back. Eventually she shoved it to the back of her mind and forgot about it.

About a year later, as she and her husband were preparing to apply for a building permit to add on a room, she had a chance to look over the abstract on the land. An abstract is a legal description of a property, which includes a complete history of how it was used and when and to whom it has been sold. As she kept turning the pages back she eventually found an entry stating that the front of her property was once a station stop for the trolley that ran from the outlying town into the city. She has been convinced ever since that what she saw that afternoon were the living, breathing people of a century ago, waiting patiently for the trolley car. I happen to think she is correct.

To gain our own wisdom of the simultaneous existence of time, we too must look at the present for glimpses of the past. We may not be as fortunate as my friend, but we can, when approaching the world in the correct frame of mind, get a feel for all that is taking place unseen around us.

Begin this exercise by strolling around a familiar neighborhood in your hometown. Relax your mind as much as is safe, but don't become so self-absorbed that you can't concentrate on traffic or other impending dangers. Begin gazing "through" the things you see. Use your magickal vision to look into and around the buildings to try and glean a hint of what is there in that exact spot beyond the veil. Depending on where you are looking, you might even find an old building still standing among the new. Note the state of any crumbling embellishments popular in ages past and try to envision what they might have looked like a hundred years ago.

Also look into the streets and up and down the sidewalk. Try to get a sense of what the people look like who are walking through you in a different time frame. Attempt to hear what they are discussing, see how they're dressed, and discover where they're heading. As you do this, try as much as possible to shove from your mind any preconceived notions that you may have gleaned during your experiments with books or television.

The next step is to find as many old photographs as possible of the area you just explored. These can be found in your local library, which will inevitably have some type of photographic archive of your hometown. Allow yourself to study the photos with your magickal senses, and try to project yourself into them as much as possible. Gaze at the people until they seem to breathe. Think about the horse pulling the wagon as being about to put that foreleg back down on the brick streets. Smell the factory, belching black smoke into the clean air. Hear the street vendors hawking their wares. After you have done this, compare all the photographed scenes to those of your earlier perceptions. Note how they compare, and then try exploring again to see if you can see any of the scenes captured in the pictures.

Another way to do this exercise is to get hold of a series of photography books called *Then and Now*, which were published by Dover Publications in the late 1970s (see Appendix C for the address). The editors of these books found old photos of familiar scenes in well-traveled places like New York and Washington, DC, then sent photographers out to attempt to take the same picture from the same place at the same time of day in the 1970s. The two pictures are placed side by side on the page, with well-researched text to help you pick out what is left of the past in the modern photos. The books are wonderfully absorbing and, if you live in or near the cities featured, you may want to take the books along while you work on this exercise. My experience has been that these ingenious books open the mind to the realities of simultaneous time in unique and pleasurable ways.

Exercise 3 — One well-known reason that it is so hard for police and lawyers to come up with reliable eye witnesses is that we all have a natural tendency to see what we want to see. We stamp these desires on our memory, and they in turn becomes the reality. The farther away from the actual event we travel in linear time, the more convinced we are of our own version of it. Eventually we adopt this personal vision so completely that even a skilled hypnotist cannot dig up the "real" memory and separate it from the "imagined" one. In other words, it backs up the old Pagan belief that thought projections can, and do, become manifest.*

Witches can use this natural ability to reshape the past in order to change the present for the better. Step one in this process is demonstrating to ourselves just how easily it works. This is different from merely reading about it. We must live the experience ourselves in order to gain real wisdom from it and to learn, on a deeper level than the merely intellectual, just how the process works.

First of all, try to think of someone you know who remembers a particular event differently than you do. If no one readily comes to mind, just get members of your family talking about past family events and you will undoubtedly come up with dozens of examples. When you have one in mind — preferably one which is not especially important to you — practice shaping your own memory of that event to match the one with which you originally disagreed. Mentally relive it the way it was told to you, rather than the way you remember it. Visualize the new information over and over to yourself, before going to bed and again upon arising. Begin to reconstruct your thinking to make this new idea part of your past reality.

After a few weeks, talk the event over again with the family member from whom you got the new version, to clear up any details you may be lacking. After a few weeks you may be surprised to discover that you are no longer able to decide which one is "true."

---

*As with any magick, this too can be abused, often by those who don't even realize what they are doing. Probably the most disturbing and profligate example of this phenomenon is seen in the current trend of therapists who "discover" (read "implant") repressed memories in the minds of their patients, leading them to believe they were molested or abused as children, sometimes in "ritual" situations. From a Pagan point of view, this can be seen both as worrisome evidence of people again refusing to accept responsibility for their own problems, and as a new tactic in the war on all groups who practice non-harmful religious rituals in secret. The saddest part is that the true victims of this practice are the family members and friends who are being falsely accused, and the real survivors of childhood abuse who are being discredited. Ethical counselors and the False Memory Syndrome Foundation (a support group for the falsely accused) assist families through these needless traumas.

Exercise 4 **(optional)** — This last experiment with non-linear time is dependent upon your skills in astral projection. When one becomes proficient at achieving this state he or she often finds it also bequeathes to them the ability to transcend time as well as space. This is partly due to the fact that time, being a creation of the physical world, has no meaning in the astral realms.

If you have experimented with astral time travel you have probably already developed an understanding of the illusory nature of time. If you are reasonably capable of projection, but have not attempted time travel, this is a good time to start.

Begin by creating for yourself a "safe spot" in the astral plane to which you can retreat if you become afraid or get that "lost" sensation. Being lost is merely a metaphor for self-inflicted mental blockages to your progress, created by the rational part of your mind constantly trying to tell you that what you are doing is impossible. When it sees that these things are possible it will often attempt to stop your inner-world adventures by making you think the astral realm is too dangerous. This safe spot can defeat the ravings of your rational mind by providing a stopping point near your physical working place to which you can return merely by willing yourself there. Your safe spot can be an astral cabin, a circle, a cave opening, a landing at the top of a large staircase, a meadow at the base of a rainbow, or any other place that feels safe to you. Make this spot the first place you travel to as soon as you are "out of body." If you wish to quickly leave whatever you are witnessing you need only think yourself back to this point, from which it is a quick trip back to normal consciousness.

While in your safe spot either summon a vision of an era you wish to see or call upon a spirit guide to escort you there. When the scene unfolds before you you may feel free to explore at will, as long as you do not violate anyone's privacy or attempt to undermine anyone's free will.

A Detailed Example of an Advanced Spell

In order to better explain the process of an advanced spell, we will follow a fictitious Witch named "Meghan" through a spell designed to bring her a home she can afford, one in which her family can be happy and safe for a long time to come. We will watch her work step by step through her advanced spell, from inception to manifestation three months later.

A Need Takes Shape — Meghan is sick of her cramped apartment. She and Martin, her lifemate, have no room, no privacy, the kids have no place to play, and they don't even have a yard for the beloved family dog. Occasionally Meghan has seen superb homes listed in the real estate section of the Sunday paper that are exceptionally nice for the money and, with a little work, could be real showplaces. Unfortunately, these don't come along very often and — worst of all — there is always something eating up the little they are able to save toward a down payment.

The need for a home of their own obsesses Meghan to the point that she knows she needs some major magickal energy to assist her. She decides to toss all that obsessive frustration into an advanced spell to begin on the next new moon. The new moon is the time of new beginnings and will make an auspicious start for a long-term home spell.

She spends several days preparing the ritualized spell so that it and all its visualizations will be exactly right.

The First Spell on the New Moon — On the night of the new moon she does her private ritual preparations (see Chapters 2 and 13), then, while inside her circle, arranges the items she has chosen for her initial spell and begins her work.

She calls a Goddess to her circle whom she knows is a patroness of new beginnings and invites her assistance by asking that her divine energy be added to the spellwork. Meghan charges the items to be used in the spell with her need, and, in the same way she drew lunar energy into her moon cords (see Chapter 9), she pulls the energy of the friendly deity into the candles she will be using.

Meghan's initial spell involves the burning of a brown candle (for home and land) and a green candle (for money), and several pictures, cut from the real estate listing service booklets, of homes she likes and can afford. Under the pictures she has her moon mirror reflecting her face surrounded by the homes. She also has a picture of her family nearby. Using the basic techniques of spellcasting (see Chapter 8) she works through her spell and links her mental imagery to the new and waxing moon.

When the spell is finished, she spends as much time chanting and visualizing her goal as she can, then releases the energy to do its work. She knows this spell is only the first of many she will have to do in order to gain her goal, and is determined to see this through.

Meghan snuffs out the candles and drapes a protective black cloth over them to hold in their growing power until she repeats the spell the next night.

Throughout the Waxing Phase — Each night until the moon is full Meghan repeats her spell in exactly the same format and—in as much as is possible—performs it at the same time of night.

During the intervening days she spends a few moments sending the spell extra energy every time the idea of owning a home even remotely crosses her mind. Meanwhile, she finds creative ways for her daily physical actions to enhance her spell.

During the waxing phase she keeps her mind focused on the gaining aspects of her goal: the gaining of money with which to make the down payment, the finding of the home, and the successful transition into it.

From the Full Moon to the Dark — After the passing of the full moon, Meghan changes her nightly spell so that it is more in tune with the energies of the waning phase of the moon. Instead of focusing the spell on the things she wishes to gain, she visualizes those things she wants to lose: her relative poverty, the crowded living conditions of her apartment, the noisy neighbors always audible through the paper thin walls, and her small communal yard. As an added measure of security, she makes sure to focus on the positive images of this separation. She visualizes a happy couple moving into the apartment who will enjoy living there and get along with the neighbors, and she sees the building secure and safe. This way she ensures that no harm will befall the structure, its owners, or those who will continue to live there.

Just as she did during the waxing phase, she performs her spell nightly.

Meghan's advanced magick is much more than just her nightly spellwork. It is a total way of living, in which the emotional intensity of her desire is carried throughout every moment of her life.

Building and Maintaining the Intensity — All Pagan magick, advanced or not, must begin with an initial visualization of the outcome, and the working of an organized spell designed to channel and focus the energy that the mind is raising on our behalf. In advanced magick, this initial fervor must continue over the long term. In other words, the operating principle of advanced magick is SUSTAINED EMOTIONAL INVOLVEMENT which, by necessity, must border on the obsessive.

In order to accomplish this, the magick must not only be visualized, but must also be woven into your everyday routine so that even the simplest task becomes an energy source that feeds the spell. Such concepts are not new; they have been part of folk magick for centuries. We often refer to the working of a spell as "casting" (from the craft of pottery making), weaving (weaving at a loom), or "spinning" (working at a spinning wheel). We also talk about "churning something up" as in butterchurning, and "furrowing," as in breaking fallow ground, to make it a fertile place to plant our "seedlings" of magick.

All of these terms came into magick from the rhythmic, repetitive actions that our ancestors used as a focus for raising energy. Extant folksongs and nursery rhymes contain hints of these old uses of everyday items. In mythology we find many spinning and weaving Goddesses who spun and wove all things into creation, usually disguised in old children's stories as spiders. Many of us learned the spinning song *Sarasponda* in summer camp, as well as others supposedly designed to make our tasks easier. In truth, they came from folk magick practices. In cultures that cling to the old ways, such as the Amish (Pennsylvania Dutch), such music is still used to accompany tasks, only now it is adapted to use as potent Christian prayers; Native Americans have long used drumming and rhythmic chants to induce altered states of consciousness in which magick can take place.

Few of us today churn our own butter or spin our own yarn, but we can still use these past techniques to help us maintain the intensity of involvement in the desired outcome by using the modern accouterments of everyday life to channel our energy into our need.

In Meghan's case, she works in an office and often uses the rhythm of the office machinery to lull her into a light trance, in which she silently chants a present-tense affirmation of her desired outcome. Martin, a construction worker, has gotten into the spirit of the spell by doing something similar with the rhythmic beat of his hammer.

No matter what your own daily routine involves, you can emulate Meghan and Martin by using your own daily habits and have-to's to channel your energy into magick. Don't worry about not remembering to do this. If you are obsessive enough about your need to embark on an advanced working, you will be obsessive enough to have the need at the forefront of your mind.

Other modern examples of incorporating your mundane life into your magickal need include:

- Chant in rhythm to machinery you work with, as long as you can do so safely.

- Use your drive to and from work as extra time to send energy to your need. Allow the vibrations of your vehicle to align with your goal and project it outward, or use the time to sing or chant.

- When at home use your usual household tasks to set up a rhythm through which you can funnel chants and songs. Use any of your former time-wasting tasks, from doing the dishes to sweeping or vacuuming.

- Use the actions of your hobbies to add to the energy flow. For example, if you do cross stitch you might want to work a design of a house you find attractive and pour the energy of your need into the effort. Or you might just want to work in a rhythm conducive to your goal. Similar actions can be performed with painting, woodworking, or needlepoint.

- Cut out pictures of your desire and place them all around you as visual reminders to focus your energy on your goal. This type of sympathetic magick is so popular that few people ever think about just where the idea came from. You can do this openly with very few questions asked; note all the people who habitually paste on their refrigerators before and after pictures of their desired bodies to help keep them on diets.

- Create and use song and story spells that not only feed energy but stimulate your inner-creative impulses and continue to serve your aims when you are not conscious of them.

Song Spells and Story Spells — Song and story spells use the power of music and myth to boost the power of magick. You don't have to have any special talent for creating and using these techniques, just the desire to direct more energy toward your goal.

You can use one or both of these spell boosters, depending on your personal tastes, but either way you will need to make two of whichever you choose — one designed for the waxing and one for the waning moon phase.

Music is a very old way of focusing magickal energies. Entire studies have been commissioned focusing on the mystical uses of sound. We all know that certain songs and sound combinations have a deep effect on our emotions and can induce potent inner-responses. If you play an instrument or compose, allow yourself to become emotionally caught up in your need, then set down your instrument and see what manifests. Even if you feel completely untalented in this direction, you can always make up word parodies for songs you already know.

The old myths and folkstories of the world are eternally fascinating. Even though they are ancient, we can still relate to them. Mythic scholars, such as famed mythologist Joseph Campbell, spend their lives studying and analyzing these stories. A story spell is simply a personalized myth with a happy ending into which you project your need. You can make up your own story, or copy your idea from another story. It is best if you write it out in your own hand. The writing process is part of investing the spell with personal energy. Feel free to use word processors and tape recorders during the creation process to make sure you have said everything you want.

In Meghan's case, she creates two simple song spells by writing a parody to the popular folksong *Oh Suzanna*. The first is to be used during the waxing moon:

> OH, I JUST FOUND MY DOWN PAYMENT FOR THE NEW HOUSE OF MY DREAMS,
> AND I JUST FOUND THE DWELLING, IT'S EVERYTHING IT SEEMS.
>> OH, MY NEW HOME,
>> A LOVELY PLACE TO SEE,
> WE NEVER WANT TO LEAVE HERE, SO HAPPY WE WILL BE.

The other version of the same song is written with the waning phase in mind:

> OH, MY BILLS ARE PAID, MY JOB IS SURE, I'M OUT OF THAT OLD BIND,
> AND IN MY MIND'S A HOME SO FINE, A PLACE I NOW DO FIND.
>> OH, SWEET FREEDOM,
>> THERE'RE NO MORE BILLS TO PAY,
> NOW I CAN BUY A NEW HOME, THIS IS MY LUCKY DAY.

Meghan sings and hums her song spells on the way to and from work, while doing housework, and any other time she thinks about them. Martin and their kids have learned the words too, and they enjoy singing together, getting excited about the new home they are soon going to find and feeding more energy into their goal.

Meghan also constructs two simple story spells by writing first about a happy family — hers — who are tired of their old residence. They find a wonderful new home that is very affordable and still everything they ever dreamed about. Although the story she writes is only four pages long, she tops it off with a "happily ever after" ending with all the force of her will. By contrast, the story spell for the waning moon focuses on the things she wishes to rid herself of in the home search: losing the bills and other financial problems preventing her from saving the down payment, and leaving the apartment and all its restrictions behind. Onto this she tacks the same happy ending since, no matter in which moon phase she is working, the ultimate goal is the same.

Meghan reads these to herself nightly, and as bedtime tales for her children.

Working In Non-Linear Time — A few weeks before Meghan began this advanced spell someone severely rear-ended her car. In the initial insurance estimate it appeared the car would be declared totaled. Meghan knows that a financial setback large enough to encompass purchasing a new car will destroy her dreams of having her own home. To counteract this, she begins a nightly meditation in which she intensely visualizes the accident as never having happened. By attempting to alter the past, she hopes to lessen its economic impact on her present. To do this she not only feeds intense personal energy into recreating the events of that disastrous day, but she also forces herself to view her current life as if the accident never occurred. This reorientation must also include the time when she is not actively working to reshape the past, such as when she must call a cab to get to work. Instead of letting herself feel inconvenienced by this necessity, she sits up proudly in the back seat and imagines being driven around in her own private limousine.

She keeps up this visualization for three solid weeks before she gets a call from her insurance adjuster, who tells her that the damage to her car turned out to be much less than first believed. The car is not totaled and all damages (minus that inevitable deductible) will be covered under her policy.

Meghan breathes a momentarily sigh of relief; the precious savings she needs for her home down payment are saved. But she cannot afford to let up on her work. There is still much more to be done.

Dream Work and Guided Meditation — The sub-conscious is easily stimulated by the powerful images of a song or story spell. When these are read or sung just prior to sleeping they stick in your mind on all levels and will be likely to manifest as dreams. In this way the energy you are investing in your spell is continuing to work for you even while you sleep. Only you will be able to determine the type of dreams you are having: wish-fulfillment, prophetic, past-life, etc. Keep in mind that if they are not what you wish them to be, strengthen the positive images in your story spell and try again. Remember that the whole purpose of magick is to change what you don't like. You always have free will, and nothing in your future is unalterable when you are forewarned.

If Meghan wanted to dream about her house and hadn't done so yet, she would fall asleep thinking about the house and the entire situation surrounding its discovery and purchase. She would give herself affirmations that she would indeed dream about the home and then awaken with full recall. After that she would fall back asleep, confident of success.

You can also use the story spell as a guided meditation (see Chapters 2, 4, and 6 for examples). Simply slow your mind and focus it on your goal, close your eyes, and see yourself living the events in the story. Like the dreams, this also strengthens your ties with your desire, and will give it an extra push. With guided meditations don't be afraid to let yourself become lost in the fantasy. As long as the images your mind conjures up are positive and in line with your goal, enjoy them.

Finding the Motivation to Continue — The vast amount of magickal energy Meghan is using on a daily basis is taking its toll. She is tired and, like everyone who embarks on an advanced spell, she is eventually tempted to let up on her efforts, or even to quit altogether. But deciding her new home is the most important thing to her and to her family, she takes steps to remotivate herself.

First, she takes a critical look at her daily schedule and rearranges it, so that she has a little more time to herself to read, play with the kids, or just relax with a cup of tea. She also evaluates her diet and adds extra grains, raw vegetables, and other proteins to counteract the depletion of nutrients caused by the extra expenditure of energy.

Next, she makes a list of the progress she has made with the spell so far. This is an important step to take before deciding whether to give up on a long-term spell. Actually seeing the evidence of your success will often give you the desire to continue. Compare the feeling to that of swimming between two distant points. If you are half-way across and want to turn back, but at the same time realize you are currently an equal distance between shores, you will usually decide to go the distance.

Meghan can cite her accomplishment with the car accident as evidence that she is succeeding. She also notes that her family's income went up when Martin got an unexpected raise only two weeks into her spell. Lastly, she can cite a call from her father telling her about a low-risk investment that required a small amount of cash for a modest return in only ninety days. She sees that this additional money will come due in another thirty days, which should increase the amount of her savings by more than five hundred dollars.

Faced with facts pointing to the eventual success of her spell, she finds her energy renewed and her motivation to continue restored.

Physical Plane Efforts — Meghan knows that she cannot sit back and expect the house of her dreams to come running to her, so she backs up her magick with practical efforts in the concrete world. She writes letters to realtors who appeal to her in the areas she would like to buy the home and outlines precisely what she wants and what she and Martin are willing to pay. She apologizes that the specifications might seem overly picky or somewhat out of range of their price restrictions, but tells them all politely that she knows such homes do come on the market from time to time and that she is not willing to look at anything that doesn't fit within her parameters. Including a day and evening contact phone number, she "draws" invoking pentagrams on each letter with her forefinger (see Chapter 2) to bring luck, and sends them out as another part of her magick.

She also contacts people who might come across her dream home in the course of their normal day. Knowing that these places do not stay long on the market, she wants to be notified immediately if something turns up for consideration. She and Martin also take advantage of weekend open houses and do as much of their own footwork as possible.

Another Cycle and Another Cycle — Meghan's dream is not realized in the first month's working of her spell, so when the moon comes new again, she begins the process all over. She also chooses to ignore realtors who attempt to get her to buy down and any people who tell her she's not being sensible. She has done her research and knows in her heart that what she wants is not unrealistic. She drops the realtors who seem unwilling to consider her needs and who seem to want only to make a quick sale.

Another month passes and still no luck, though more and more of the homes they look at are coming closer to her ideal. While she has often been tempted to stop the obsessive spellwork, she decides that the goal is worth the effort. Each "almost right" house she sees renews her determination.

The Manifestation — Finally, at the end of the third cycle, the place she wants at the price she can afford comes available. Through her networking contacts, she learns of the home early and she and Martin are the first to see it. They love it and make an offer on the spot.

Thanks to her visualization, the closing and move go smoothly, and Meghan and Martin know they will be happy in their new home for a long time to come.

Advanced Magick for the Half Moon

You can also align your advanced magick to work on only one phase of the moon, taking the other off to see if it will manifest. This works especially well with spells designed to lose, decrease, or banish something, since a large part of eliminating anything from your life is accomplished through putting it out of your mind. Examples of such magick would be spells designed to help you break a bad habit or to erase the memory of someone from your life.

To make this work for you, you would follow all of the above steps for advanced magick, but only perform them throughout the waning phase. Then, as the moon begins to wax, you would stop filling the spell with energy and try to put it out of your mind (but do mark the day after the full moon on your calendar so that you will remember when to start your spell again if needed).

These advanced banishment spells work exceptionally well with time manipulation techniques. For instance, it would certainly help erase someone unpleasant from your memory if you relived the event and altered it so that you either never met the person in the first place, or, if you did, you chose not to become emotionally involved.

How To Construct
Your Own Rituals

'Tis wise to learn;
'Tis God-like to create.
                    — John Godfrey Saxe

Using rituals and spells found in other Pagan books and grimoires is fine, but nothing can substitute for those you have created yourself, based on your knowledge, need, and personal affinities. The creative process for accomplishing this is much easier than it might first appear. There are few hard-and-fast rules, but there are generally accepted methods of approach that will not only root your ritual and magick deeply in the western Pagan tradition, but also bend your ritual practice into forms that have proven themselves successful for many centuries.

Constructing Pagan Rituals

How many times MUST you hit the snooze alarm before you finally drag yourself out from under the warm covers? Are you the sort of person who can't wait to brush away the dragon in your mouth each morning? Without fail, do you jog before breakfast? Can you not make pleasant conversation until you have that first cup of coffee? Do you feel compelled to rehang the toilet paper if you think it has been put up "backward?" Do you insist on putting on both socks and then both shoes, or must you do one foot at a time?

We construct and follow rituals for ourselves every day of our lives. Most of the time we don't even recognize them as such. Yet, if deprived of these daily guideposts, we feel a sense of disorientation, of something being amiss, as if we got up "on the wrong side of the bed."

Familiar rituals trigger something instinctive within us. They send signals to our subconscious mind that something special is about to happen. For example, that first cup of coffee tells your mind and body that a hectic new day is about to begin. With that first sip you unconsciously begin to regroup your inner-energies and mentally prepare yourself for what what lies ahead. The same process is true in the Pagan ritual experience. Rituals let your deep mind know that you are taking it into another realm and that it must prepare for the journey.

By its very nature, ritual must contain a certain amount of repetition, but it need not be so self-same that it becomes automatic, unthinking, and — eventually — meaningless. Whether you are a solitary or part of a large group (there are some covens with fifty or more persons who put on rituals like well-rehearsed theatrical productions), you should always feel free to add something new. This addition can be as simple as allowing someone to read a moving piece of ritual poetry they have written or found, or trying out a new song or a new way of raising power.

In any case, your rituals should always be *written out and memorized*. The reasons for this are very practical.

- It ensures that everyone involved in the rite gets at least a small role, and that no one is unintentionally overlooked.

- It eliminates needless worry for shy, unconfident, or self-conscious people who might fear they will be suddenly asked to do or contribute something for which they do not feel prepared.

- It ensures that no part of the ritual is omitted, and also provides a double-check that all equipment is inside the circle before the rites begin.

- It serves as a blueprint, so that no one spoils the mood or hampers the power you are attempting to raise by wondering what he or she should do next.

- It allows for a smooth flow of action. When each person knows his or her part, all participants are able to focus on the deeper meaning of the ritual, enhancing it for everyone.

Solitaries often question why they need to write out their rituals, since they will be the only person participating. The reasons for doing so are similar to those for covens. You need to focus on the ritual, not on worrying about what comes next. You are not putting on a school pageant; you are worshipping and aligning with your Goddesses and Gods and/or trying to raise power for magick. Random thoughts and mundane worries have no purpose in ritual.

Certainly solitaries have greater latitude for last-minute changes; this is a big plus cited by many people who are solitaries-by-choice. But having a written ritual to follow should not hamper spontaneity. You can still feel free to perform that dance you are moved to do, or chant the words that come whispered to you on the night air, but you will be working them in around your planned rites, not pulling them from a random bag of tricks like a stage magician pulls impossible items from a silk top hat.

The following is a step-by-step guide for creating Pagan rituals that can be adapted to almost any need, and that can work for both covens or solitaries.

1. Have firmly in mind the EXACT PURPOSE of your ritual. This need not be a lofty goal, but you must know why you want to do a ritual in order for it to be coherent, meaningful, and/or successful. You can also combine goals. For example, you may wish to honor the Goddess of the full moon AND do a ritualized spell for your mother's health. The two need not be mutually exclusive.

2. Begin writing a rough ritual outline, the details to be filled in later. Decide what direction you want the rite to take, what repetition from other rituals you want to keep, or what you want to discard. After you have made your outline, set it aside for a few days and let the details take shape in your mind as you go about your daily affairs.

3. When you are ready to flesh out the details of the ritual, read back over your outline and decide if it is in its final form, or if you want to make changes. You can rearrange, discard, or add elements. Nothing is ever set in stone. If you are part of a coven, everyone should have a say in this final draft.

4. If you are working with a group, assign roles that everyone will memorize. If you are alone, make sure you are familiar with exactly what you want to do; memorize any speeches, invocations, or other words you wish to speak aloud.

5. Set up your working area. While an altar is not absolutely necessary, it is useful for providing a focus for the growing energy you will raise and for providing a safe place to set candles and other accouterments used in the rites. To focus the group mind and add a festive atmosphere, it helps to have the altar set with symbols of the season: acorns, apples and gourds in fall; flowers in spring; herbs, fruits or greenery in summer; holly and evergreen in winter, etc. You can also add objects or colors that correspond to the moon, the lunar month, or to any deities you may wish to call upon. The direction your altar faces is up to you. Every coven and solitary has a view on this; many will change these orientations with the seasons.

6. Cast a circle of protective energy with an athame (ritual knife), your creative mind, your forefinger, or with any other ritual tool you feel comfortable using. See it clearly in your mind as a perimeter of protective blue-white light rising around you. In some covens everyone is asked to lend energy to the creation of this sacred space.

7. State aloud the purpose of your ritual: Sabbat/Esbat observance, personal enrichment, rite of passage, honor of a deity, magick, or whatever. This will help you fully align all levels of yourself with the purpose.

8. Call on the directional quarters, watchtowers, or other sentient energies if you wish, and light a candle to honor them. Many traditions call in these living spirits of the elements and do not feel a rite can be complete without them. Be sure to walk clockwise as you call the quarters. The direction with which you choose to begin is a personal choice, though some traditions will dictate it for you.

9. You may invite, but never command, friendly spirits, faeries or other elementals to join you.

10. It is nice to use a candle or some other symbol to honor each deity invited to your circle. Goddess candles are traditionally white, God candles orange or red. You can use white, red, and black candles for the Triple Goddess. Once again, only you can decide this matter. If you have only plain, white candles available, use them for both the God and Goddess, marking them with male and female symbols for distinction.

11. Evoke (call to you) or invoke (call into you) any deities you wish at this time. This includes the rite of Drawing Down the Moon. Offer food or honors to the deities as befits your tradition and/or personal practice.

12. Begin with the body of your ritual work, performing first any set procedures you or your tradition deem necessary. Your ritual can enact scenes from mythology, honor deities, celebrate the season or moon phases, or commemorate virtually any meaningful event.

13. Sing, dance, chant, meditate, and/or offer praise and thanks to your deities. Let the words come from your heart. Singing (please feel free to make up your own words and melodies as you go along) can quickly tap you into your inner-state of consciousness, and dancing (you can improvise here also) can raise your personal power and energies.
    Now is the time to try new songs, dances, stories, seasonal poetry, etc, with which you want to experiment. Allow everyone who is interested to add something to this phase of the ritual. Avoid becoming critical of other's choices in this matter. Remember that the way we choose to express our spiritual impulses is highly personal, and in a sacred space like the circle all views should be respected. You may find that you get more out of this spontaneous offering than from your well-prepared speeches. Don't let this concern you. Rejoice in it! If you find you have done something you or your coven really like, then by all means write it down after you have closed the circle so that it can be repeated.
    When the improvisation is over return to your ritual script to avoid confusion.

14. If your ritual purpose is a rite of passage, initiation, or some other special memorial, you should already have worked out with the family of those involved what words, gestures, or materials will be used. Keep these as simple as possible, without losing the meaning of the event. Solitaries can also do rites of passage; do not feel you need anyone else's permission to honor your dead, initiate yourself, etc.

15. Ritualizing spells greatly improves their efficacy simply because you are putting more forethought and zeal into them. If you do choose to work magick in this ritual, have with you whatever materials you need for your spell(s). Once a circle is cast, it is unwise to break it until it is grounded. Making a "hole" in the protective sphere allows

the energy you've raised to seep out, and can allow who-knows-what to enter. Don't learn the hard way. The energy you raise may attract things you don't want around. Always respect your circle.

16. Raise and send your "cone of power." If you have no immediate magickal need for it, you might send it out to heal the polluted and ailing Mother Earth. If you have just celebrated a rite of passage, send this loving energy to the person(s) or spirit involved.

17. If you are having a ritual feast, such as the Ceremony of Cakes and Ale, you can conclude the rites with the blessing of the food. Don't forget to set aside a libation for the faery folk or any other beings you have called to your circle.

18. Release any invoked energy (i.e.; reverse the Drawing Down the Moon process).

19. There need be no rush to close the circle once you have finished your ritual. You may sit inside it and sing, meditate, feast, do divinations, or just feel yourself in communion and at peace with nature and your deities. The circle is always conceptualized as being the center of the universe, a point from which you can connect with all that is. Just being in this sacred space has a positive and healing effect on both the mind and the body.

20. When you are ready to close the circle, thank the elementals and spirits who have joined you, and then thank the deities who have blessed your rites.
   If you have previously called the quarters, you need to dismiss them. Do this by moving in a counterclockwise direction, starting at the point with which you ended the construction of the circle. Dismiss all the elementals, etc., you have called upon with the traditional phrase, "Merry meet, merry part, and merry meet again."

21. Ground the energy from your circle — always! Undo it the opposite way you constructed it. Walk counterclockwise around the inner perimeter, returning the raised power to the ground. See and feel it dissipate and return to the earth.

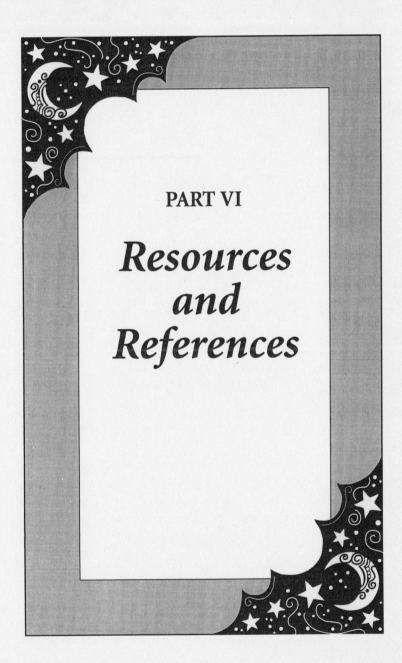

PART VI

Resources and References

Appendix A

Moon Goddesses and Gods
From Around the World

The following is a list, by no means exhaustive, of Moon Goddesses and Gods from around the world. Because of the moon's relationship to the female fertility cycle, the majority of the deities are feminine, although please note that male deities are well-represented. Gods have been continuously worshiped for thousands of years by cultures that hung on to their male moon deities long after most of the west had adopted the Greco-Roman view of moon = feminine, sun = masculine. It is also interesting to observe that the majority of moon deities still known to us today come from civilizations which have preserved their original lunar calendars (i.e.; The Middle East, Africa, Polynesia, China). Most of these cultures lie on or near the Equator, where lunations assumed greater importance in yearly cycles than sun phases.

Aega (Greek) — A very beautiful moon Goddess who was viewed as being the daughter of the sun. Gaia, the earth Goddess, hid her in a cave during a Titan attack on the Olympic deities so that she would not be stolen away.

Aine (Irish) — Aine is a cattle, sun, and fire Goddess who is still very popular in her native Munster, where she is honored at Midsummer. She was also a minor moon Goddess who might have been the origin of the virgin Goddess Anu.

Al-lat (Arabian-Chaldaean) — A moon and Underworld Goddess. In Arabic, her name means "Goddess." The masculine version of the name, meaning "God," is familiar to people today as Allah, the God of Islam.

Alignak (Inuit) — A moon God who was one of the first people on the earth. The other was his sister. After they created all life through their union, they were banished for their "crime" of incest. He then became the moon, and she, the sun.

Anahita (Persian) — A river Goddess who was also a Goddess of Venus and the moon. In Persian mythology she is the mother of Mithras, a God widely worshiped throughout the Middle East.

Anna Perenna (Roman) — A Goddess of grains and of the turning of the year, honored at the full moons and on New Year's Day.

Andromeda (Greek) — Although seen today as a stellar Goddess, many scholars believe that Andromeda was a pre-Hellenic moon deity.

Annuit (Babylonian) — A Goddess of the moon and of the evening star who later became known as Ishtar.

Anu (Irish) — A maiden Goddess linked to the moon, sometimes thought to be a maiden form of the great Celtic mother Goddesses, Dana (Gaelic) and Don (Brythonic).

Aponibolinayen (Philippino) — A moon Goddess who wore a fertile vine wrapped around her ample waist. During the day she lived in the "house of the sun," where she gave birth to the sun's children through her fingertips.

Aradia (Roman) — A moon and earth Goddess, the daughter of Diana.

Arianrhod (Welsh) — A Goddess of the moon whose symbol is the silver wheel. She is one of the children of the powerful mother Goddess Don, and of Beli, the God of death.

Ariel (European) — A faery Goddess/queen linked to the magickal power of the full moon.

Artemis (Greek) — She is the Greek version of the Roman waxing moon Goddess Diana. Like her Roman counterpart, she is also a Goddess of the hunt and of romance.

Artimpassa (Scythian) — A Goddess of the moon and of love.

Ashima (Samaritan) — A moon Goddess.

Athenesic (Native North American) — A moon Goddess of several north central Native American tribes, particularly the Iroquois and Huron.

Athergatis (Syrian) — A Goddess of the moon and fertility, symbolized by the fish.

Athtor (Egyptian) — This Goddess was called by the name "Mother of the Night." She may have also been a moon Goddess.

Auchimalgen (Native South American) — A moon Goddess who was also a deity of divination and a protectress from evil spirits.

Baiame (Aboriginal) — This Australian God was the lover of the sun and the inspiration of all fun and mischief-making.

Belili (Middle Eastern) — A Goddess of the moon, love, the planet Venus, sacred wells, and trees.

Bendis (Greek) — A moon Goddess who was the consort of the sun God Sabazius. Her cult flourished in Athens during the fifth century BCE.

Bong (Punjabian) — A former sun Goddess with her twin sister Bomong. When the creatures of the earth realized they could not live with two suns, each one shining for twelve hours every day, they decided to kill Bong. The plan backfired when Bomong, grieving for her sister and fearing for her own life, went into hiding, leaving the earth in perpetual darkness. The earth beings, realizing they needed the balance of both night and day, recreated Bong as the moon, the light of the night sky.

Britomartis (Crete) — A moon Goddess who was the patron deity of Creten sailors.

Callisto (Greek) — A moon Goddess whose name means "the most beautiful." Bears were sacred to her.

Candi (Aryan) — The consort of the moon God Chandra. The two of them took turns ruling the night sky.

Cerridwen (Celtic) — This crone, grain, sow, and moon Goddess is most famous for her cauldron of wisdom. She was the mother of the great bard Taliesin, and is deeply linked to the image of the waning moon.

Ch'ang-O (Chinese) — Symbolized by the frog, this moon Goddess was once the wife of an archer who was forced to flee to the moon after stealing a magickal potion which granted immortality.

Chandra (Aryan) — A moon God who took turns with his consort, Candi, in ruling the night. Chandra was born after his mother swallowed the moon (Candi).

Chia (Native South American).— Another name for Huitaca.

Chup-Kamui (Japanese) — This deity was once the Goddess of the moon, but she begged the male sun to change places with her.

Coatlicue (Aztec) — A moon and earth Goddess whose name means "the skirt of the serpent." She was associated with flower festivals, planting rites, and the stars.

Coyalxauhqui (Aztec) — A moon Goddess whose name means "golden bells." A huge shrine to her was unearthed during a 1978 archaeological dig near Mexico City.

Cynthia (Greek) — Another name for Artemis.

Dae-Soon (Korean) — A Korean moon Goddess.

Delia (Greek) — Another name for Artemis.

Diana (Greek) — The Goddess of the waxing moon and of the hunt who is deeply associated with the rest of her Triple Goddess form, Selene the mother and Hecate the crone. A feminist Witchcraft tradition bears her name. She is symbolized by the bow and arrow, and is also a Goddess of love, sometimes equated with Eros/Cupid.

Eithne (Irish) — This Goddess of death and the moon is believed to have originally come from the Middle East, her image and myth having traveled westward with the Celts. Her name means "nutmeat."

Epona (Gaulish-Celtic) — A horse Goddess associated with the night and dreams, who has lunar attributes. In western Ireland, legends still abound of hearing the hoof-beats of her horse as she rides west to escape the rays of the rising sun. She is also a Goddess of magick and feminine power.

Eterah (Semitic) — The moon God, husband of a sun Goddess.

Eri of the Golden Hair (Irish) — Eri was a virgin Goddess of the divine/faery race known as the Tuatha De Danann. One day, while at the bank of a river, a man in a golden boat floated down to her on a beaming ray of sunlight. They fell into the boat, made love, and conceived the God/hero Bres. Eri's energy as moon Goddess, consort to the sun image presented here, marks her as a form of the feminine principle of creation.

Europa (Creten) — This Goddess was the namesake of the European continent. Though she is also seen as an earth/fertility Goddess whose consort is the bull, she has many lunar attributes.

Fati (Polynesian) — A moon God, the son of Taoniui, the Goddess of the stars.

Fleachta of Meath (Irish) — A moon Goddess associated with the Irish stronghold at Tara, possibly a fertility deity of the High Kings, and Goddess of divination for the Druids.

Freya (Norse) — Also called Frigg and Freya. This supreme warrior Goddess of the Nordic pantheon is the mother of Baulder, the sun God, and the wife and sister of Odin. She is often depicted driving her chariot across the night sky. Though not originally a moon deity (the earliest Teutonic moon deities were male), she often fills this role in modern Norse traditions. The last weekday, Friday, is named in her honor.

Gnatoo (Polynesian) — This moon Goddess is prevalent in native legends as the "woman in the moon," the equivalent of the "man in the moon" in Anglo-American folklore.

God D (Mayan) — A moon God who was seen as an old man. His name was thought to contain so much power that its utterance was prohibited. Hence, his name was lost in time. The appellation God D was assigned to him by an anthropologist studying Mayan culture.

Gou (Benin) — A moon God, the brother of the mother Goddess Lissa.

Gungu (Aryan) — A new moon Goddess.

Gwen (Anglo-Welsh) — A minor sun/moon Goddess and Goddess of light.

Hanwi (Native North American) — This moon Goddess of the Oglala Sioux once lived with the sun God Wi. Because of a transgression, she was forced by him to become a creature of the night. This myth shows how the night and its feminine attributes have been systematically devalued in patriarchal culture.

Hecate (Greek) — A crone Goddess deeply associated with the waning and dark moons. She is depicted as haunting crossroads with her two large hounds, and carrying a torch, symbolic of her great wisdom. Many scholars believe she is a very old deity who far predates the rest of the Greek pantheon. She is usually worshiped with the rest of her triplicity, Diana the maiden, and Selene the mother.

Helen (Greek) — Before she became a mythic heroine, she was the Goddess of vegetation, birth, and the moon.

Helle (Middle Eastern) — Though her name suggests links to the Underworld/ Otherworld, she was worshiped as a fertility/earth Goddess in her native Boeotia. Writer and scholar Robert Graves has suggested that she was originally a moon Goddess who ruled the tides.

Helice (Greek) — Another name for Callisto.

Hermes (Greek) — Hermes has many attributes, one of which is that of a moon God.

Hina (Polynesian) — This Hawaiian moon Goddess' name means "woman who works the moon." She is a Triple Goddess — maiden, mother, and crone — unto herself. Native myth says she got tired of working for her brother and fled to the moon to live in peace.

Holle (Teutonic) — A moon Goddess who has come down in popular legend as a Witch or faery. She is also the Goddess of snow.

Huitaca (Native South American) — Also known as Chia, this moon Goddess was native to Colombia. She was a protectress of women as well as a deity of pleasure and happiness who is always battling her male counterpart Bochica, a God of hard work and sorrow.

Hun-Apu-Atye (Guatemalan) — A moon Goddess who is the wife of the sun. Her sacred animal is the nocturnal tapir, a long-nosed, pig-like mammal native to Central and South America.

Hunthaca (Native South American) — The Chibcha Indians believed this one-time wife of one of their heroes became the moon as a punishment for causing the great flood of their land. Such deluge stories are a worldwide mythical phenomenon.

Hypnos (Greek) — A God of sleep and the night, sometimes given lunar attributes.

Ida (Aryan) — This moon Goddess of the Indian tradition is also an earth Goddess and Goddess of divination, fire, and communication.

Ilmaquh (Middle Eastern) — A moon God.

Inanna (Sumerian) — A moon Goddess later known as Ishtar.

Io (Greek) — This pre-Hellenic moon Goddess was also a cow deity. On the isle of Iona she was venerated as a Goddess of grain, fertility, and abundance.

Ishtar (Babylonian) — A moon Goddess with roots in the Sumerian deity Inanna. Some myths say she is the daughter of the moon, others the mother. It is likely she was a triplicity unto herself — all three faces in one entity. She is also a Goddess of fertility, storms, love, and sexual unions.

Isis (Egyptian) — This powerful and widely worshiped Goddess was not only a moon deity, but a Goddess of the sun as well.

Itzamna (Mayan) — A moon God who was the father of all the other Mayan deities. He ruled the western sky and was credited with teaching agriculture and writing to his people. Rodents were sacred to him and were often sacrificed in his honor.

Ix Chel (Mayan) — A Central and South American moon Goddess and the lover of the sun. Poisonous snakes are her totem animal.

Ix-Huyne (Native Central American) — A moon Goddess from the Panama region.

Izanami (Japanese) — A moon and sea Goddess. She also had control over the tides, fishing, and all destructive sea phenomena.

Jacy (Native South American) — A moon God from the Amazonian region who was the creator of plants.

Jarah (Hebrew) — A Goddess of the new moon who was seen as the bride of the sun. She was the prototype for the Shekinah, the feminine half of the Jewish God, who is today honored (but never worshiped) by Jews as the "Sabbath Queen." She was once the sun Goddess, with the moon being a masculine figure in early Semitic mythology. Jarah was originally a masculine deity.

Jezanna (Central African) — A Goddess of the moon and healing.

Juno (Roman) — A Goddess of the new moon and sky, worshiped largely by women.

Jyotsna (Aryan) — A Hindu Goddess of twilight and the autumn moons.

Ka-Ata- Killa (Native South American) — A moon Goddess worshiped in the Lake Titicaca region.

Khonsu (Egyptian) — A moon God who was the son of the God of the air, Amun, and a mother Goddess named Mut. His name means "he who travels the heavens." He was associated with bloody sacrificial rites and is sometimes depicted as having the head of a hawk. A huge temple was erected to him at Thebes.

Komorkis (Native North American) — A moon Goddess of the Blackfoot tribe.

Kuan Yin (Chinese) — A Buddhist Goddess. Modern feminist Pagans believe she far pre-dates Buddhism's origins. She was a Goddess of the moon, compassion, and healing, whose confusing myths have been greatly altered over time.

Kuhu (Aryan) — A new moon Goddess.

Kuu (Finnish) — A moon Goddess from the northern Baltic region.

Lalal (Etruscan) — A moon Goddess.

Lasya (Tibetan) — A Goddess of the moon and beauty, symbolized by a mirror.

Levannah (Canaanite-Hebraic) — A moon Goddess similar to the early Hebrew Jarah, and to the Jewish Shekinah, in that she was viewed as fully one-half of the creative divine.

Losna (Etruscan) — A moon Goddess.

Lucina (Roman) — A Goddess of light with both solar and lunar attributes. She was Christianized as St. Lucia, a saint honored at Yule in many parts of Europe.

Luna (Roman) — A very old moon Goddess, the namesake for the Latin word luna meaning "moon." Her name is also the root of the English words "lunar" and "lunatic."

Mah (Persian) — A Goddess of the moon and time who is associated with the growth cycles of plants.

Mait Carrefour (Haitian) — A moon God of the Voudon tradition, rooted in Africa.

Mama Quilla (Incan) — A moon Goddess, the protectress of married women. A large temple to her was erected at the Incan capitol of Cuzco. She was associated with the metal silver. Eclipses were said to occur when she was eaten and then regurgitated by the Jaguar Woman.

Mani (Nordic) — A moon God linked to old stellar creation myths.

Mari (Basque) — The supreme being of the pre-patriarchal Basque people. Mari was not only a moon Goddess, but also the ruler of the sun, rain, and stars, the mother who gave birth to them all. She was Christianized as the Virgin Mary.

Mawu (African) — A moon Goddess who ruled the sky with her twin brother, the sun God Lisa.

Menu (Lithuanian) — A moon God.

Menulis (Proto-IndoEuropean) — Once a moon God, s/he is now seen as a Goddess in all but the Lithuanian tradition, which is attempting to go back to its proto-IndoEuropean Pagan roots.

Metzli (Aztec) — A mother moon Goddess who leaped into a blazing fire in order to give birth to the sun and the sky.

The Morrigan (Celtic) — A triplicity of crone Goddesses who represent battle, death, destruction, and strife. They are linked with the waning and dark phases of the moon. The three Morrigan are Badb, Macha, and Nemain.

Muireartach (Irish-Scottish) — A sea and battle Goddess associated with the waning moon. In modern Scottish folklore, an entire race of sea faeries bears her name.

Myestas (Slavic) — A moon God who each spring would wed the sun Goddess. In later myth he became Myestyas.

Myestyas (Slavic) — A moon Goddess who is eternal. She marries the sun each spring and holds him lovingly as he dies in autumn. In older stories it was she who gave him rebirth at Yule (Midwinter).

Mylitta (Assyrian) — A Goddess of love, prosperity, and the moon. In patriarchal times she became linked with institutional prostitution.

Nair (Irish) — A Goddess of both fertility and regicide (ritual, periodic king-killing), associated with the exact moment of the dark moon.

Nanna (Sumerian) — A moon God, son of grain Goddess Ninlil. He was originally thought to have been one and the same as the Goddess Nina.

Nannar (Chaldaean) — A moon God from Ur who is often equated with Sin.

Nina (Sumerian) — A moon Goddess, replaced in popular mythology by her brother Nanna.

Nuah (Babylonian) — A mother and moon Goddess associated with deluge myths. Irish Witches and writers Janet and Stewart Farrar hypothesize that the story of the Judeo-Christian deluge hero, Noah, was grafted from her myths.

Pandia (Greek) — A full moon Goddess.

Pandion (Greek) — A full moon God.

Persea (Greek) — A pre-Hellenic moon Goddess.

Perone(Greek) — A pre-Hellenic virgin Goddess of the moon and of beauty.

Pheraia (Thessalian) — A moon Goddess whose myths have been lost, but whose image remains. She is depicted carrying a torch and riding a bull.

Phoebe (Greek) — Another name for Artemis.

Prosymna (Greek) — A new moon Goddess.

Pythia (Greek) — A serpent Goddess, daughter of the earth mother Gaia, who has both lunar and earth attributes. Also a Goddess of fertility.

Rabie (Indonesian) — This lovely young girl of myth lived in an Indonesian village with her parents in the time before there was a moon. The sun God Tuwale saw her and demanded she become his bride. Her parents refused to give her up and tricked Tuwale into taking a pig instead. In revenge, he took Rabie and placed her in the night sky as the moon. She was usually worshiped at moonrise.

Raka (Aryan) — A full moon Goddess.

Re (Phoenician) — A moon Goddess whose name is thought to mean "light." Scholars often try to link her with the myths of the Egyptian sun God Ra.

Rhiannon (Welsh, Cornish) — A Goddess of fertility, the moon, night, and death whose name means "high queen." She married the Irish-Manx sea God Manann, and was falsely accused of eating her baby son. She is often equated with Epona.

Samas (Semitic) — A moon God.

Sams (Semitic) — A moon Goddess.

Sardarnuna (Sumerian) — A new/waxing moon Goddess.

Sefkhet (Egyptian) — A moon Goddess, sometimes said to be the wife of Thoth. She was also the deity of time, the stars, and architecture. Her aid was invoked when temples and palaces were being planned and constructed.

Selene (Greek) — A mother Goddess linked to the full moon. She is widely worshiped by Pagans today, especially within the Dianic tradition. Selene is shown wearing wings and a crown with an upturned silver crescent, an old and potent moon symbol. She is deeply linked to the rest of her triplicity, Diana the maiden, and Hecate the crone.

Sin (Assyrian) — A moon God, the son of the storm God Enlil. He was worshiped at a sacred site in what is now the city of Ur. Myth tells us he gave birth to the sun God, Shamash.

Sina (Polynesian) — The moon Goddess who was the sister of the sun God Maui. She is sometimes called Ina.

Sirdu (Chaldaean) — A moon Goddess wed to the sun God Shamash.

Sister Moon (Native North American) — A term of endearment for the moon, used during ritual and personal spiritual quests. The sun was Brother Sun.

Soma (Aryan) — A God of the moon and the stars. He married twenty-seven Goddesses who, by him, gave birth to all things, including soma juice, a drink sacred to Vedic deities. He is the consort of the star Goddess Tara. He came into the Hindu religion as Somanatha.

Somanatha (Aryan) — This "Lord of the Moon" came from Aryan Pagan myth to be worshiped within the Hindu religion. He is often equated with Shiva, the supreme God of that faith.

Tanit (Phoenician) — A moon and fertility Goddess. Many scholars and mythologists believe she came into the Celtic pantheon as Dana or Don, both mother Goddesses. She was worshiped as Tanat in Cornwall on the Bealtaine Sabbat (May 1).

Tapa (Polynesian) — A moon Goddess, equated with Hina.

Taukiyomi (Japanese) — A moon God married to the sun Goddess Amaterasu. Both of these Pagan deities are still worshiped in the Shinto religion.

Teczistecatal (Aztec) — A male version of Metzli. He is depicted as an old man carrying the burden of a huge conch shell on his stooped back.

Teczistecatl (Native Central American) — A Mexican moon Goddess.

Telita (Babylonian) — A moon deity dubbed "Queen of the Moon."

Thoth (Egyptian) — This God has many aspects, one of which is lunar deity.

Titama (Polynesian) — A Goddess of moonset.

Titania (Roman) — Associated with Diana, this virgin moon Goddess came into modern lore as a faery queen, possibly the prototype of the faery Goddess known as Ariel. Titania's faery aspect was immortalized in Shakespeare's *A Midsummer Night's Dream*.

Tlaculteutl (Aztec) — A Goddess of sex, symbolized by the four phases of the moon: dark, waxing, full, and waning.

Triple Goddess (Universal) — While some cultures view feminine deities as fourfold, the majority see their moon Goddesses as a triplicity, three beings in one: maiden, mother, and crone. She is symbolized by the three faces of the moon.

Tsuki Yomi (Japanese) — A Shinto moon God born when the great mother washed his right eye. His name means "moon who counts the months"; he is also a deity of time. Shrines and temples to him are still kept in the towns of Ise and Kadono.

Ursula (Slavic) — A moon Goddess whose feast day was October 21. She became Christianized as St. Ursula.

Varuna (Aryan) — A Hindu moon God. He was the son of the great mother, Aditi, who gave birth to all things.

White Shell Woman (Native American) — A virgin moon Goddess.

Woman-Light of Shadows (Egyptian) — The Goddess of the dark side of the moon, the half that can never be seen from earth, but on which the sun still shines.

Xochhiquetzal (Aztec) — A moon and magick Goddess, also the deity of flowers, spring, sex, love, and marriage. She was the wife of storm God Tlaloc. She took several divine lovers and gave birth to the widely known and worshiped hero/God/messiah, Quetzalcoatl.

Yellow Woman (Native North American) — This Pueblo moon Goddess had a brother who searched for her through melon rinds during her dark time. The rinds symbolized her new waxing crescent.

Yemanja (Native South American) — This Brazilian ocean Goddess is symbolized by a waxing crescent moon.

Yohuatlicetl (Native Central American) — A Mexican moon Goddess.

Yolaikaiason (Native North American) — A Navajo moon Goddess fashioned from an abalone shell by her sister Yolkai, the Goddess of the sky.

Zarpandit (Babylonian) — A Goddess of moonrise.

Zirna (Etruscan) — A Goddess of the waxing moon. She is always depicted with a half-moon hanging from her neck, indicating that she was probably honored at the beginning of the second quarter phase.

Appendix B

Major Moon Festivals and Holidays

The following is a list of some of the major moon festivals or holidays which either honor the moon itself or are timed by her appearance. The list includes celebrations from both the past and the present, most of these from cultures which still rely on lunar calendars. The majority of these civilizations are in areas where there is little differentiation in the solar year; therefore the moon naturally became of greater importance to them. Other cultures converted old moon festivals to solar dates many centuries ago; in most cases, the original lunar dates have been lost to us.

Ancestor Moon (Chinese) — The new moon of the tenth month of the Chinese lunar year, usually falling in November or December, is a time to honor the dead. The eldest living male in the family leads the procession to the burial ground, where the family picnics with the spirits of departed loved ones.

Anthesterion (Greek) — This three-day festival of wine takes place on the full moon closest to the Spring Equinox. It was once a festival of fertility and, like Bealtaine in modern Witchcraft, celebrated the sacred marriage of the Goddess and God.

Artemis, The Feast of (Greek) — On the full moon before Midsummer Artemis, the Goddess of fertility and of the hunt, was honored in an all-night gala that involved many fertility rites.

Baba Yaga, The Feast of (Russian) — Baba Yaga was a crone Goddess who has become, in modern times, a wicked old witch whose image is used to frighten errant children. At one time she was honored for her wisdom and healing skills at the full moon of November.

Birth Moon (Japanese) — In Japan, the first new moon after Midwinter begins the New Year. It is also considered to be the official birthday for everyone over the age of sixteen. Divination, feasting, and rituals for luck and health are popular events.

Blue Moon (Solar Calendar Cultures) — In cultures using a twelve-month solar calendar the thirteenth moon of the year must necessarily fall within a month which already has a full moon. This is known as the Blue Moon, an infrequent occurrence that used to be thought of as a time of blessing and prosperity. The popular catch phrase "once in a Blue Moon" derives from this yearly event.

Chinese New Year (Chinese) — The Chinese calendar is arguably the oldest continuously used lunar calendar in existence. Their festive New Year's celebration begins on the first new moon after the sun enters the sign of Aquarius. The clearing of debt before this holiday is an important part of its observance.

Cituua (Native South American) — A spring fertility festival celebrated at the full moon nearest the Autumn Equinox.

Ciuateotl, The Night of (Aztec) — The full harvest moon of the Aztecs was a time to appease the Goddess of strife, misfortune, and labor whose name means "the great bath of sweat."

Dark Moon (Aztec) — The Aztec priests believed that it was necessary to offer inducements to the dark moon in order to cause her rewaxing each month. Offerings usually took the form of human sacrifice performed at the famous Temple of the Moon. The ancient Temple still stands.

Disirblot (Norse) — The full moon following the Autumn Equinox once began the Nordic New Year, an attribute later given over to the solar date we call Midwinter. On this night, great family feasts were held which featured foods sacred to the Autumn deities.

Divali, The Feast of the (Indian) — This celebration of lunar light takes place on the night when the moon turns from dark to new, at the beginning of the tenth month. Bonfires, candle lightings, and the sharing of sweets are part of the celebration, which may have had roots in harvest rites of the past.

Easter(Christian) — Based upon Middle Eastern and European Pagan rites, this holiday, celebrating the resurrection of Jesus from the dead, falls on the first Sunday after the first full moon after the Spring Equinox and retains much of the Pagan symbolism upon which it was built.

Edfu (Egyptian) — The full moon after Midsummer is the date of the Feast of Hathor-Tiamet, one of the most widely known and worshiped Goddesses of the Egyptian pantheon. She arrives at the communal feast site by boat and is celebrated in a joyous ceremony venerating her fertility, beauty, and power over romantic love.

Festival of New Wine, The (Greek) — The first new moon after Midwinter was a minor festival to Dionysus, the God of wine, who was more fully celebrated in autumn.

Festival of Saravati, The (Indian) — The glory of this Goddess of communication was celebrated at the first appearance of the waxing crescent moon before the Spring Equinox.

Full Moon (Australian Aboriginal) — The Aborigines have many very old Pagan observances, most of whose meanings are still not clear to outsiders. Their season circles around the moons of their year. Like other native peoples, they named their moons and held feasts and dances in their honor.

Full Moon (Celtic) — The Celts honored the full moons as an integral part of their Wheel of the Year. A popular tree calendar was created in the early part of this millennium, attributing a sacred tree to each lunar month.

Full Moon (Central African) — Most African tribes named the full moons and honored them as representations of either Goddesses or Gods. Each one calls for a special type of ritual celebrated by the entire community.

Full Moon (Native North American) — Many Native North American tribes assigned names and attributes to the full moons and honored them — female or male — accordingly, with rituals and magick appropriate to the season.

Full Moon (Polynesian) — The people of the south sea islands honor their full moon as a mother figure who can grant fertility to barren couples and bring fish back to their shores.

Hanna Matsuri (Korean) — This four-day festival begins at the start of the second quarter of the fourth month of the Korean year. It celebrates spring flowers and fertility and is also one of the times to honor the dead.

Harvest, The Feast of the (Russian) — At the start of the second quarter in the month of September, Russians once honored the Goddess and God of the harvest season. Modern folklore claims this as the birthday of the harvest deities, celebrated today with corn dollies in a manner similar to the celebration of Imbolg and Lughnasadh in the Celtic year.

Harvest Moon (Native North American) — The first full moon after the Autumn Equinox was the day on which the last of the harvest had to be gathered. Later, feasting and dancing honored the Grandmother Moon.

Harvest Moon (Celtic, Early American and Canadian) — The harvest moon was the last full moon before Samhain (Halloween). It was considered a blessing to have her light to see by, in order to work later into the evening to gather in the last of the harvest. This night evolved into a community celebration involving the folksy customs of corn husking, quilting, and thanksgiving-style feasting.

Herb Festival (Chinese) — Some of the oldest-known herbal medicine and magick comes from China, where a day was once set aside to pay homage to these herbs. The principal herb honored was mugwort, valued in both Asia and Europe for its healing powers as well as for its usefulness in many magickal spells. The festival takes place on the new moon of the fifth month of the Chinese year.

Homage to Ch'ang-O, The (Chinese) — This moon Goddess has her festival on the full moon nearest the Autumn Equinox. The number thirteen, which represents the number of full moons in a solar year, figures heavily in the symbolism of the holiday, which is celebrated with feasting, dancing, divination, and the recitation of her myths.

Homage to Chung K'ui, The (Chinese) — On the full moon of the fifth month of the year, honor is paid to this God of protection, whose image is still used to banish and ward off evil.

Homage to the Wealth Gods, The (Chinese) — The Chinese still make a pilgrimage to the shrine of their Gods of prosperity on the last full moon before their New Year.

Hunter's Moon (Slavic) — The last full moon before the Summer Solstice is the night of the Hunter's Moon in Slavic Pagan traditions. In the not-too-distant past this was the night to honor the Goddess of the hunt; hunting parties set out in search of fresh spring game for a communal feast.

Kalends of Januarius (Roman) — The first new moon after Midwinter was the start of the Roman year, a significance which was eventually transferred to the Winter Solstice. The Romans turned it into a political holiday which involved electioneering and government convocations.

Kwan Yin, The Festival of (Chinese) — This important Goddess has been honored both in Pagan times and in the Buddhist religion which today dominates China. She has been adopted by modern feminist Pagans as a Goddess of protection, healing, and feminine power. The celebration takes place at the beginning of the fourth quarter of the eleventh month of the Chinese year.

Lantern Festival, The (Chinese) — This holiday takes place on the last full moon before the New Year. The festival involves the hanging of colorful lanterns in every conceivable space. In the distant past this was an act of sympathetic magick intended to lure the waning sun back to the earth, much as Imbolg is celebrated in modern Wicca.

Luna, Feast of (Roman) — A festival to honor the primal waxing/full moon Goddess of ancient Rome. Her temple on Aventine Hill was the site of worship, feasting, and wild dancing orgies. The untamed character of those abandoned revelries was the source of our word "lunatic."

Makara (Indian) — Makara, the Indian New Year, begins on the fifth day after the first new moon after the sun enters the sign of Capricorn. Goddesses of spring, fertility, and prosperity are honored at this time.

Mama Paca (Native South American) — The Indians of the Andes Mountains celebrate this earth Goddess on the full moon after the Autumn Equinox. This is the start of their planting season, a time when the newly tilled earth has to be blessed and consecrated in her honor. As an act of faith in her benevolence, the majority of foodstuffs remaining from the previous year are eaten in a communal feast.

Mother Moon Pilgrimage, The (Maori) — The native people of New Zealand honor the full moon after the Autumn Equinox as the patroness of the coming harvest. She is the power who can awaken and unite the sleeping Goddess and God of the earth and ensure the fertility of the island. The Maoris seek out the highest mountain available and make offerings to her.

New Moon (Lithuanian) — For centuries the Lithuanians have retreated to their Pagan roots on the New Moon, recalling their folktales of her and honoring her and her God-consort with prayer.

New Year for Cattle (Canaanite-Babylonian) — On the new moon of the twelfth month of the old Babylonian calendar (around August), cattle were honored. Cattle have been sacred to Pagan Goddesses in many, many cultures.

New Year for Kings (Canaanite-Babylonian) — A lunar festival to honor male rulers that has come into modern Judaism. It is likely that this festival once honored Middle Eastern moon God/desses.

New Year for Trees (Canaanite-Babylonian) — The New Year for Trees was celebrated on the full moon of the fifth month of the old Babylonian lunar calendar (around February). Both the calendar and the festival have been adopted into modern Judaism. The holiday is celebrated in Israel by the planting of new trees, usually in memory of a person or to commemorate a happy event of the previous year.

Osiris and Isis, The Feast of (Egyptian) — The full moon of the twelfth month of the year honored the Underworld and harvest God Osiris and his Goddess consort Isis.

Powamu (Native North American) — The Hopi Indians of the American southwest dedicated the full moon of the second month of their year to ceremonies encouraging crop growth and honoring their grain deities.

Purim (Jewish) — The full moon of the sixth month of the Jewish year commemorates the fall of Haman, the wicked Grand Vizier who advised his Persian King to destroy all the Jews in the realm. The Jews were saved through the heroic efforts of the Jewish Queen, Esther. The holiday is celebrated with costumes and candy, much like Halloween.

Ramadan (Islamic) — Unlike many lunar calendars, the Islamic one makes no adjustment for the solar year. Months can fall in any season, each festival coming at a slightly earlier time each year. Ramadan is one of the oldest of the holy observances in Islam and probably has roots in long-forgotten, moon-centered worship. Today Ramadan takes place during the entire ninth month of the year — the same month in which Islam's chief prophet, Mohammed, received his revelations from Allah (God) — and is solemnized by prayer and daytime abstinence from food, drink, smoking, and sex.

Rosh Hashanna (Jewish) — The Jewish New Year comes each fall at the beginning of the month of Tishri, in accordance with Judaism's lunar calendar. Rites of atonement and blessings for the year ahead are a part of the solemn occasion which begins a ten-day period known as Yamim Nora'im (the Days of Awe). At the end of this period, Jews believe their God has decided who will live and prosper, and who will die, in the year to come.

Rosh Hodesh (Jewish) — Rosh Hodesh is the name of the first day of each Hebrew month. Their lunar calendar is Babylonian in origin, making it very old and very Pagan. Although Rosh Hodesh was once held in reverence as a holy day for women, today it is celebrated in the male-dominated synagogues with special prayers and holy readings.

Seventh Moon, The (Teutonic) — The seventh full moon of the year falls close to the time of Midsummer. Once it was probably a major Pagan festival time, but from the late dark ages on it was considered a night for rampant evil, witches, and baneful faeries. Persons living in the Black Forest regions still believe that venturing forth on this night is unwise.

Starvation Moon (Native North American) — The Indians of many North American tribes called either the first or second month after Midwinter by this ominous name. During this time game was scarce and food stores of grains from the previous year's harvest grew thin. Rituals were held to lead the tribe's hunters to fresh game.

Sukkot (Jewish) — At the start of the waxing quarter of the second month of the Hebrew year, an eight-day harvest festival, similar to Lughnasadh in the Celtic year, takes place. Today it is celebrated both in the synagogue and outdoors in temporary huts. Sukkot honors the fruits of the harvest.

Virgin, The Feast of the (Italian) — This Christianized Pagan festival honors the Virgin Mary, who was believed to have appeared in the village of Carmine many centuries ago. The celebration takes place at the first full moon in the month of July.

Youth, The Festival of (Southeast Asian) — This autumn celebration honors the living spirit of children. On this night they are given sole possession of the powers of light. In honor of this responsibility parades are held, in which children carry lanterns they have made themselves. The festival occurs at the full moon of the eleventh month of their year.

Appendix C

Resources and Merchants Guide

The following businesses stock and sell wares or operate organizations of interest to Pagans. When contacting any of these merchants/organizations by mail, be sure to enclose a self-addressed stamped envelope (SASE), or an International Reply Coupon (IRC) when addressing mail to a foreign country (any country other than the one in which you live).

At the time of this writing all of the following organizations are active and all of the merchants are in business, and most of them are reputable and on a solid footing. However, keep in mind that groups and businesses can move, and even the best of them can fail. Call directory assistance or the Better Business Bureau in the respective towns if you need further assistance.

Herbs, Oils, and Incenses

American Herb Association
P.O. Box 353
Rescue, CA 95672
This umbrella body does not sell herbs, but instead seeks to promote knowledge and use of herbs. They can recommend reliable herb dealers throughout the United States.

Balefire
6504 Vista Avenue
Wauwatosa, WI 53213
This mail-order company carries a large stock of brews, oils, and incenses designed for specific Pagan needs, such as scrying, spirit contact, and spellwork. Write for a free catalog.

Capriland's Herb Farm
Silver Street
Coventry, CT 06238
Write for free price list of dried herbs and herbal books. Capriland also holds special classes on herb use and has herbal lunches at various times throughout the year. Reservations are a must!

Companion Plants
7247 N. Coolville Ridge Road
Athens, OH 45701
Catalog $2.00.

Co-Op Essentials
5364 Ehlich Road, Suite 402
Tampa, FL 33625
Sells fine essential oils. Prices vary by demand. Send $1.00 for most current price list.

Dreaming Spirit
P.O. Box 4263
Danbury, CT 06813-4263
Natural, homemade incenses, resins, and oils, and tools for using them. Dreaming Spirit welcomes queries about custom blends of incenses or oils. The $2.00 for their catalog is refundable with your first order.

Halcyon Herb Company
Box 7153 L
Halcyon, CA 93421
Sells not only magickal herbs, but also staffs, brooms, cloaks, drums, and other items of interest to Pagan folk. Current catalog $5.00.

Herbal Endeavors
3618 S. Emmons Avenue
Rochester Hills, MI 48063
Catalog $2.50.

Indiana Botanical Gardens
P.O. Box 5
Hammond, IN 46325
Sellers of herbs, teas, charcoal blocks, herbal medicines and some books on alternative health care. Request free catalog.

Marah
Box 948
Madison, NJ 07940
Sellers of herbs, incenses, oil blends, and other tools. Catalog, $1.00.

Mountain Butterfly Herbs
106 Roosevelt Lane
Hamilton, MT 59840
Write for current information and prices.

Leydet Oils
P.O. Box 2354
Fair Oaks, CA 95628
Sellers of fine essential oils. Catalog and price list is $2.00.

Sandy Mush Herb Nursery
Rt. 2, Surrett Cove
Lancaster, NC 28748
Has over 800 in-stock herbs, dye plants, and other foliage. Catalog contains helpful herbal tips as well as recipes. Catalog $4.00, refundable with your first order.

Wildwood Fragrances
717 Spruce Street
Boulder, CO 80306
Creates and sells oils, perfumes, potpourris, incenses, oils, etc.; many constructed to align with the energies of deities or festivals. Also offers a mail-order course in blending ritual oils, incenses, etc. Catalog is $2.00, refundable with your first order.

Stones and Stone Information

Lapidary Journal
P.O. Box 80937
San Diego, CA 92138
This is a publication for rock collectors, containing information on stone origins and their lore. It also has ads from companies which sell stones, tumblers, jewelry mountings, etc. Write for subscription information.

Pagan Music

Circle Sanctuary
P.O. Box 219
Mt. Horeb, WI 53572
Circle sells printed and recorded music written by and for Pagans. Request a sample copy of their excellent periodical for more information. Sample copy $4.50.

Green Linnet Records
70 Turner Hill
New Canaan, CT 06840
Sells recorded Celtic music. Request free catalog.

Postings
Dept. 654
P.O. Box 8001
Hilliard, OH 43026-8001

Send $3.00 for a year of video and audio catalogs. They are sellers of videos and off-beat audio tapes and CD's. Their audio catalog usually includes a good selection of folk and ethnic music.

Southern Music Company
1100 Broadway
San Antonio, TX 78212
(210) 226-8167

Publishers and sellers of printed music, including folk and ethnic music. They publish no catalog, but stock virtually everything that is in print. Contact by phone for information on placing orders.

Soaring Spirit (formerly *Winners!*)
P.O. Box 683
Ashland, OR 97520-0023

Publishers and sellers of New Age music and of mind/body video and audio tapes, including tapes to aid meditation, past-life recall, dream programming, and astral projection. First copy of their mag-a-log is free upon request, and will continue to be sent free for up to a year if you order from them.

Books

Dover Books
31 East 2nd Street
Mineola, NY 11501

Dover will send a free catalog upon request. Titles cover a broad range of subject matter including mythology, needlecraft, art, celebrations, nature crafts, music, etc., and reprints of works of Pagan historical interest such as the *Malleus Maleficarum*. They also publish collections of old photography including the *Then and Now* series mentioned in Chapter 12.

Llewellyn's New Worlds of Mind and Spirit
(Formerly *New Times*)
P.O. Box 64383
Dept. 269
St. Paul, MN 55164-0383

This informative catalog is produced by one of the world's largest and oldest sellers and publishers of books on metaphysics, magick, Paganism, astrology, and alternative spirituality. This mag-a-log contains book reviews, articles, interviews, and a list of upcoming events, as well as order forms for their large line of excellent publications. One year's subscription is $10.00.

Pyramid Books
P.O. Box 3333
Altid Park
Chelmsford, MA 01824-0933
Sellers of metaphysical, Pagan, magick books, and beautiful Pagan jewelry and statuettes. Catalog $2.00.

Magickal, Ritual, Pagan Supplies, Jewelry, and Odds and Ends

Abyss
RR #1, Box 213 F
Chester, MA 01011
(413) 623-2155
or fax at (413) 623-2156
Everything in Abyss is perfectly beautiful! Request this free large catalog of magickal supplies including candles, books, jewelry, statuary, and other ritual items.

Aphrodite's Emporium
628 N. 4th Avenue
Tucson, AZ 85705
Sells books, jewelry, oils, candles, and gifts with a Pagan focus. Catalog, $3.50.

Compass Grove
Box 100
Hartland Four Corners, VT 05049
The full color catalog is worth the $5.00 asking price. Offers a wide range of Pagan products.

The Flame
P.O. Box 117
Korbel, CA 95550
The Flame bills its catalog as "complete." They carry all manner of ritual and magickal items. Catalog, $2.00.

Gypsy Heaven
115 S. Main Street
New Hope, PA 18938
(215) 862-5251
Bills itself as "THE Witch Shop of New Hope." Request catalog of magickal supplies, oils, jewelry, statues, cards, etc.

Isis Metaphysical
5701 E. Colfax
Denver, CO 80220
(303) 321-0867

Write for information, catalog price varies. Isis carries jewelry, incense, oils, herbs, books, and periodicals. They carry a wide stock of books on all metaphysical topics, and what they don't carry they will gladly order for you. It is also a pleasant gathering center for local Pagans and other "New Age" thinkers. Be sure to obtain a list of their upcoming workshops, lectures, and classes. A few years ago Isis was the target of arson by an unknown party. As Isis continues to grow as a gathering place for those seeking alternative spirituality, the threat of repeat violence is likely. Any protective energy you can send their way would no doubt be greatly appreciated.

McNamara's Green
P.O. 15822
Seattle, WA 98115

This catalog carries art, jewelry, stickers, sun-catchers, and jewelry with a Celtic flair. Most of it is rather inexpensive. I have ordered from them for years and have always been happy with their products. Catalog and annual supplements, $2.00.

The Magic Door
P.O. Box 8349
Salem, MA 01971

All manner of magickal and ritual supplies. Request free catalog and ordering information.

Moon Scents and Magickal Blends, Inc.
P.O. Box 1588-C
Cambridge, MA 02238

Sells all manner of magickal paraphernalia and books. Request free catalog.

Mythic Force
92-734 Nenelea Street
Ewa Beach, HI 96707
(808) 672-3988

Jewelry, art, t-shirts, glassware, and notecards copied from Pagan designs and ancient museum pieces. Catalog is $1.00, and will be credited against your first order.

Nature's Jewelry
27 Industrial Avenue
Chelmsford, MA 01824-3692

Sellers of seasonal and nature-oriented jewelry at very reasonable prices. Certain items come and go seasonally, and new items are always being added to the basic stock. Very environmentally aware. Designs include moons, suns, autumn leaves, faeries, snowflakes, cornucopia, jack o'lanterns, dolphins, snakes, and holly. A recent catalog included a set of dangling pewter earrings shaped like brooms, and a silver "father of the wind" ring. Also an excellent source for gift exchange items for Pagans gatherings and festivals. Write to request a free catalog.

POTO
11002 Massachusetts Avenue
Westwood, CA 90025-3510
(310) 575-3717

POTO is short for "Procurer of the Obscure." Their mail order catalog features services, rare books, and herb for those in the magickal life. Special orders and requests always welcome. Send $5.00 for current catalog and ordering information.

Sacred Spirit Products
P.O. Box 8163
Salem, MA 01971-8163

Sellers of books, magickal tools, herbs, incense, and other occult items. Catalog $3.00

Sidda
1430 Willamette #119
Eugene, OR 97401

Crafters of ritual blades and magick mirrors. Send $1.00 for brochure.

Pagan Periodicals

Circle Network News
P.O. Box 219
Mt. Horeb, WI 53572

This quarterly Pagan publication is nothing less than excellent. It is full of well-written articles and contacts. *Circle* sponsors Pagan gatherings throughout the year and helps Pagans all over the world connect with one another. At this writing a one-year subscription is $15 by bulk mail to USA addresses, $20 first class to USA, Canada, and Mexico, and $27 elsewhere. Payment must be in U.S. funds. Write for other subscription information, or request a sample copy, currently priced at $4.50.

The Cauldron
Caemorgan Cottage
Caemorgan Road
Cardigan, Dyfed
SA43 1QU
Wales

Send one IRC for updated subscription information on this quarterly which covers many nature spirituality paths.

The Green Egg
P.O. Box 1542
Ukiah, CA 95482

This was the reigning queen of Pagan periodicals in the early 1970s, and has been successfully revived. Contains beautiful artwork and well-researched articles. Deliciously controversial! Subscriptions to this quarterly are $15 in the USA and $21 in Canada. Write for other subscription information. Sample copy, $4.95.

Hecate's Loom
Box 5206, Station B
Victoria, BC
Canada V8R 6N4

A quarterly journal of Paganism. Yearly rates for US subscriptions, $18. Write for full information.

Llewellyn's New Worlds of Mind and Spirit
(Formerly New Times)
P.O. Box 64383
Dept. 269
St. Paul, MN 55164-0383

See description above under "Books."

Meade
American Meade Association
P.O. 206
Ostrander, OH 43061

This organization promotes and keeps alive the art and lore of meade, the rich honey-ale long associated with Bealtaine, the full moon, and handfasting rites. It also provides access to various recipes and meade-making supplies. Membership is $10 a year.

Seasonal/Ritual Art and Poetry

Circle Network News
P.O. Box 219
Mt. Horeb, WI 53572

See description under "Pagan Periodicals."

Ideals Magazine
P.O. Box 148000
Nashville, TN 37214-8000

Ideals has been publishing beautiful seasonal material since just after World War II. They publish eight standard issues a year plus some specialty issues. Current copies can be found in most bookstores, and back issues in many second-hand bookstores.

National/International Pagan Organizations

In addition to the large organizations listed below, many regions have smaller organizations which provide support, networking, and a sense of community to solitary Pagans. Please look in the pages of Pagan publications for these addresses.

The Fellowship of Isis
Clonegal Castle
Enniscorthy
County Wexford, Ireland
This is an international organization of Goddess-worshippers with a membership of around 10,000. Send one IRC for response to inquiries.

International Wiccan/Pagan Press Alliance
P.O. Box 1392
Mechanicsburg, PA 17055
A membership in the WPPA is open to all, not just to writers and publishers, for $18.00 a year. The monthly newsletter, *The Midnight Drive,* discusses trends and news from the Pagan publishing industry, keeps you abreast of the current state of legal problems and other issues facing the Pagan community, and provides ordering information for books from small presses that are hard to find elsewhere.

The Pagan Federation
BM Box 7097
London WC1N 3XX
England
Founded in 1971, this British-based organization seeks to make itself a forum for all European Pagan traditions, and to promote understanding, networking, and exchange of ideas between these diverse groups. Send one SASE or two IRCs for membership information.

Pagan Spirit Alliance and Lady Liberty League
c/o Circle Sanctuary
Box 219
Mt. Horeb, WI 53572
For membership application to PSA, send SASE to Circle. LLL involves itself in aiding Pagans who face legal difficulties due to their religion.

Witches' Anti-Defamation League
c/o Black Forest Publishing
P.O. Box 1392
Mechanicsburg, PA 17055
Modeled on the very effective Jewish Anti-Defamation League, this group actively combats discrimination against persons involved in nature religions. Include SASE for response.

Witches' League for Public Awareness
P.O. Box 8736
Salem, MA 01970
Include a business-sized SASE for response. This organization seeks to educate the public about nature religions and tackles discrimination issues.

Witches Today
Box 221
Levittown, PA 19059
An organization whose goal is helping to educate the general public about Witchcraft and Paganism, and in maintaining religious freedom for everyone. If you are interested in aiding their efforts, please write.

Glossary

Alchemy (AL-kem-ee) — A branch of High Magick developed in the Middle Ages that sought to magickally and/or chemically turn base metals into gold. Part of its focus was the elevation of the human soul to a more God-like existence through the role of creation. Alchemists have always referred to the practice of their tradition as "The Great Work." Alchemy is also a branch of High or Ceremonial Magick in which the elements and spirits are manipulated to do the will of the magician.

Alignment/Attunement — The art and practice of placing our spiritual and mental selves in sync with the energies of an astronomical event (i.e.; a full moon) or another being (i.e.; a God or Goddess.) This can be achieved through mental exercises, evocation, invocation, or ritual.

Altered State of Consciousness — See **Meditation**.

Amulet — A natural object that is reputed to give protection to the carrier. Amulets are such things as stones or fossils and are not to be confused with human-made talismans.

Archetype — Universal symbols, defined by Funk and Wagnalls as a "standard pattern" or a "prototype." Archetypal symbols speak to all of us in the ecumenical language of the sub-conscious. They are the images that cloud our dreams, the inherent power of our deities, and the machinery that makes all forms of divination possible. Archetypal images are used heavily throughout pathworking, for this is the only language our sub-conscious (sometimes called our super-conscious or deep mind) can understand and utilize, and with which it communicates back to our conscious minds.

Aspect — 1. The particular principle or part of the Creative Life Force being worked with or acknowledged at any one time. For example, Brigid is a Mother aspect of the one Goddess, Thor is one aspect of the God, and both are merely single aspects of the Creative Life Force. 2. The relationship between any two planets as calculated on a conceptualized, earth-centered, horoscope drawing of the heavens at any given moment. The number of degrees separating the planets determines how they aid or contradict each other's influences.

Astral Plane — A place which is generally conceptualized as an invisible parallel world that remains unseen from our solid world of form. The vast majority of Pagans believe this plane can be entered, with practice, through conscious effort.

Astral Projection — The art of "leaving one's body," or "lucid dreaming," whereby someone in a trance state visits other locations, realms or times. This is often referred to as traveling on the astral plane, a place generally conceptualized as an invisible world parallel to our world of form.

Astrology —The study of and belief in the effects the movements and placements of planets and other heavenly bodies have on the lives and behavior of human beings.

Athame (ATH-aah-may)—The ritual knife often associated with the element of air and the direction of the east, though some traditions attribute it to fire and the south. The knife was traditionally black-handled, but many modern Pagans seek handles of natural wood.

Aura — The life-energy field surrounding all living things. The aura can be seen by those who train themselves to see it or by using special photographic techniques.

B.C.E. —"Before the Common Era." This is a designation scholars often use to denote dates synonymous with B.C., but without biased religious implications. It is sometimes abbreviated BCE, without the periods between the letters.

Besom (BEE-sum or BAY-shum) — An old English word for the Witch's broomstick. European folklore tells of Witches riding their besoms through the sky, which many feel is an uninformed explanation of astral projection. As a magickal tool, the besom is used to sweep a sacred area, ground a circle, or to brush away negative influences. Besoms were often mounted and "ridden" over crops in fertility rites.

Bless — To bless something or someone is to set it apart as sacred, or, as the dictionaries prefer, to make it "holy." The word is sometimes used synonymously with "consecrate."

Book of Shadows — Also called the Book of Lights and Shadows, it is the spell book, diary, and ritual guide used by an individual Witch or coven. Some believe the name came from having to hide the workings from early church authorities, and others say it means that an unworked spell or ritual is a mere shadow, not taking concrete form until performed by a Witch.

The Burning Times — The years from the the Spanish Inquisition through the last outbursts of persecution and Witch killings in the mid-nineteenth century (though murderous persecutions began as early as the twelfth century). The last known capital sentence for Witchcraft in the west took place in Scotland in the early 1800s. Figures vary concerning how many were killed during this hysteria; estimates range from 50,000 to as many as 9 million. Regardless of the number of lives actually lost, these murders for the sake of religious persecution should never be forgotten. The Jewish Holocaust of this century frighteningly shows us that such atrocities can occur in any age, to any of us.

Cauldron — Linked to Witchcraft in the popular mind, this primal Goddess image is used like a chalice or cup. This was a common magickal instrument in the Celtic traditions because it was a practical object as well, which could be used for cooking or washing as well as making brews and magick potions. In many of the mythological stories from Ireland and Britain, the cauldron is symbolic of the womb of the Mother Goddess in which all life begins, ends, and regenerates.

C.E. — "Common Era." This term is often used by scholars to denote dates synonymous with A.D., but without a religious bias. It is sometimes abbreviated as CE, without periods between the letters.

Ceremonial Magick — A highly codified magickal tradition based upon Kaballah, the Jewish-Gnostic mystical teachings. The magickal emphasis is on summoning and controlling demons, angels, and other entities, who are then commanded to do the magician's bidding.

Circle — The sacred space wherein all magick is to be worked and all ritual contained. The circle both contains raised energy and provides protection for the Witch, and is created and banished with her/his own energy. Many books on magick go into circle lore and practice heavily; it is recommended that students of Paganism study these carefully.

Cone of Power — The cone of energy ritually raised within the circle by an individual or by a coven. When the energy reaches its peak, it is released to do its work.

Consecrate — To consecrate something is to dedicate it to a sacred or higher purpose. The word is often used synonymously with the term "bless."

Coven — A group of Witches who worship and work together. A coven may contain any number of Witches, both male and female, but the traditional number of members is thirteen, reflecting the thirteen moons in the solar year, or three persons for each season plus a priest/ess.

Craft, The — A phrase used to denote Witchcraft as a complete spiritual system. Just when the word was first applied to Pagan practice is unknown. Some give the term claims to antiquity, others say it was a creation of the late Victorian period. Masonic orders also use this term for their practice.

Crone — That aspect of the Goddess that is represented by the old woman. She is symbolized by the waning moon, the carrion crow, the cauldron, and the color black.

Dark Moon — The moment when the moon is positioned so that no sun is reflected from its surface to the earth. The dark moon is poised at the precise instant that the moon ceases waning but has not yet begun moving into the waxing phase.

Deity — An inclusive name for a Goddess or God.

Deosil (JES-ul)— The act of moving, working, or dancing in a clockwise direction. This is the traditional direction one works with for creative magick or magick for increase. Deosil is also called sunwise or going to the right. Remember that a movement performed clockwise is not inherently good or positive.

Divination — The act of divining the future by reading potentials currently in motion. Divination can be done through meditation, scrying, astral projection, with cards, stones, or any of a myriad of means. The most popular forms of divination today are Tarot, Runes, pendulums, scrying, automatic writing, dream-working, and using the controversial Ouija Board.

Drawing Down the Moon — Ancient Pagan ritual enacted at the Esbats to draw the powers of the full moon, in her aspect as Great Mother Goddess, into the body of a living Witch, usually a female. This ritual's alter-ego, Drawing Down the Sun, is an act usually reserved for males.

Elements, The — The four alchemical elements once thought to make up the entire universe. These are earth, air, fire, and water, plus the fifth element of pure spirit which exists in, of, and outside them all. Each Pagan tradition has its own, slightly differing directions, tools, and correspondences for each element.

Enchanting — The act of empowering an herb, stone, or other magickal object with one's own energies directed toward a magickal goal. Enchanting is synonymous with charging, empowering, or energizing.

Ephemeris (Eff-uh-MARE-us) — A book containing charts which detail planetary movements. The word comes from the same root word as "ephemeral" meaning "to last for only a short while."

Evocation — The act of summoning the presence of deities, friendly spirits, or elementals to your circle or home.

Folklore — The traditional sayings, cures, fairy tales, superstitions, and folk wisdom of a particular locale which may be separate from their body of mythology.

Full Moon — The moment when the full face of the moon is illuminated by the sun as seen from earth. The full moon comes at the precise time when the moon has completed its waxing phases but has not yet begun to wane.

Grimoire (GREEM-warr) — A book of magickal spells and rituals. Some claims to theirantiquity are highly suspect, and those that are truly ancient contain much apocryphal material. However, this does not invalidate the spells or rituals in the newer ones—it just means they are not old. Any Book of Shadows is also a grimoire.

Grounding — To disperse excess energy, generated during any magickal or occult rite,by sending it into the earth. It can also mean the process of centering one's self in the physical world both before and after any ritual or astral experience.

Guided Meditation — Though the term comes to Paganism from ceremonial magick, Pagans use it to define a guided journey into the realm of the unconscious, or astral plane, for the purpose of acquiring a lasting change in both the conscious and sub-conscious mind of the seeker. The term is synonymous with pathworking. Good storytelling often leads the listener on an unconscious guided meditation.

Herbalism — The art of using herbs to facilitate human needs, both magickally and medically.

Invocation — The act of drawing the aspect of a particular deity into one's physical self. The rite of Drawing Down the Moon is an example of invocation.

Karma — A Hindustani word which reflects the ancient belief a person's good and evil actions will return to be visited on him or her, in either this life or a succeeding one.

Law of Responsibility, The — This is an often repeated corollary to the other laws of Paganism. It simply means that if you inadvertently violate someone's free will or harm them in any way, you will accept responsibility for your action and seek to make restitution. This does not apply in cases in which you have used magick to protect yourself from someone seeking to harm you.

Libation — A ritually given portion of food or drink to a deity, nature spirit, or ghost.

Lunar Calendar — A system of keeping time by the phases of the moon. Each month in the calendar begins at a new moon and ends twenty-nine days later with the dark moon. There are approximately thirteen lunar months in each solar year.

Lunation — A single cycle of a lunar month from the new to dark moon.

Magick — Spelled here with a 'k' to differentiate it from the magic of stage illusions. The best definition of magick was probably invented by infamous ceremonial magician Aleister Crowley: "Magick is the science and art of causing change to occur in conformity to will." The word came into English from the Greek *magikos* meaning "power of the magi (magicians)." The Greeks took it from an even older Persian term meaning "to control the elements."

Maiden — The youngest aspect of the Triple Goddess, also known as the virgin. She is represented by the waxing moon and the colors white and blue.

Major Arcana — The twenty-two principle cards of the Tarot deck which symbolize human spiritual progress and outline the culmination of life experiences.

Matrifocal — Also matricentric. A term used to denote pre-patriarchal life, when familial clans centered around and lived near one clan matriarch. While in certain temperate regions these female-headed tribes were exceptionally peaceful and egalitarian, others were not. Generally, tribes and clans living in colder regions were more war-like. Anthropologists cite the seasonal unavailability of vital natural resources as a possible reason for this differentiation.

Meditation — Meditation can be defined in many ways. For many it is a sustained thought process during which the mind is clearly focused, to the exclusion of all else. For others, mostly from Asian traditions, it is the complete and controlled absence of thought. In either case, it involves altering one's normal state of consciousness to a slower, more receptive level. In simplest terms it is a deliberate attempt to slow the cycles-per-second of one's brain waves in order to generate a consciously controlled sleeping state.

Mother — One of the aspects of the Triple Goddess., representing motherhood, mid-life, and fertility. She is represented by the full moon, the egg, and the colors red and green.

New Moon — The phase of the moon when she has just begun to wax. The energy of the new moon is thought to last from the moment she begins to wax until the slender, waxing crescent appears about four days later.

Occult — The word occult literally means "hidden" and is broadly applied to a wide range of metaphysical topics which lie outside of the accepted realm of mainstream theologies. Such topics include, but are not limited to, divination, hauntings, spirit communication, natural magick, ceremonial magick, alternative spirituality, psychic phenomena, alchemy, astrology, demonology, the study of the spiritual practices of ancient civilizations, and the study of any of the above mentioned topics as applied to mainstream religions.

Pagan — Generic term for anyone who practices an earth or nature religion. The word is sometimes used synonymously with Witch, but not all Pagans are known as Witches. However, all Witches are Pagan.

Pagan Rede, The — This is the basic tenet of Witchcraft: "as ye harm none, do what thou will." The Rede prohibits Pagans from harming any other living thing, or from violating anyone's free will. The Rede is sometimes called the Witches' or Wiccan Rede.

Pantheon — The major deities in any religious system that make up the "whole" deity, or the complete power source.

Pathworking — See **Guided Meditation.**

Patriarchal — A term used to designate a society or political unit dominated by males. In general, patriarchy became the norm in most cultures somewhere between 5,000 and 7,000 years ago.

Pentagram —The five-pointed star which has come to symbolize western Paganism. It is an ancient symbol with multiple meanings. It is always seen with its apex up. It can represent the four elements headed by the fifth element of spirit, or it can represent a human with arms and legs spread to represent mind over matter. It can also represent the creative principle over all creation. Sometimes it is encased in a circle; then it is properly called a pentacle. Satanic cults often take the pentagram and invert it to signify matter over spirit in much the same way that they pervert the meaning of the Christian cross. "Pentegram" is an alternate spelling.

Power Hand — For purposes of magick, this is the hand which is dominant, usually the one with which you write.

Receptive Hand — For purposes of magick, this is the hand which is non-dominant, usually the one that you do not use for writing.

Reincarnation — A basic tenet of Paganism, the belief that the souls of human beings return to the earth plane in another human body, or even in another life-form, after death. There are many theories of how reincarnation works, but the largest division is between those who believe that all our lives are lived in one great omnipresent now, and those who believe we live a linear succession of many lives.

Ritual — A systematic, formal or informal, prescribed set of rites whose purpose is to imprint a lasting change on the life and psyche of the participant.

Ritual Tools — A general name for magickal or ritual tools used by a Witch or magician. These tools vary by tradition and usually represent one of the elements. Ritual tools can also be called magickal tools or elemental weapons.

Runes — A divination device consisting of twenty-four stones upon which are carved a single letter of the Elder Futhark, an old Nordic alphabet. There is also a blank stone. Since writing was considered a sacred act in most cultures at the time this lettering was used, they have become a method for reading the potentials which shape our futures and hold the secrets of our pasts.

Sabbat — Any of the eight solar festivals or observances of the Pagan year. The word is derived from the Greek word *sabatu* meaning "to rest." The eight Sabbats of Witchcraft are Samhain (October 31), the Winter Solstice, Imbolg (February 1 or 2), the Spring Equinox, Bealtaine (May 1), the Summer Solstice, Lughnasadh (August 1 or 2), and the Autumn Equinox. Not all traditions celebrate all of these Sabbats, and some include others not listed here.

Scrying — The divinatory act of gazing at an object or candle until prophetic visions appear.

Sigil — A symbol with occult meaning. The term comes from the Latin *sigillum,* meaning "a sign." More specifically, a sigil is a drawing used in ceremonial magick to identify a power or being which is captured and controlled through manipulating its sigil.

Skyclad — Ritual nudity, common practice within the Gardnerian tradition of Wicca. Contrary to popular belief, going skyclad is not the norm among many Pagans working in group situations. Going skyclad is a personal choice, and should not be made mandatory, especially since there is little or no evidence to suggest that this was common practice in ancient Paganism. Gerald Gardner got the idea from an Italian monograph written in the late medieval period by a Pagan woman. While it may be warm enough in sunny Italy to run around naked most of the year, that was and is not the case in most of northern and western Europe and was probably not a part of general practice in those areas.

So Mote It Be — A very old affirmation of an act completed. Mote is an obsolete term for the word "must." When uttered after an invocation, spell, etc., it seals the intent by voicing it as a *fait accompli,* something that is now part of reality rather than an unformed wish. The words are used widely in all traditions of modern Paganism.

Solar Calendar — A system of keeping time based on the movements of the earth in relation to the sun. The twelve-month Common Era calendar is a solar calendar.

Solitary — A Pagan who works and worships alone, without the aid of a larger coven.

Solitary by Chance — A solitary Pagan who would rather be part of a larger group, but has not found one which is compatible. Be cautioned about jumping into a coven just because you want desperately to be a part of one. Be sure first that your ideologies are in sync, or you could find yourself in a miserable situation.

Solitary by Choice — A Pagan who practices alone because this is how the person feels most comfortable expressing his or her spirituality. Being solitary has certain advantages, but can lead to feelings of isolation or loneliness. You might want to consider attending a Pagan festival or gathering once a year or so just to have the support and companionship of like minds.

Spell — A specific magickal ritual designed for the purpose of obtaining, banishing, or changing one particular thing or condition. Synonyms for making spells are spell weaving, spellcraft, casting, and spinning.

Sub-conscious Mind —That part of the mind functioning below the levels we are able to access in the course of a normal, waking day. This area stores symbolic knowledge, dreams, and the most minute details of every experience ever had by a person. In Paganism this is sometimes referred to as the super-conscious mind.

Sympathetic Magick — A concept of like-attracts-like. The best example of sympathetic magick was in the hunting dances of Native America. Hunters would dress as the animals they sought and enact their own slaying. Sympathetic magick is the most common method for working spells.

Talisman — An object reputed to offer protection or other magickal service to the carrier. It differs from an amulet by being constructed and charged by the Witch, rather than being found in nature.

Tarot — A set of seventy-two cards containing potent symbols that can be read by the sub-conscious in order to do divination. The origin of the cards is unknown, but some guess that they originated in the Middle East approximately three thousand years ago.

Threefold Law, The — The karmic principle of Paganism. It states that any energy released by the Witch or magician (or anyone else), either positive or negative, will return to the sender three times over.

Tradition — The branch of Paganism followed by any individual Witch or coven. There are hundreds of these traditions, most drawn along ethnic or cultural lines, but several are modern amalgamations. The word "traditions" in this case is synonymous with path, ie; Wicca is one tradition of Paganism.

Triple Goddess — The one Goddess in all of her three aspects: Maiden, Mother and Crone. This triple theme of feminine deity has been found in nearly every known culture on the planet.

Wand — Another ritual tool brought into the Craft through ceremonial magick. A wand can symbolize either the element air and the direction east, or south and fire.

Waning Moon — The phase of the moon from the time it is full until it is dark.

Waxing Moon — The phase of the moon from the time it is new until it is full.

Wheel of the Year — A conceptualization of the eternal cycle of time. In Pagan mythology the Goddess turns the Wheel of the Year, bringing everything to its season. The Wheel of the Year is symbolized by either a wreath, a ring, a snake holding its tail in its mouth, or an eight-spoked wheel.

Wicca — A modern term for Witchcraft. Wicca is an Anglo-Saxon word meaning "to bend," a term which, in the 1950s, was first used to label the Craft as it was practiced in England, Wales, and the continental region known as Saxony. Wicca has erroneously become a generic catch-all phrase for nearly all Witchcraft traditions.

Widdershins — This word is from the Teutonic (Germanic) Pagan tradition. It literally means "to go backwards," and it is the act of moving, working or dancing counterclockwise in order to banish, diminish or counter some negative force. While widdershins is the term most commonly used to denote this movement, other names are tuathail, against the sun, walking to the left, and reverse. Remember that a movement performed counterclockwise is not inherently negative or evil.

Zen — A tradition of the Buddhist religion, featuring work with altered states of consciousness to attain total inner-peace and connection with divinity. Many students spend their lives studying with Asian Zen Masters who have developed the capability to spend hours in deeply altered states of consciousness, characterized by the complete absence of thought.

Annotated Bibliography
and Selected Reading

Adler, Margot. *Drawing Down the Moon*. (Revised and Expanded Edition) Boston: Beacon Press, 1986.

An interesting look at expressions of modern Pagan traditions in the United States.

Asimov, Isaac. *The Clock We Live On*. New York: Abelard-Schuman, 1959.

Blum, Ralph. *The Book of Runes*. New York: St. Martin's Press, 1982.

Usually sold with a complete Rune set, this book teaches the use and meanings of this oracle.

Brennen, J. H. *Astral Doorways*. Wellingborough, Northamptonshire: Aquarian Press, 1986.

In my opinion, this is one of the two best books on astral projection ever written. It approaches the subject from a practical point of view, relates actual experiences, and teaches safety and "rescue" techniques.

Buckland, Raymond. *Practical Color Magick*. St. Paul, MN: Llewellyn, 1987.

An excellent guide to incorporating the strong symbols of color into any magick rite.

Budapest, Zsuzsanna E. *Grandmother Moon*. San Francisco: HarperCollins, 1991.

A look at Pagan moon celebrations from a feminist viewpoint.

Chaundler, Christine. *The Book of Superstition*. Secaucus, NJ: Citadel Press, 1970.

Chaundler covers many different types of fearful folk belief, including moon lore.

Cunningham, Scott. *The Complete Book of Incense, Oils and Brews*. St. Paul, MN: Llewellyn, 1989.

A well-researched compilation of formulas and recipes for all magickal and ritual needs. Among the topics discussed are formulas for flying ointments and ritual oils for lunar and solar rites.

———. *Cunningham's Encyclopedia of Crystal, Gem and Metal Magic*. St. Paul, MN: Llewellyn, 1986.

This book covers the mineral world and its relationship to ancient and modern magick. Included are tables of correspondences to help you pick out stones that would work well in moon-centered rituals.

———. *Cunningham's Encyclopedia of Magical Herbs*. St. Paul, MN: Llewellyn, 1986.

This book has almost become the bible of the modern magickal herbalist. It contains extensive listings of herbs and their traditional associations, as well as tables for helping you choose herbs whose energies work best in moon rituals, or in spells for any other magickal need. Excellent.

Cunningham, Scott. *Earth, Air, Fire and Water: More Techniques of Natural Magic.* St. Paul, MN: Llewellyn, 1991.
  A sequel to *Earth Power.* Contains spells for natural magick.

———. *Earth Power: Techniques of Natural Magic.* St. Paul, MN: Llewellyn, 1987.
  A good basic guide to the methods of natural magick. Included are numerous step-by-step spells.

———. *The Magic In Food.* St. Paul, MN: Llewellyn, 1991.
  A great source for Sabbat and Esbat recipes, hints on kitchen Witchery, and help in identifying foods with specific planetary associations.

Denning, Melita and Osborne Phillips. *Astral Projection.* St. Paul, MN: Llewellyn, 1979.
  In my opinion, this is one of the two best books written on astral projection. A very practical guide covering everything from preliminary exercises, to what you may expect to encounter in advanced projections.

———. *Creative Visualization* (second edition). St. Paul, MN: Llewellyn, 1983.
  A practical, informative guide to learning to visualize anything at any time.

———. *Psychic Self-Defense and Well-Being.* St. Paul, MN: Llewellyn, 1980.

Fitch, Ed. *Magical Rites From the Crystal Well.* St. Paul, MN: Llewellyn, 1986.

Frazer, Sir James. *The Golden Bough* (Abridged Edition). New York: Macmillian, 1956.
  A good sourcebook, though Frazer is at times condescending to magickal thought. This backlash usually occurs at points at which it is clear that he is quite taken with all he has read, studied, and seen.

Gamow, George, and Harry C. Stubbs. *The Moon* (Revised Edition). New York: Abelard-Schuman, 1971.
  A layman's text on the science of the moon.

George, Demetra. *Mysteries of the Dark Moon.* San Francisco: HarperCollins, 1992.
  This book explores the crone or dark Goddesses and discusses their powers of inner-healing. Though the perspective is feminist, the writing and themes should not be unpalatable to male Pagans.

Glass-Koentop, Pattalee. *Year of Moons, Season of Trees: Mysteries and Rites of Celtic Tree Magic.* St. Paul: Llewellyn, 1991.
  A look at the tree/lunar calendar system of the Celts.

Gray, Eden. *Mastering the Tarot.* New York: Signet Books, 1971.
  This fully illustrated mass-market paperback manages to teach in detail all of the basics of Tarot. The text is easy to follow and has many examples to clarify points. Excellent.

Guiley, Rosemary Ellen. *Moonscapes.* New York: Prentice Hall Press, 1991.
  This book on the moon uniquely approaches her from both scientific and mythological viewpoints.

Leek, Sybil. *The Complete Art of Witchcraft.* New York: Harper and Row (Signet Imprint), 1971.
  A look at the life of a hereditary Witch who practiced before the repeal of England's Anti-Witchcraft laws. Provides a good introduction to Pagan ethics and ideology.

Llewellyn Publication's Annuals. *Daily Planetary Guide* and *The Moon Sign Book.* St. Paul, MN: Llewellyn, (each published annually).

These two annuals are indispensable if you want to know what astrological aspects are at work any time of the night or day. Both are accurate and heavily oriented towards the influences of the moon.

Ludzia, Leo F. *The Space/Time Connection.* St. Paul, MN: Llewellyn, 1989.

Discusses in depth the use of time perceptions in creative visualization.

McCoy, Edain. *How to Teach Yourself Automatic Writing.* St. Paul. MN: Llewellyn, 1994. Teaches this divination technique step by step.

———. *Celtic Myth & Magick.* St. Paul, MN: Llewellyn, 1995.

Contains detailed information on invocation and evocation techniques.

Modrzyk, Stanley J. A. *Turning of the Wheel: A Wiccan Book of Shadows for Moons and Festivals.* York Beach, ME: Samuel Weiser, Inc., 1993.

RavenWolf, Silver. *To Ride a Silver Broomstick.* St. Paul, MN: Llewellyn, 1993.

In my opinion, this metaphysical bestseller is one of the best introductions to Witchcraft ever written.

Richardson, Alan. *Earth God Rising.* St. Paul, MN: Llewellyn, 1992.

Rush, Anne Kent. *Moon, Moon.* New York: Random House, 1976.

Goddess lore, moon lore, ritual and poetry jointly published by Random House and Moon Books, an "independent women's publishing company."

Sabrina, Lady. *Reclaiming the Power: The How and Why of Practical Ritual Magic.* St. Paul, MN: Llewellyn, 1992.

This work is completely devoted to examining and teaching the use of ritual in Pagan practice. Well-written by a long-time priestess, the guide is a must read for all Witches who take their ritual seriously, or who wish to understand more fully how ritual affects consciousness and spellwork.

Stein, Diane. T*he Women's Spirituality Book.* St. Paul, MN: Llewellyn, 1988.

———. *Casting the Circle.* Freedom, CA: The Crossing Press, 1990.

Starhawk. *The Spiral Dance.* San Francisco: Harper and Row, Publishers, 1979.

Stepanich, Kisma. *Sister Moon Lodge.* St. Paul, MN: Llewellyn, 1993.

A book about women's cycles and their attunement to the phases of the moon.

Valiente, Doreen. *Natural Magic.* Custer, WA: Phoenix Publishing Inc., 1980.

A guide to natural magick focusing on the psychology and cause/effect of spellwork.

Walker, Barbara G. *The Crone: Woman of Age, Wisdom, and Power.* San Francisco: HarperCollins, 1985.

A wonderful little book that looks at the crone and how she has been systematically devalued, hated, and hidden for centuries. Walker is a practitioner of a womanspirit Pagan tradition.

———. *Women's Rituals: A Sourcebook.* San Francisco: HarperCollins, 1990.

Wallis, Wilson D. *Religion in Primitive Society.* New York: F. S. Crofts and Co., 1939.

> Although this book often adopts a condescending tone, it is a basically well-written study of religious views and practices in isolated or very early societies.

Waring, Phillipa. *A Dictionary of Omens and Superstitions.* New York: Ballantine Books, 1979.

Weinstein, Marion. *Earth Magic: A Dianic Book of Shadows.* Custer, WA: Phoenix Publishing Inc., 1980.

> A lovely but slim book which contains a short discussion/ritual on cord magick.

———. *Positive Magick.* Custer, WA: Phoenix Publishing Inc., 1978.

> Weinstein's book, fast becoming a modern classic, discusses and teaches magick, divination, and Pagan ethics.

Wilson, P. W. *Romance of the Calendar.* New York: W. W. Norton Company, Inc., 1937.

Index

☾ Reach for the MOON

Llewellyn publishes hundreds of books on your favorite subjects!
To get these exciting books, including the ones on the following pages,
check your local bookstore or order them directly from Llewellyn.

Order by Phone
- Call toll-free within the U.S. and Canada, 1-800-THE MOON
- In Minnesota, call (651) 291-1970
- We accept VISA, MasterCard, and American Express

Order by Mail
- Send the full price of your order (MN residents add 7% sales tax)
  in U.S. funds, plus postage & handling to:

  Llewellyn Worldwide
  P.O. Box 64383, Dept. 0–7387–0092–4
  St. Paul, MN 55164–0383, U.S.A.

Postage & Handling
- **Standard** (U.S., Mexico, & Canada)

If your order is:
  $20.00 or under, add $5.00
  $20.01–$100.00, add $6.00
  Over $100, shipping is free
(Continental U.S. orders ship UPS. AK, HI, PR, & P.O. Boxes ship USPS 1st class. Mex. & Can. ship PMB.)

- **Second Day Air** (Continental U.S. only): $10.00 for one book + $1.00
  per each additional book
- **Express** (AK, HI, & PR only) [Not available for P.O. Box delivery. For
  street address delivery only.]: $15.00 for one book + $1.00 per each
  additional book
- **International Surface Mail:** Add $1.00 per item
- **International Airmail:** Books—Add the retail price of each item;
  Non-book items—Add $5.00 per item

Please allow 4–6 weeks for delivery on all orders.
Postage and handling rates subject to change.

Discounts
We offer a 20% discount to group leaders or agents. You must order a minimum of 5 copies of the
same book to get our special quantity price.

Free Catalog
Get a free copy of our color catalog, New Worlds of Mind and
Spirit. Subscribe for just $10.00 in the United States and Canada
($30.00 overseas, airmail). Many bookstores carry New Worlds—
ask for it!

Visit our website at www.llewellyn.com for more information.

Sabbats
A Witch's Approach to Living the Old Ways

EDAIN MCCOY

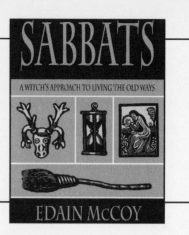

Sabbats offers many fresh, exciting ways to deepen your connection to the turning of the Wheel of the Year. This tremendously practical guide to Pagan solar festivals does more than teach you about the "old ways"—you will learn workable ideas for combining old customs with new expressions of those beliefs that will be congruent with your lifestyle and tradition.

Sabbats begins with background on Paganism (tenets, teachings, and tools) and origins of the eight Sabbats, followed by comprehensive chapters on each Sabbat. These pages are full of ideas for inexpensive seasonal parties in which Pagans and non-Pagans alike can participate, as well as numerous craft ideas and recipes to enrich your celebrations. The last section provides sixteen complete texts of Sabbat rituals—for both covens and solitaries—with detailed guidelines for adapting rituals to specific traditions or individual tastes. Includes an extensive reference section with a resources guide, bibliography, musical scores for rituals, and more.

This book may contain the most practical advice ever for incorporating the old ways into your Pagan lifestyle!

1–56718–663–7
320 pp., 7 x 10, illus., photos   **$17.95**

To order, call 1-800-THE MOON

Prices subject to change without notice

Making Magick
What It Is and How It Works
EDAIN McCOY

How do I raise and send energy? What happens if I make a mistake in casting a spell? What is sex magick all about? What is the Moon's role in magick? Which magickal tools do I need the most?

Making Magick is a complete course in natural magick that answers these and hundreds of other questions. Through exercises designed to develop basic skills, *Making Magick* lays a firm foundation of elemental magickal wisdom. The first chapters begin with an introduction to magick and how it works. You will study Craft tools, learn to connect with the elements—the building blocks of magick—and delve into the intricacies of spell construction and timing. The last half of the book will take you into the advanced magickal arts, which rely on highly honed skills of meditation, astral projection, visualization, and sustaining of creative energy. A special chapter on the tattwas will show you how to use these ancient Hindu symbols as gateways into the astral worlds.

1–56718–670–x
304 pp., 6 x 9, illus., photos

$14.95

To order, call 1-800-THE MOON

Prices subject to change without notice

Bewitchments
Love Magick for Modern Romance

EDAIN McCOY

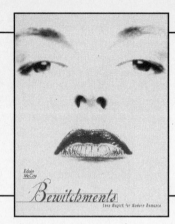

The simple act of braiding your hair can be a potent spell for love—that's why Celtic women had to wear their hair loose at their weddings. Eat a pineapple, long a symbol of friendship and unity, and watch new friends come into your life. Whether you're looking for a new friend or a lifelong mate, *Bewitchments* can help you narrow the focus of the search and show you how to attract, sustain, or refine these relationships with its grimoire of over ninety spells. Drawing on both multicultural folk magick and new scientific discoveries about the chemical process known as "falling in love," *Bewitchments* shows, step by step, how to bring the ancient spells into the present and make them work.

1–56718–700–5
264 pp., 7 ½ x 9 ⅛, illus. $14.95

To order, call 1-800-THE MOON
Prices subject to change without notice